An Introduction to Instructional Services in Academic Libraries

Elizabeth Connor, MLS, AHIP
Editor

Routledge
Taylor & Francis Group
NEW YORK AND LONDON

First published 2008
by Routledge
270 Madison Ave, New York, NY 10016

Simultaneously published in the UK
by Routledge
2 Park Square, Milton Park, Abingdon, Oxon OX14 4RN

Routledge is an imprint of the Taylor & Francis Group, an informa business

© 2008 Taylor & Francis

Printed and bound in the United States of America on acid-free paper by
Sheridan Books, Inc.

Trademark Notice: Product or corporate names may be trademarks or
registered trademarks, and are used only for identification and explanation
without intent to infringe.

Library of Congress Cataloging in Publication Data
    An introduction to instructional services in academic libraries /
Elizabeth Connor, editor.
        p. cm.
    Includes bibliographical references and index.
    SBN: 978-0-7890-3707-7 (hbk: alk. paper)
    ISBN: 978-0-7890-3708-4 (pbk: alk. paper)
    1. Library orientation for college students—Case studies. 2. Academic
libraries—Relations with faculty and curriculum—Case studies. 3.
Information literacy—Study and teaching (Higher)—Case studies. I.
Connor, Elizabeth, MLS.
    Z711.25.C65I58 2008
    025.5'677-dc22

                                                        2007033978

ISBN 10: 0-7890-3707-6 (hbk)
ISBN 10: 0-7890-3708-4 (pbk)
ISBN 10: 0-2038-8936-3 (ebk)

ISBN 13: 978-0-7890-3707-7 (hbk)
ISBN 13: 978-0-7890-3708-4 (pbk)
ISBN 13: 978-0-2038-8936-7 (ebk)

Elizabeth Connor, MLS, AHIP
Editor

An Introduction to Instructional Services in Academic Libraries

*Pre-publication
REVIEWS,
COMMENTARIES,
EVALUATIONS . . .*

"These case studies and narratives provide new ideas and a strong foundation for successful library instruction. Librarians seeking to broaden or just liven up their instruction repertoire would benefit from this superb collection. Librarians will be inspired by their colleagues' success and will have many examples of tried and true techniques from which to choose."

Helene E. Gold, MLS, MEd
*Electronic Services Librarian/Associate Professor, Eckerd College,
St. Petersburg, Florida*

"Provides a current overview of attempts to integrate information literacy skills across curricula. Each chapter discusses a unique, contextualized approach to embedding information literacy instruction in curricular content. . . . An admirable job collecting a diverse, yet coherent, group of case studies—contributors speak with a common voice throughout the collection. . . . All librarians who administer or provide instructional services in academic settings will find something of value here."

Mark A. Spasser, PhD
*Director of Research Services,
Palmetto Health Richland,
Columbia, South Carolina*

More pre-publication
REVIEWS, COMMENTARIES, EVALUATIONS . . .

"If you are looking for detailed, practical examples of proven activities to use in your academic library instructional services program, then this is the text to consult. . . . Clearly written. . . . A reliable resource for putting instruction ideas into action. . . . More than 'How I did it good' literature—contributors have been careful to provide thorough literature reviews, and in some cases, small scale evaluation research. . . . A welcome foundation for academic librarians to build upon their local concepts, adapt, and use in their libraries. The variety of academic institutions (community college, four-year liberal arts, health-related specific professions, etc.), and the diversity of faculty and students academic librarians serve are well represented in this text. . . . A resource the instructional services librarian should not be without."

Lorna Peterson, PhD
Associate Professor,
University at Buffalo

"All librarians have to teach, but librarians in academic institutions have to teach more advanced information literacy skills than most. Here is a score of real-life reports of such instruction in a wonderful variety of methods, models, and media."

Michelynn McKnight, PhD, AHIP
Assistant Professor,
School of Library and Information Science,
Louisiana State University

An Introduction
to Instructional
Services in Academic
Libraries

CONTENTS

PART C. LIBRARY INSTRUCTION IN HEALTH SCIENCES UNIVERSITY SETTINGS

ABOUT THE EDITOR

Elizabeth Connor, MLS, AHIP, is Associate Professor of Library Science and Science Liaison at the Daniel Library of The Citadel, the Military College of South Carolina. Since earning her MLS at the State University College at Geneseo in 1978, Ms. Connor has worked as a community college librarian, medical librarian at teaching hospitals and medical schools in three states (Maryland, Connecticut, and South Carolina), and two foreign countries (Kingdom of Saudi Arabia and Commonwealth of Dominica), and is employed as an academic librarian at the Military College of South Carolina in Charleston. She is a distinguished member of the Academy of Health Information Professionals (AHIP), serves as the book review editor of *Medical Reference Services Quarterly,* and co-edits *Journal of Electronic Resources in Medical Libraries*. Research interests relate to how scientists develop habits of mind and how case studies can be used to engage and sustain science learning, especially in undergraduates. Recent publications include *A Guide to Developing End User Education Programs in Medical Libraries; Planning, Renovating, Expanding, and Constructing Library Facilities in Hospitals, Academic Medical Centers, and Health Organizations; An Introduction to Reference Services in Academic Libraries;* and *Evidence-Based Librarianship: Case Studies and Active Learning Exercises.*

CONTRIBUTORS

Laura Aaron, PhD, RT (R)(M)(QM), is Assistant Professor in the College of Nursing and Program Director of the Radiologic Technology Program at Northwestern State University of Louisiana in Shreveport.

Shelley Arlen, MA, Library Science, **MA,** English, **MA,** Anthropology, (shelarl@uflib.ufl.edu), is Interim Assistant Director for Public Services at George A. Smathers Libraries at the University of Florida in Gainesville.

James Andrew Buczynski, MLIS, (james.buczynski@senecac.on. ca), holds an MLIS and BA in Urban Studies from McGill University and is employed as Campus Librarian (Seneca@York Library and Computing Commons) at Seneca College of Applied Arts and Technology in Toronto, Ontario, Canada.

Joanna M. Burkhardt, MLS, MA, BA, (jburkhardt@mail.uri.edu), is Professor and Head Librarian at the University of Rhode Island Providence Campus Library. She coordinates the Information Literacy program at the Providence Campus.

Leslie Bussert, MLIS, (lbussert@uwb.edu), is Reference and Instruction/Ethics & Humanities Librarian at the University of Washington Bothell (UWB).

Sally Carroll-Ricks, MLS, MM, AHIP, (scarroll@tlu.edu), is Assistant Professor at Blumberg Memorial Library at Texas Lutheran University, Seguin. Formerly, Ms. Carroll-Ricks was Head Librarian at Northwestern State University of Louisiana's Nursing Education Center Library.

Merrie Davidson, MLS, (merdavi@uflib.ufl.edu), is Psychology/Sociology Librarian at George A. Smathers Libraries at the University of Florida in Gainesville.

An Introduction to Instructional Services in Academic Libraries

Chelsea Dinsmore (chedins@uflib.ufl.edu) is International Documents Librarian at George A. Smathers Libraries at the University of Florida in Gainesville.

Anthony J. Frisby, PhD, (Tony.Frisby@jefferson.edu), is Director of Academic and Instructional Support and Resources at Scott Memorial Library of Thomas Jefferson University in Philadelphia.

Carmen Genuardi, MLIS, (carmen.genuardi@senecac.on.ca), is Health Sciences Librarian at Seneca Libraries at Seneca College of Applied Arts and Technology at King Campus in Ontario, Canada.

Diane Graham-Webb, MSN, RN, CNE, is Associate Professor in the College of Nursing at Northwestern State University of Louisiana.

Jill Gremmels, MLS, (jigremmels@davidson.edu), former College Librarian at Wartburg College in Waverly, Iowa, is now Library Director at Davidson College in Davidson, North Carolina.

Tammy S. Guerrero, MLS, (guerrero@calumet.purdue.edu), is Assistant Professor of Library Science at Purdue University Calumet in Hammond, Indiana.

Kristin M. Harkin, MA, is Assistant Director of Orientation at Purdue University Calumet in Hammond, Indiana.

Patricia C. Higginbottom, MLIS, AHIP, (phiggin@uab.edu), is Assistant Professor and Associate Director for Public Services at Lister Hill Library of the Health Sciences at the University of Alabama at Birmingham.

Beth Hill, MLS, (bhill@kmc.org), is Library Manager at Kootenai Medical Center in Coeur d'Alene, Idaho. Formerly, Ms. Hill was Assistant Professor, Reference Librarian, and Outreach and Distance Education Librarian at University of Idaho Library in Moscow.

Christopher V. Hollister, MLS, (cvh2@buffalo.edu), is Information Literacy Librarian at Oscar A. Silverman Undergraduate Library at the University of Buffalo in Buffalo, New York.

Emily Johnson, PhD, (johnson.emil@uwlax.edu), is Chair, Psychology and Director, General Education at the University of Wisconsin-LaCrosse.

Kathryn E. Kerdolff, MLIS, AHIP, (KKerdo@lsuhsc.edu), is Distance Education Coordinator and School of Medicine Liaison at

Isché Library at Louisiana State University Health Sciences Center in New Orleans.

Daniel G. Kipnis, MSI, (dan.kipnis@jefferson.edu), is Senior Education Services Librarian at Scott Memorial Library of Thomas Jefferson University in Philadelphia.

Maureen M. Knapp, MA, (MKnapp@lsuhsc.edu), is School of Allied Health Liaison and School of Graduate Studies Liaison at Isché Library at Louisiana State University Health Sciences Center in New Orleans.

Margy MacMillan, MLS, BA, (MMacMillan@mtroyal.ca) is Instructional Services Librarian at Mount Royal College in Calgary, Alberta, Canada.

Iona R. Malanchuk, **MLS, MA,** (ionmala@ufl.edu), is Head, Education Library at the University of Florida in Gainesville.

Lucretia McCulley, MSLS, (lmcculle@richmond.edu), is Head, Outreach and Instruction Services at the University of Richmond Libraries in Richmond, Virginia.

Debbie Moore, MSN, RN, is Assistant Professor in the College of Nursing at Northwestern State University of Louisiana.

Megan Oakleaf, MLS, PhD, (moakleaf@syr.edu), formerly the Librarian for Instruction and Undergraduate Research at North Carolina State University in Raleigh, is Assistant Professor in the iSchool at Syracuse University.

Suzan Parker, MLIS, (sparker@uwb.edu), is the Reference and Instruction/Social Sciences Librarian at the University of Washington Bothell (UWB).

Susan T. Pierce, EdD, RN, CNE, is Associate Professor in the College of Nursing at Northwestern State University of Louisiana.

Diane Prorak, MLS, (prorak@uidaho.edu), is Reference Librarian at the University of Idaho Library in Moscow.

Cristine Prucha, MALS, MA, (prucha.cris@uwlax.edu) is Information Literacy Librarian at Murphy Library at the University of Wisconsin-LaCrosse.

Justin Robertson, MLIS, AHIP, (jroberts@bbl.usouthal.edu) is Assistant Director of Public Services at the Biomedical Library at the University of South Alabama in Mobile.

Petra M. Roter, PhD, (roterp@uwosh.edu), is Vice Chancellor for Student Affairs at the University of Wisconsin Oshkosh. Formerly, Dr. Roter was Senior Student Affairs Officer at the University of Wisconsin-LaCrosse.

Linda Roussel (lroussel@usouthal.edu) is Clinical Assistant Professor in the College of Nursing at the University of South Alabama in Mobile.

Ellen Sayed (els2026@qatar-med.cornell.edu) is employed by Weill Cornell Medical College in Doha, Qatar. Formerly, she was Head of Collection Management at the Biomedical Library at the University of South Alabama in Mobile.

Randall Schroeder, MA, (randall.schroeder@wartburg.edu), is Information Literacy Coordinator and Librarian at Wartburg College in Waverly, Iowa.

Julia Shaw-Kokot, MSLS, AHIP, (jsk@med.unc.edu), is Assistant Department Head, User Services at the Health Sciences Library of the University of North Carolina at Chapel Hill.

Debra Shelton, MSN, APRN-CS, CNA, OCN, CNE, EdD, (sheltond@nsula.edu), is Associate Professor in the College of Nursing at Northwestern State University of Louisiana.

Mark Szarko, MSLIS, MA, (szarko@mit.edu), is Instruction Coordinator for the Humanities Library at the Massachusetts Institute of Technology (MIT). Formerly, he was Humanities Librarian at the University of Washington Bothell (UWB).

K. T. L. Vaughan, MSLS, (KT_Vaughan@unc.edu), is Pharmacy Librarian at the Health Sciences Library and Clinical Assistant Professor in the School of Pharmacy of the University of North Carolina at Chapel Hill.

Martha E. Verchot, MS, MLS, (mverchot@uab.edu), is Associate Professor, Reference Librarian, and Senior Web Editor at Lister Hill Library of the Health Sciences at the University of Alabama at Birmingham.

Lee A. Vucovich, MS, MLS, AHIP, (lvucovi@uab.edu), is Instructor and Assistant Director for Reference Services at Lister Hill Library of the Health Sciences at the University of Alabama at Birmingham.

Janelle L. Wertzberger, MLIS, MA, (jwertzbe@gettysburg.edu), is Director of Reference & Instruction at Musselman Library, Gettysburg College, Gettysburg, Pennsylvania.

Nancy J. Young, MLS, JD, (nyoung@uidaho.edu), is Reference and Instruction Librarian at the University of Idaho Library in Moscow.

Preface

Teaching is an inherent part of reference services provided by librarians. Over time, the librarian's teaching role, especially in academic settings, has become more formalized and involves considerable preparation, collaboration, and understanding of pedagogical principles that underpin effective instruction. The shift away from showing and telling toward using active learning approaches such as problem solving, case studies, and small group discussions has resulted in library sessions that engage participants by requiring critical thinking and application of new knowledge beyond the assignment at hand.

How do librarians become effective teachers? Faced with planning and teaching library instruction sessions, some librarians may experience degrees of fear and trepidation. Other librarians relish their time on the instructional stage and may be reluctant to alter time-honored traditions and teaching methods. Some institutions give librarians "one shot" to orient and teach groups of incoming students. In other academic settings, librarians have been successful teaching first-year experience courses and/or integrating library instruction into course curricula. Such experiences offer unparalleled insight into how students use the literature to learn new material and complete course assignments beyond the basic skills necessary to navigate library catalogs and article databases. Some studies have examined and systematically reviewed the effectiveness of library instruction[1] and assessed learning outcomes in information literacy instruction.[2] Librarians can learn a great deal from practice-based research published in the library literature and related fields.

This book presents case studies from a variety of academic library settings in the United States and Canada of interest and value to experienced and inexperienced librarians alike. This book is divided into three main sections (college libraries, university libraries, and health sciences university settings). This work is supplemented by exercises

An Introduction to Instructional Services in Academic Libraries

that can be used in library education programs, staff development, on-the-job training, and continuing education situations.

The chapters in Part I relate to library instruction in small to medium-sized college library settings. Wartburg College colleagues Gremmels and Schroeder report the integration of information literacy into the college curriculum. Buczynski and Genuardi use a train-the-trainer approach to implementing information literacy instruction at a Canadian community college. McCulley relates the development of basic library skills workshops as a graduation requirement at the University of Richmond. Wertzberger uses clicker technology to enhance the learning of library skills at Gettysburg College.

The chapters in Part II involve library instruction in university libraries. Bussert, Parker, and Szarko at the University of Washington Bothell relate collaborative efforts to use problem-based learning methods in an interdisciplinary course. At the University of Idaho, the development of Core Discovery courses prompted librarians Young, Prorak, and Hill to develop an information literacy tutorial and research guides. Librarian Guerrero and colleague Harkin collaborate in the planning of freshman orientation at Purdue University Calumet. Hollister uses a compelling case study to spark critical thinking in University of Buffalo students. Johnson, Prucha, and Roter use problem-based learning in a freshman information literacy seminar at University of Wisconsin-LaCrosse. Arlen, Dinsmore, and Davidson use contemporaneous documents to bring library instruction alive to undergraduate students at the University of Florida. MacMillan collaborates with chemistry and journalism faculty members at Mount Royal College to incorporate information literacy principles into library instruction. Malanchuk works with University of Florida English-as-a-second-language students to impart confidence and skills mastery. Oakleaf explains the planning and development of a library tutorial at North Carolina State University. Burkhardt details information literacy instruction for nontraditional students at the University of Rhode Island.

Part III concerns library instruction in health sciences university settings. In their chapter about the University of Alabama at Birmingham's Lister Hill Library, Higginbottom, Vucovich, and Verchot detail how an education strategy team approach was used to extend teaching responsibilities to a wider group of health sciences librarians. Kerdolff and Knapp examine the effectiveness of library instruction delivered to medical students at Louisiana State University Health Sciences Center. Kipnis and Frisby explain the development of an information literacy curriculum for Thomas Jefferson University graduate students. Shaw-Kokot and Vaughan describe the development of online assignments for pharmacy students at the University of North Carolina at Chapel Hill. Carroll-Ricks and former colleagues at Northwestern State University of Louisiana explain the importance of information literacy instruction for nursing students. Robertson, Sayed, and Roussel give a fascinating glimpse into librarian involvement and leadership in distance nursing education at the University of South Alabama in Mobile.

Consistent themes throughout this work are that successful students are information literate and librarians contribute considerable energy, knowledge, and leadership to academic success. What can librarians do to help a typical student extend this basic set of skills (formulating questions, choosing databases, formulating search strategies) to other subjects and situations? How does an information-literate student become a lifelong learner? Challenges remain related to how best to teach information literacy skills to students hooked on Google.[3] Educational Testing Service (ETS) <http://www.ets.org/> issued some sobering results from their Information and Communication Technology (ICT) Literacy assessments <http://www.ets.org/Media/Products/ICT_Literacy/pdf/2006_Preliminary_Findings.pdf>. This literacy assessment asked test takers to define, access, evaluate, manage, integrate, create, and communicate information through the use of lifelike scenarios. Based on the pilot study administered at sixty-three high schools, two-year colleges, and four-year colleges in February 2006, ETS surmised that "few test takers demonstrated key ICT literacy skills" as evidenced by difficulties choosing a thesis statement related to a class assignment; evaluating a Web site for objectivity, authority, and timeliness; narrowing search results; and focusing on relevant information when making an argument. Rockman and Smith suggest ways these data can be used to assess knowledge.[4]

Use and adapt the ideas and approaches contained in this work to build, improve, and/or assess library instruction. Relate library instruction to the greater whole by working closely with and collaborating with other teaching faculty. Become involved in scholarship of teaching and learning activities on campus. Attend continuing education programs such as ACRL's information literacy immersion course <http://www.ala.org/acrl/events>. Think reflectively about what works and does not work well when teaching others. Incorporate assessment methods into instruction planning,[5] and continuously collect data about student learning outcomes and teaching effectiveness. Share your ideas and work products (handouts, syllabi, exercises) with others in cooperative and collaborative ways. The academic success and satisfaction of your faculty colleagues and students depend on it.

NOTES

1. Koufogiannakis, Denise and Wiebe, Natasha. "Effective Methods for Teaching Information Literacy Skills to Undergraduate Students: A Systematic Review and Meta-Analysis." *Evidence Based Library and Information Practice* 1, no. 3 (2006): 3-97.

2. Carter, Elizabeth and Jefferson, Renee N. "Collaborating on Information Literacy." In *Revisiting Outcomes Assessment in Higher Education,* edited by Peter Hernon, Robert E. Dugan, and Candy Schwartz. Westport, CT: Libraries Unlimited, 2006, pp. 303-325.

3. Martin, Pamela. "Google as Teacher: Everything Your Students Know They Learned From Searching Google." *College & Research Libraries News* 67, no. 2 (2006): 100-101.

4. Rockman, Ilene F. and Smith, Gordon W. "Information and Communication Technology Literacy: New Assessments for Higher Education." *College & Research Library News* 66, no. 8 (2005): 587-589.

5. Carter, Elizabeth W. "Outcomes Assessment in a College Library: An Instructional Case Study." In *Outcomes Assessment in Higher Education,* edited by Peter Hernon and Robert E. Dugan. Westport, CT: Libraries Unlimited, 2004, pp. 197-217.

Recommended Reading

Bilal, Dania and Kirby, Joe. "Differences and Similarities in Information Seeking: Children and Adults as Web Users." *Information Processing & Management* 38, no. 5 (2002): 640-670.

Cody, Dean E. "Critical Thoughts on Critical Thinking." *Journal of Academic Librarianship* 32, no. 4 (2006): 403-407.

Connor, Elizabeth. "Using Clinical Vignette Assignments to Teach Medical Informatics." *Medical Reference Services Quarterly* 22, no. 4 (2003): 31-44.

Connor, Elizabeth. "Engaging and Sustaining Information Fluency in Science Students." Paper presented at 2006 Annual Meeting of the Special Libraries Association, Baltimore, Maryland. Available: <http://units.sla.org/division/dbio/Baltimore/infofluency.pdf>. Accessed: November 1, 2006.

Fenci, Heidi and Scheel, Karen. "Engaging Students: An Examination of the Effects of Teaching Strategies on Self-Efficacy and Course Climate in a Nonmajors Physics Course." *Journal of College Science Teaching* 35, no. 1 (2006): 20-24.

Grassian, Esther. "Building on Bibliographic Instruction." *American Libraries* 35 (October 2004): 51-53.

Hutcherson, Norman B. "Library Jargon: Student Recognition of Terms and Concepts Commonly Used by Librarians in the Classroom." *College and Research Libraries* 65, no. 4 (2004): 349-354.

Islam, Ramona L. and Murno, Lisa Anne. "From Perceptions to Connections: Informing Information Literacy Program Planning in Academic Libraries through Examination of High School Library Media Curricula." *College & Research Libraries* 67, no. 6 (2006): 492-514.

Jones-Wilson, T. Michelle. "Teaching Problem-Solving Skills Without Sacrificing Course Content: Marrying Traditional Lecture and Active Learning in an Organic Chemistry Class." *Journal of College Science Teaching* 35, no. 1 (2005): 42-46.

Lang, James M. "Beyond Lecturing." *Chronicle of Higher Education* 53 (September 29, 2006): C1.

Munro, Karen. "Reading and Technology: The Bigger Picture." *College & Research Libraries News* 67, no. 5 (2006): 312-313.

Pullman, Ethan. "Experiencing ACRL's Immersion Program: Learning Outcomes for Future Participants." *College & Research Libraries News* 67, no. 10 (2006): 631-633.

Smith, Stefan A. "Designing Collaborative Learning Experiences for Library Computer Classrooms." *College & Undergraduate Libraries* 11, no. 2 (1994): 65-83.

Sutton, Shan and Knight, Lorrie. "Beyond the Reading Room: Integrating Primary and Secondary Sources in the Library Classroom." *Journal of Academic Librarianship* 32, no. 3 (2006): 320-325.

Walter, Scott. "Instructional Improvement: Building Capacity for the Professional Development of Librarians as Teachers." *Reference & User Services Quarterly* 25, no. 3 (2006): 213-218.

Ward, Dane. "Revisioning Information Literacy for Lifelong Meaning." *Journal of Academic Librarianship* 32, no. 4 (2006): 396-402.

Willis, Carolyn N. and Thomas, Wm. Joseph. "Students as Audience: Identity and Information Literacy Instruction." *Portal: Libraries and the Academy* 6, no. 4 (2006): 431-444.

Yu, Fei, Sullivan, Jan, and Woodall, Leith. "What Can Students' Bibliographies Tell Us? Evidence Based Information Skills Teaching for Engineering Students." *Evidence Based Library and Information Practice* 1, no. 2 (2006): 12-22.

PART A:
LIBRARY INSTRUCTION
IN COLLEGE LIBRARIES

Chapter 1

Creating an "Information Literacy Across the Curriculum" Program from Scratch

Jill Gremmels
Randall Schroeder

INTRODUCTION

In ten years, the information literacy program at Wartburg College has been transformed from a peripheral library service to a program central to the college's curriculum. Wartburg, a baccalaureate general college of 1,800 students, affiliated with the Evangelical Lutheran Church in America (ELCA), and located in Waverly, Iowa, is best known nationally for its music and athletics programs. The top six majors, in terms of enrollment, are business administration, communication arts, education, music, psychology, and biology. In 1994, when Jill Gremmels was hired as college librarian, the library was underutilized, unpopular with students and faculty, and disconnected from the educational enterprise. Library staff were unenthusiastic and considered information literacy a nonessential service. In addition, the library building was not conducive to information literacy activities. Gremmels was hired with an administrative mandate to "provide leadership for integration of information literacy into teaching and learning for students and faculty,"[1] and Randall Schroeder was brought on board a year later. By 2005, information literacy was the stated mission of the library as well as a formal part of the college's general education curriculum, and business in all areas of library service had boomed (see Figure 1.1). This case study takes a thematic approach in describing the transformation.

REDEFINING POSITIONS

In August 1994, the Wartburg Library had a new director, a vacant public services position, and the start of the academic year just a month away. To meet the immediate need and preserve flexibility, Gremmels decided to advertise locally for a temporary assistant public services librarian to work from September 1994 through May 1995. Duties would include reference, departmental liaison for book selection, helping with interlibrary loan overload, and supervising the curriculum library. A suitable candidate was found, and the year began.

The position announced in March 1995 was quite different. Titled "Information Literacy Librarian," it listed the following responsibilities:

> Develop and promote the library's information literacy program with its emphasis on project-centered, collaborative learning; work with classroom faculty to design and co-teach resource-based learning experiences; organize human, printed, and multimedia resources for training students, faculty, and staff in the use of campus information tools (in partnership with Computing Services); participate in the delivery of reference service, including one evening per week; oversee curriculum materials center; participate in library planning and direction-setting.[2]

As a result of this search, Schroeder began work in the summer of 1995. The next opportunity arose in 1999, although in an unfortunate way. In July, the senior public services librarian passed away unexpectedly. Again, a local search was done for a temporary person, and the job description was reworked in preparation for a search in the early months of 2000. The second information literacy librarian position was conceived as a partner to the first. Schroeder would coordinate instruction to groups (classes) and the new person would handle instruction to individuals (reference and consultations). As a result of this search, the second information literacy librarian joined the staff in the summer of 2000.

	Then (1994/1995 unless otherwise indicated)	**Now** (2005/2006 unless otherwise indicated)
Enrollment (FTE)	1,347	1,772
Information Literacy Sessions	20	135 (2004/2005)
Reference Questions	1,804 (1998/1999)	4,220 (2004/2005)
Circulation	34,052	48,714 (2004/2005)
Reference Librarian Available	Five days a week (Monday-Friday only)	Six days a week (Sunday-Friday)
Facility	Engelbrecht Library 42,000 sq. ft. underutilized	Vogel Library 71,000 sq. ft. heavily used
Library Staff (FTE)	8.5	9.5
Librarians (FTE)	4.5	5.5

FIGURE 1.1. The Wartburg Library—then and now.

The third information literacy librarian position was the result of the library's first personnel increase in over ten years. By this time, the library's Web page had become an integral part of instruction and service, so virtual instruction became the obvious area of coordination for this position. As a result of this search, the third information literacy librarian joined the staff in July 2005. Three of the library's 5.5 Full-Time Equivalent (FTE) librarians then held the official title of information literacy librarian, and the inexorable trend toward deploying human resources in direct support of the library's mission was evident.

THE END OF THE SELF-PACED WORKBOOK

Bibliographic instruction at Wartburg had long been conducted primarily through a self-paced workbook, created by a librarian in 1980. Updated annually, the workbook was modeled after materials developed at University of California at Los Angeles (UCLA) and Penn State University. Like many bibliographic instruction efforts of its day, it was completely tool-oriented, acquainting students with the card catalog, indexes and abstracts, bibliographies, and other kinds of material. A search strategy was recommended only in lesson fourteen, after the student had used the various tools and found his or her way around the collection. Students completed the workbook as part of a first-year general education course, but by the mid-1990s, changes in pedagogy, student learning styles, and libraries in general had made the workbook unpopular. By 1994, the librarians were already rethinking its use. New leadership and emerging concepts of information literacy would show the way to a different strategy.

DESIGNING A BUILDING TO SUPPORT INFORMATION LITERACY

In 1994, the Wartburg library facility comprised a 1956 core building with a 1972 wrap-around addition. By the late 1980s, the inadequacies of the building were already apparent, and in the early 1990s, an architect was engaged to draw up plans for another renovation and addition. The library staff were excited, but then their hopes were dashed when the Board of Regents decided the plans were not forward-looking enough to serve the college in the twenty-first century.

Gremmels and Schroeder were hired, in part, because of previous building experience. Soon after Gremmels' arrival, she and the then academic dean developed a vision statement for the library, with dual purposes: to define goals for the building project and to gauge faculty support. The fine-tuned and revised statement became the conceptual framework for the building program, issued in May 1996. Distinctly inspired by Barr and Tagg[3] and called *The Learner's Library: A Library for the Future* (1996), the program statement depicted a building with an information literacy foundation. (Please note that in the following excerpt, the emphasis is original):

> A library designed to produce learning differs from traditional libraries in a variety of ways. The mission of a learning library is to produce learning by creating *powerful public learning environments in which communities of learners discover and construct knowledge.* Librarians collaborate with faculty and students . . . to improve the quality of learning. Learning libraries specialize in "just-in-time" services to support the information literacy needs of learners. Faculty and librarians are designers of "deep"

learning experiences which begin in the library space and extend into the campus and the world. The learner's library is a *library for the future.*[4]

The planners realized that only in the library do learners, experts, and tools all come together. To those ends, flexibility and utility in design were emphasized. The desired ambience was described:

> The building should reflect the buzz of intellectual involvement. This is a space for humans to connect with each other and with information, and everything about it should be in the service of learning. People should feel welcome, comfortable, and stimulated in the building. . . .[5]

Perhaps the design decision that made other innovations possible was the choice to put the entire circulating collection in compact shelving on the lower level. In addition to a philosophy of "let the warehouse be a warehouse," the intention was to make the collection geographically close with an obvious arrangement to make it as easy as possible for users to find materials. The placement also had the advantage of leaving two other floors free for users and showing through architecture that the library was dedicated to people, not materials.

The new library, gutted and enlarged from 41,000 to 72,000 sq. ft., opened in September 1999. A large information laboratory, featuring eighty computers and the reference collection, occupies much of the main floor, adjacent to the service desk. Two classrooms, used exclusively for information literacy instruction, border the lab, allowing librarians to teach concepts and demonstrate sources in the classrooms, then send students out into the lab to work and, finally, reconvene to debrief the lesson.

The upper floor of the library is mostly user space, with six ten-person group study rooms, ten six-person rooms, lounge furniture in nooks and groupings, and a quiet study wing. The designers' goal was to support as many learning styles as possible, hence the variety in group spaces and the diversity of furniture in the quiet study wing: lounge furniture, tables, and even a few atypical carrels. There are also five individual study rooms for people who crave solitude.

INFORMATION LITERACY
AS THE LIBRARY'S MISSION

That the library's mission would have something to do with information literacy was never in doubt under the new leadership. The nature of the emphasis and the boldness of the statement, however, evolved over time. The 1996 *Learner's Library* document tied the library's mission to the college's and affirmed, "The library's mission is to prepare students to be lifelong learners who can and do solve information problems by answering five critical questions: (1) What do I need? (2) How do I find it? (3) Is it reliable? (4) What does it mean? and (5) How do I use it?"[6] This statement was a departure from vague boilerplate statements about "supporting the curriculum" so common in college libraries, but it still delineated a fairly narrow scope and claimed responsibility only for "preparing" students.

In 2001, the librarians wrote a fuller, more confident statement (see Appendix 1.1). Inspired by Barr and Tagg's[7] paradigm shift from "providing instruction" to "producing learning," the librarians explicitly claimed "educating information-literate lifelong learners" as the library's mission and expounded upon that claim in three principal statements: "Educating students is our priority. . . . Information literacy is our foundation. . . . Producing lifelong learners is our objective."[8] The document further clarified that this is the mission of the entire library, not just the public services or information literacy staff.

In preparation for the Best Practices Initiative application, the librarians wrote an information literacy mission statement (see Exhibit 1.1). Almost a manifesto, this statement outlines core beliefs about information literacy, its place in a Wartburg education, and the role of librarians and classroom faculty.

Revision of the General Education Program

In 1999 the faculty approved a sweeping revision of the nineteen-year-old general education program. Suddenly, the library teaching team faced a blank college curriculum page. The team realized it had a once-in-a-lifetime opening to infuse information literacy into the college's curriculum. The combination of administrative support for information literacy, a new building, and the revision of the general education curriculum resulted in a challenging opportunity for librar-

EXHIBIT 1.1. Information Literacy Mission Statement

Vogel Library's mission is to educate information-literate lifelong learners. Our information literacy program is the flagship of that effort, but other library operations also contribute toward this goal. The information literacy program is designed to embody leadership and visibility in promoting the library's mission of educating students. As such, our information literacy mission closely reflects that of the Library. We embrace the National Information Literacy Competency Standards for Higher Education <http://www.ala.org/ala/acrl/acrlstandards/informationliteracycompetency.htm> and that document's definition of information literacy: *"a set of abilities requiring individuals to 'recognize when information is needed and have the ability to locate, evaluate, and use effectively the needed information.'"*

We believe that information literacy is so fundamental that it is an integral part of the academic experience in and out of the classroom.

We believe course-integrated instruction connected with a real academic need is more effective than stand-alone information literacy courses or disconnected tours and library orientations.

We believe in a planned curriculum with distinct, sequenced information literacy content that allows practice and reinforcement without duplication.

We believe that our information literacy instruction and any subsequent activity must help to achieve a faculty member's course objectives.

We believe that professors and students must be guided toward the understanding that the librarians' goals are interconnected with their own course goals and curricular needs.

Above all, we emphasize the teaching of concepts over skills as a means to achieve our information literacy mission of educating information-literate lifelong learners.

We also educate individual students and faculty at the reference desk and in individualized consultations by appointment. We strive to make each of these encounters an educational experience. In these settings we reinforce information literacy concepts from prior instruction and give students further opportunities for guided practice.

ians and faculty to set a new course for information literacy, a course that might successfully overcome the languor of past practice and resistance to change.

If the classroom faculty were to be persuaded that a new Information Literacy Across the Curriculum (ILAC) program should become a general education requirement, the library instruction team had to demonstrate that ILAC would provide a quality program that would meet a need not previously met. As Lakos and Phipps pointed out, libraries can learn much from the business concept of "total quality management," which is defined by Oxford University Press's *A Dictionary of Business,* as "an approach to management that seeks to integrate all the elements of an organization in order to meet the needs and expectations of its customers."[9] Put another way by Lakos and Phipps, "libraries must transform themselves into organizations that support the values of quality and quality management."[10] The old general education program contained no formal information literacy requirements. The library was simply not an integral part of most courses. Faculty requests for instructional support were almost always the result of informal conversations with librarians. Furthermore, any given student might have similar lessons about reference sources in three different classes because three different faculty members requested the same instruction. Lessons had no logical sequence and were frequently repetitive. This situation stretched the patience of students, instructors, and librarians to the limit.

Campus-wide curriculum revisions can be vicious turf battles, but the librarians took advantage of their invitation to serve on the planning committees. It was a five-year process that witnessed one general education plan rejected by the full faculty before the current requirements, the Wartburg Plan of Essential Education, were approved in 1999. The plan required five classes of all students before graduation. These five classes were to be taken primarily during the first two years at Wartburg. Two of the required five classes—IS101: Asking Questions, Making Choices, and IS201: Diverse World—were to be created out of whole cloth. The other three Essential Education courses were already in the books. The Information Literacy coordinator secured an invitation to be on the design team for the IS101 class required of first-year students.

In addition, the Wartburg Plan of Essential Education required an information literacy strand in each major. The philosophy was that the information literacy needs of, for example, a biology major would differ from the needs of an art major. Each information literacy strand had to be reviewed and approved by the college's Educational Policies Committee. With librarians well integrated into the design process of the new curriculum, the creation of ILAC was secure. Other key aspects of ILAC success were the development of a curriculum map and the design of a rigorous assessment program to assure quality to the college community.

Using a Curriculum Map to Navigate Organizational Culture

As Lakos and Phipps pointed out, "libraries must develop internal organizational systems that enable successful assessment and evaluation of their services and processes to achieve positive outcomes for customers."[11] In other words, if a library is to make the case to infuse information literacy into any academic endeavor—a class, a departmental major, or a curriculum—the justification lies in a "culture of assessment." Frequently, a culture of assessment will be at odds with an institutional culture because it challenges long-held assumptions. Institutional culture represents the accumulated learning of the group; it is stable and difficult to change. Assessment within the program is a key lever for creating a culture of improvement and quality.[12] The ILAC team could guide students and classroom faculty with the curriculum map and prove the quality of the program with a culture of assessment.

In other words, ILAC's success at Wartburg College depended on achieving buy-in from classroom faculty. The buy-in was further complicated by institutional culture that did not necessarily value information literacy. The ILAC team had a limited opportunity to show its customers a full plan that would be rigorously assessed to show that it made a difference. A plan plus a culture of assessment shifted the institutional culture to a new paradigm.

The curriculum map[13] was created using the Information Literacy Competency Standards for Higher Education. The ILAC team created a committee composed of librarians and interested general education faculty to review every indicator and outcome to see where it was taught in the Wartburg General Education Program. A summary of the map was presented at a full faculty meeting in 2000. Some members of the faculty objected, saying that the summary did not provide enough details. At the following meeting of the full faculty, all were presented with the full twenty-two-page curriculum map. Some faculty responded that the map had too much detail. The ILAC team referred those faculty members to the previous summary. Despite some objections, the curriculum map was approved by the Wartburg College faculty and became the template of the ILAC program. The team knew, however, that it had a limited amount of time to convince reluctant faculty that ILAC would make a difference, even with a curriculum map.

Culture of Assessment

The proof of ILAC effectiveness lay in assessment. Best practices encourage direct assessment done at multiple times in multiple formats. Wartburg librarians embraced assessment, not to satisfy the administration or prepare for accreditation, but to gain important insights about the library and its new initiatives, particularly the information literacy program. Questions included,

- Does the information literacy instruction result in the desired outcomes?
- Do group lessons effectively meet student and classroom faculty needs?
- Are students able to apply in practice the concepts learned in the information literacy classroom?
- Do individual reference consultations and the library Web page strengthen the mission of the information literacy program?

Most important, perhaps, for a small college with limited resources, assessment also helps the library make informed decisions about the most effective use and placement of those resources. Creating a culture of assessment ensures that initiatives will be ongoing, iterative, and lasting in their impact.

The nature of the program makes ILAC's assessment different from others across-the-curriculum literacies; there is no single course dedicated solely to information literacy. Lessons are delivered in a partnership between library and classroom faculty. Librarians also work with and through the classroom faculty to deliver and assess instruction. Using this partnership, the librarians administer an information literacy pretest to new first-year students on the first day of fall term in the English composition classes and a posttest in the required sophomore seminar classes. The pretest/posttest sequence provides a baseline for librarians and classroom faculty to examine student information literacy achievement during the first year. Some individual classes are assessed through information-seeking logs to provide evidence of robust student search strategies and evaluation of information. Assessment in the majors occurs through posttests and evaluation of senior project bibliographies using primary trait analysis.

Change Is a Constant in the Culture of Assessment

The results of the assessment tools are reported to the appropriate committees on a regular basis. In addition, the ILAC coordinator writes and posts a report of direct assessment results on the library Web page.[14] Assessment lives up to its full potential only when its results are used to change and improve the delivery of instruction. The information literacy portion of IS101, Wartburg's foundational first-year class, is on its third iteration in five years because pretest results have indicated that student understanding of the information universe is changing, as indicated by the following:

- The first lesson was an Internet toolkit, but it became apparent over time that students were increasingly familiar with the Internet. This may seem self-evident now, but the reader should remember that the Internet has a very short history and that, even a few years ago, access at home or school could not be assumed.
- In response to pretest answers indicating difficulty selecting good subject headings for searches, the librarians changed the lesson to teach the role of overview sources and thesauri in choosing subject headings. Because of the required tie-in to convocations and the obscurity of convocation speakers, the lesson did not work as well in practice as hoped, and the response of IS101 faculty was not as positive as the librarians would have liked.

Pretest data also showed that, while students frequently used the Internet and were confident of their Internet searching abilities, their understanding of the information universe beyond the Internet was incomplete, especially print and scholarly resources. Another factor was anecdotal reports of overlap between the IS101 and the required English composition course lessons. Consequently, the IS101 lesson was revised yet again, to cover the information universe and a beginning strategy for evaluating information. It is currently tied to any information-gathering exercise chosen by the instructor. Changes were made to create the best ILAC lesson plans possible. Although it may seem that constant change would be problematic for the classroom faculty, it was welcomed as a visible sign that the ILAC team took its culture of assessment seriously. In a course-integrated program, librarians have limited opportunities to instruct.

CREDIBILITY ON CAMPUS AND OFF

As the program grew and gained some notoriety within librarianship, the librarians discovered an ironic trend: there continued to be some drag within the classroom faculty at the college. ILAC still had the benefit of early adopters in the teaching faculty, and there were some who did not see any utility to the ILAC program at all. The largest group, however, was the reluctant middle who, while not outwardly hostile to ILAC, were not very supportive.

That equation changed in 2002 when a team of three Wartburg librarians, the dean, and a professor applied for and were accepted to the Best Practices in Information Literacy Programming Invitational Conference in Atlanta. The conference, sponsored by Association of College & Research Libraries (ACRL), brought together ten academic libraries, of all types and sizes, which represented the best practices in information literacy. Participation in this elite event opened the doors to many other opportunities for Wartburg librarians to present aspects of the ILAC program to national audiences. Invitations to conferences sponsored by ACRL, Library Orientation Exchange (LOEX), Association of American Colleges and Universities, American Association for Higher Education, and Council of Independent Colleges cemented Wartburg's national reputation. It should be noted that the venues were not just for librarians but included conferences and workshops for classroom faculty and administrators.

Sometimes external validation is instrumental in gaining respect within an institution. The Best Practices conference and its aftermath appeared to give the ILAC program some "street cred" with Wartburg's own faculty. It is not unusual for classroom faculty to discuss information literacy needs in faculty and department meetings without any prompting from the librarians.

LESSONS LEARNED

One of the lessons learned is also the caveat for this section. There is always a context. Institutional culture can help or hinder a library's transformation, and, while cultures can change, there is a limit to what one can reasonably hope to achieve counterculturally. The wise leader makes a priority of discovering as much as possible about the culture and choosing carefully before committing to an institution. Wartburg's mostly egalitarian culture and a pivotal moment of readiness for change made a fertile field for innovation.

Leadership and vision are essential, and librarian leadership is the most important of all. Librarians are the people with information literacy specialties; they should not hesitate or wait to let their programs be defined by others. Seeking input judiciously is important, but too much involvement can slow down the process or derail it entirely.

Opportunities should be seized as they arise. At Wartburg, librarians got involved in efforts to revise the general education curriculum, thus positioning themselves to make sure an information literacy component was included. Schroeder was elected to and currently sits on the college's Educational Policies Committee, ensuring librarian input into curricular matters. Librarians were early and enthusiastic adopters of assessment, using it as intended to improve their own practice. In addition, their success with assessment made them campus leaders and pleased academic deans who had been their proponents.

Assessment of student learning is a formative, not summative activity; its purpose is feedback for improvement, not judgment. It should be embraced, not feared or loathed. Assessment may reveal that some lessons do not work as intended, but ignorance of that fact only obscures the problem and delays the solution. The use of assessment in information literacy shows librarians to be educators who face and overcome the same challenges as their peers in the classroom. It shows that information literacy makes a difference.

Finally, once an information literacy program has found its feet, librarians need to publish and speak at conferences and workshops. This is the same challenge that classroom faculty face in their own disciplines. It seems to be the quickest way to gain faculty respect, especially among those who are not information literacy enthusiasts.

APPENDIX 1.1
VOGEL LIBRARY MISSION STATEMENT

Vogel Library's mission is to educate information-literate lifelong learners. **This means:**

1. **Educating students is our priority.** It is the focus of all we do. While our information literacy program is the flagship, our more traditional library operations also contribute toward this goal:
   - Information literacy instruction provides an opportunity to make appropriate information choices and to evaluate the quality of information.
   - Reference service reinforces classroom learning in the context of answering individual questions and providing one-on-one guidance to students and staff.
   - Interlibrary loan gives students access to a world of materials and ideas.
   - Acquisitions/cataloging develops the collection which supports student and faculty learning.

   Wartburg librarians are partners with classroom faculty in the college's educational enterprise. Our information literacy expertise complements the subject specializations of classroom faculty to create an integrated learning environment for students.

2. **Information literacy is our foundation.** We embrace the National Information Literacy Competency Standards for Higher Education <http://www.ala.org/acrl/ilcomstan.html> and that document's definition of information literacy:

   . . . a set of abilities requiring individuals to "recognize when information is needed and have the ability to locate, evaluate, and use effectively the needed information."

   In keeping with the standards, we emphasize the teaching of enduring concepts, not skills that obsolesce with changes in the next version of familiar software.

3. **Producing lifelong learners is our objective.** We intend to instill and reinforce in our students the abilities and habits of information-literate lifelong learning. To evaluate and improve our performance, we continually create assessments that measure the capability of our alumni and current students in this area.

   The skills and knowledge we teach make Wartburg College graduates the future leaders and responsible citizens our country needs.

This is the library's contribution to the college's mission as expressed in the Wartburg College Catalog: challenging and nurturing students for lives of leadership and service as a spirited expression of their faith and learning.

NOTES

1. "Wartburg College 1994-95 Faculty Positions." *Chronicle of Higher Education,* January 5, 1994.

2. Wartburg College. "Notice of Faculty Position Vacancy," position announcement, March 7, 1995.

3. Barr, Robert B. and Tagg, John. "From Learning to Teaching—A New Paradigm for Undergraduate Education." *Change* (November/December 1995): 13-25.

4. Gremmels, Jill and Pence, James. *"The Learner's Library: A Library for the Future."* Waverly, IA: Wartburg College, 1996.

5. Ibid.

6. Ibid.

7. Barr and Tagg, *"From Learning to Teaching."*

8. Gremmels et al. "Vogel Library Mission Statement." Waverly, IA: Wartburg College, 2001.

9. *A Dictionary of Business.* Oxford University Press, 2002.

10. Lakos, Amos and Phipps, Shelley. "Creating a Culture of Assessment: A Catalyst for Organizational Change." *Portal: Libraries and the Academy* 4 (2004): 345-361.

11. Ibid.

12. Ibid.

13. Gremmels, Jill, Lehmann, Karen, and Schroeder, Randall. "Vogel Library Curriculum Map of the *Information Literacy Competency Standards for Higher Education.*" Waverly, IA: Wartburg College, 2003. Available: <http://www.wartburg.edu/library/infolit/>. Accessed: March 12, 2006.

14. Schroeder, Randall. "ILAC Assessment at Vogel Library." Waverly, IA: Wartburg College, 2005. Available: <http://www.wartburg.edu/library/infolit/>. Accessed: March 12, 2006.

Chapter 2

Experiential Learning: Teach Them and They Will Come

James Andrew Buczynski
Carmen Genuardi

INTRODUCTION

Information literacy goals need not be limited to the parameters of the information literacy standards developed by the Association of College & Research Libraries (ACRL). These standards can be used to meet library "bottom line" goals such as increasing *collection usage.* "Build it and they will come," the one-sided library philosophy of program accreditation boards everywhere, was challenged at Seneca College of Applied Arts and Technology in Toronto, Ontario, Canada. Programs had a "right" to adequate holdings but there would be a "responsibility" attached to using the collections. Using information literacy as the catalyst for combining collections with curricula, faculty were given professional development mini-sessions at the beginning of each semester and insight into integrating library research and resources into their courses. All Seneca students, each September, are given an introductory class to review research basics and orient them to their discipline's literature. When compared with work completed by students in years prior to the instruction classes, faculty reported that students were integrating a greater variety and diversity of sources that were more authoritative, more current, and more international in scope. This information literacy program has successfully increased collection usage and increased student success in program coursework.

An Introduction to Instructional Services in Academic Libraries

SETTING

Founded in 1967, Seneca College of Applied Arts and Technology is Canada's largest community college, with approximately 700 faculty, 90,000 part-time students, and 17,000 full-time students. The college has the largest enrollment of international students attending college in Canada and more than seventy-five countries are represented in Seneca's student population, mirroring the diverse cultural mosaic of Toronto. The college's ten campuses are spread throughout the Toronto (Ontario, Canada) and the greater metropolitan area. Students can choose from more than 260 careers and receive academic foundation, workplace experience, and practical training needed to succeed. Beginning in 2002, the college began offering baccalaureate degree programs in addition to diploma, post-diploma, and graduate certificate programs. Ontario's twenty-four community colleges have a long history of being market-driven, occupation-focused, and balanced between skills training with theory, and their graduates are behind much of Ontario's economy. In terms of analogy, community colleges today serve the same role of preparing people for work as high schools did in the early twentieth century in a less technology-intensive era.

LIBRARY DESCRIPTION

Each of the college's four main campuses has its own library. Professional staff includes ten librarians and thirty-three library technicians. All librarians have faculty status and participate in library and college committees. No technicians are involved in information literacy activities. Not all librarians have teaching or instruction responsibilities. At the time of this writing, information literacy is not mentioned directly in the college's mission statement, strategic plans, or annual operational plans. In practice it falls under the college's strategic commitment to providing "quality education experiences" for all students and student "retention/success" goals and objectives. Information literacy is incorporated into various courses in each academic program under the umbrella of "employability skills." Graduates of each program are expected to demonstrate skills and knowledge about: communication, numeracy, critical thinking and problem solving, information literacy, and interpersonal/intrapersonal skills. Information literacy curricular learning outcomes and teaching practices at Seneca vary by program, department, school, and campus. Some schools or programs have a history of focusing on information literacy while others do not. Some professors have taken the initiative to incorporate information literacy objectives into their courses and have strong relationships with their liaison librarians, while others assume it is covered elsewhere and that their students already have the skills and knowledge. There are no standard information literacy practices across the college, unlike information technology basic skills and knowledge, which are delivered via a required first-year course.

Seneca Libraries has emphasized information literacy in its mission statement:

> To enhance and support the varied teaching and learning, research and information needs of our scholarly, academic community through innovative services, information resources, and the promotion of information literacy and lifelong learning.

Seneca Libraries' staff have worked actively and cooperatively with faculty to address information literacy concerns. Given this needs-based approach to increasing information literacy instruction opportunities, it is not surprising that implemented solutions are on a continuum from in-library tours/demonstrations to in-class lectures and demonstrations to hands-on computer lab workshops. Given limited staffing and workshop computing facility access, a Web-based information literacy tutorial was developed and customized to meet the needs of various programs. The "Research for Success" tutorial is widely used in large first-year courses at Seneca College and is licensed for use at other Ontario community colleges as well. Information literacy participation rates vary from school-wide (e.g., School of Business and all its programs) to program-wide to single courses. The point of entry is generally through first-year courses, and through final year courses with significant literature research review outcomes.

PROJECT PARTICIPANTS

The Corporate Communications[1] Program is run by the School of English and Liberal Studies, and prepares graduates for public relations management careers in business, government agencies, public relations consultancies, professional associations, and nonprofit organizations. Graduates generally begin their careers in entry-level public relations and promotional positions before moving on to communication careers in areas such as issues management, crisis communication, employee relations, fund-raising, media relations, financial relations, government relations, speech writing, special event planning, and spokesperson training. Some graduates apply the knowledge gained in this program to careers other than public relations. The program is the only public relations program in Canada and one of only eleven in North America to be certified by the Public Relations Society of America (PRSA), the world's largest professional organization for public relations practitioners. It is also officially recognized by the Canadian Public Relations Society and the International Association of Business Communicators. The program is one of the smallest programs at Seneca College, with a median annual enrollment of 105 students.

The program employs active experiential learning and emphasizes excellent management, research, writing, technical, speaking, and social skills, allowing public relations graduates to become productive quickly, without requiring much supervision. Students are expected to work productively and closely with each other as well as the professors to learn the skills, and build the knowledge base necessary to pursue their chosen careers. The curriculum has been developed based on the recommendations and standards of the PRSA and the International Public Relations Association. Research skills and knowledge play a pivotal role in the program.

Corporate Communications students are generally found to have already completed an undergraduate degree prior to entry into the program. They usually possess good information research skills and experience, compared with the average student at Seneca College. Like many students new to a discipline, these students lack a cognitive map of the discipline's structure, and are relatively unaware of key research tools and core titles of professional trade and research literature. Offered at the college's technology-centric campus, Seneca@York, the program is supported by extensive library collections, that were started in 1999, with the opening of the campus. The collections are strong in current resources, with some weaknesses in older, out-of-print materials. Fortunately, the Seneca@York campus is located on the main campus of York University, and Seneca students have limited access to York University's many libraries with relevant holdings dating back over four decades.

PROJECT DESCRIPTION, PLANNING, AND DELIVERY

Program accreditation requires among other things, a significant investment in information resources to support the curriculum. Seneca's extensive collections include monographs, serials, periodicals, practitioner manuals, and audiovisual materials. Many of the titles are not held by other academic libraries, both locally and regionally. The program's faculty has continually lobbied for a larger funding allocation to develop broad and deep collections to support their multidisciplinary curriculum. In fall 2003, a multiyear collection development and management plan[2] was developed and approved, to address the goals of the faculty.

Given the magnitude of the commitment, years of past experience servicing this program, and the powerful gravity of Google and its peers, information literacy was identified as critical to the success of the collection development initiative. "Build it and they will come," the one-sided library philosophy of program accreditation boards everywhere, was challenged by Seneca Libraries. The program had a "right" to adequate holdings but there would be a "responsibility" attached to using the collections. Low use would trigger cuts to the funding allocation. Outreach initiatives could be deployed to ensure the collections were used, and were not just for "show" or "just-in-case." Information literacy, faculty professional development, and communication with faculty were vital to the collection development initiative's success.

The faculty wanted the students to rapidly acquire research skills and experience, while Seneca Libraries sought to maximize the use of expensive collections. Information literacy can do both. Since August 2003, corporate communications faculty have been given professional development mini-sessions at the beginning of each semester, lists of key library resources (search aids, periodicals, practitioner manuals, etc.), and insight into integrating library research and resources into their courses. All corporate communications students, each September, are given an introductory class to review research basics and orient them to corporate communications related literature.

Seneca Libraries sought to integrate information literacy into numerous courses where appropriate, in a face-to-face setting with students. A constant theme in information literacy research and best practices literature is the concept of "timing instruction" to the point of need in a course.[3,4] For students to be motivated they need to see a clear link between information literacy instruction and classroom assignments.[5] As Mackey and Jacobson explain:

> We are at a juncture in information literacy education that demands the development of fully integrated, comprehensive programs. If our students are going to build on a foundation of information skills, they must continue to have experience with information literacy activities throughout their college careers.[6]

ACRL's *Information Literacy Competency Standards for Higher Education* demonstrate the progressive nature of acquiring information literacy skill sets and knowledge.[7] It is not something that can be acquired in one lecture or one course. In the planning phase, it was obvious that from a practical perspective, multiple class sessions were not possible. Class meeting time is limited and synchronizing schedules is almost impossible given the range of librarian responsibilities and workloads.

Two solutions were used to address this challenge. First, Seneca librarians would orient faculty to library resources, on a regular basis, to ensure that they could successfully integrate information literacy skills and knowledge into their classes when and wherever appropriate. A "train-the-trainers" mind-set was used. At the beginning of each semester, librarians attend corporate communications faculty meetings in order to offer information literacy professional development sessions, outline new library initiatives, overview both the corporate communications collections and newly purchased materials, and finally request suggestions for material purchases. These meetings are especially useful to new faculty and part-time faculty. Rather than claiming information literacy as the domain of Seneca Libraries, or the domain of librarians, it was set free. Librarians would take a supporting role in aiding faculty who were interested in adding information literacy outcomes to their courses.

Second, an information literacy foundational class was developed and delivered to all incoming students in CCM 747: Introduction to Research. The description for this course reads:

> This mostly self-directed subject provides an opportunity for students to explore qualitative and quantitative public research techniques, and decide which method would be most appropriate for their own research project. Students will become investigators and develop a problem statement and methodology, and construct a research proposal.

In the following semester students use their research skills and knowledge to actually carry out a research project from the beginning to the publication stage. The class was developed to encourage students to develop their own concepts of information literacy. Building on the program's experiental learning philosophy,[8] the one-shot two-hour class provides students with the solid foundation necessary for self-directed and peer-based information literacy learning.[9] Experiential learning in its simplest form is learning by doing or from experience, and is closely related to the concept of active-learning.[10,11] Consequently, the reference desk becomes an extension of the classroom where information literacy skills are supported through teaching, and students are encouraged to be active participants in the research process. This self-directed learning mind-set is especially important for this group of students who will find that their careers require continuous investment in research capabilities.

The two-hour CCM 747 information literacy class uses a combination of lecture, demonstrations, and hands-on active learning exercises in a computer lab classroom in the library. Students are provided with lists of core periodical titles and online information services for the discipline and the profession. The exercises address the course's first assignment as well as deliverables required in other courses. The learning objectives include the ability to:

- identify keywords, synonyms, and related terms for the information needed;
- identify potential authoritative sources of information, given the discipline's poor bibliographic control and multidisciplinary nature;

- efficiently retrieve information from identified sources, both on-line and in the real world;
- identify the purpose and audience of potential sources;
- differentiate between primary and secondary sources; and
- broaden the information-seeking process beyond local resources.

Corporate communications, and more specifically the specialty of public relations, is a difficult discipline to cover from an information literacy perspective. The literature has poor bibliographic control, is not available through traditional commercial publication channels, and is not collected by libraries extensively. Many key sources remain unavailable online and consequently are "invisible" to students. In an information universe chock full of search engines, the lack of searchable indexes makes teaching information literacy skills to this group of students quite challenging. Program faculty initially tried to address this challenge by demanding that all corporate communications materials be held physically separate from the library's general collection. They actually tried to put it all into the "reserve collection," behind the circulation desk. In time, however, they began to recognize that the students would not learn the research skills they needed if this practice continued. Information literacy instruction could not be "engineered" out of the curriculum.

Besides face-to-face instruction and practice exercises, students are provided with lists of core periodical titles as well as professional practice manuals to provide starting points to identify relevant sources needed in their learning and future professional activities. Students are also taught how and when to broaden the information-seeking process beyond local resources to include, for example, other libraries, and people with specific expertise, corporate operation responsibilities, and experience. Many of these students will go on to pursue a master's degree in public relations, and it is not surprising that they often asked whether additional public relations education contributed to career success. Clearly, talking to practicing professionals will yield more current, locally context-sensitive, and deeper answers to the question than searching trade literature. Building a knowledge base of contacts for information, advice, and assistance is vital to career success. Students leave the information literacy class knowing who and where they can go to seek assistance in identifying and accessing information resources needed in their assignments and self-learning activities.

RESULTS

Seneca Libraries has started to develop a culture of assessment in information literacy activities. As a result, the initiative was planned and delivered without a formal assessment plan. The information literacy project focused on improving both usage of the quickly growing corporate communications collections and the quality of student work submitted to corporate communications faculty. In terms of collection usage, circulation statistics were used to measure the success of faculty and student information literacy initiatives. After the first year, the usefulness of the measure was challenged. Anecdotal evidence from circulation staff, reshelvers, and the reference desk staff suggested that the formerly "dusty" materials were being used, compared with the past where only a few selected periodical titles were used. Materials, however, were not being signed-out, rather they were consulted in-house. Although the vast majority of the collection circulates, students, working in teams, used the materials in the library. Signing materials out is the exception rather than the rule. Students do not want to carry books with them. Circulation statistics are a key accountability measure for the library, and this behavior is common among students in many programs with the exception of computer studies. At this time, the library's Integrated Library System (ILS) lacks the functionality to efficiently scan items being sorted for reshelving, and the library lacks the staffing necessary to do so. Possible solutions remain in the committee debate phase. As a surrogate measure for usage, faculty feedback about student success has value in assessing usage.

Student success in the corporate communications program was the key motivation for faculty support of the information literacy initiative, both from the standpoint of their own professional development, the ability to integrate information literacy outcomes into their courses, and improving the quality of work submitted by students. Meeting with corporate communications faculty each semester provided a venue for both continuing professional development centering on library resources and services, and discussion about student usage of library resources. When compared with work completed by students in years prior to the instruction classes, longtime faculty and one part-time instructor reported that students submitted vastly improved literature reviews. They integrated a greater variety and diversity of sources, and used more authoritative, more current, and more international sources. As a broad generalization, faculty reported that students were more "turned on" to research, a mind-set considered pivotal to academic success.

Faculty said that students reported a better grasp of the big research picture compared with their university experience where libraries were a place to just get "something on your topic," copy, print, and "get out." Students really appreciated getting to know "their librarian." It greatly influenced the quality of their library experience. It is not uncommon to receive thank-you letters via e-mail from students after the class, at the end of the semester or upon graduation from the program.

Reference desk staff reported that the sophistication of reference questions from corporate communications students, improved since the information literacy classes were launched in 2002. Student motivation was vastly superior and there was less resistance to suggestions of using specific print resources. Unfortunately, those students who did not attend the class or tuned out, lagged behind their peers.

Seneca@York campus librarians discontinued the use of formal one-page instruction evaluations in 2002, due to low response rates and the generally poor attitude of students toward them. Students are unwilling to reflect and fill out a paper-based survey, and bolt for the door. Given this assessment challenge, librarians delivering the class ask questions as a form of formative assessment and walk around to each and every student during the hands-on portion of the class to make sure they have grasped the essential concepts. Online real-time in-class surveys are being considered given their success at Seneca in distance education live online classroom environments. The ability for students to anonymously answer short polls about how the class is going (too fast, too slow, I'm lost, That's amazing!, I have a question, etc.), as it is being delivered, is extremely attractive as an assessment instrument.

CHALLENGES

The corporate communications information literacy program faces three challenges: assessment, part-time faculty buy-in, and gaining access to students in upper-level classes. Informal assessment suggests faculty/student satisfaction and that the program meets its objectives in terms of collection usage and student success. What remains unknown is how far students and faculty are progressing in developing their information literacy skills and knowledge. They might be satisfied because they are unaware of the full breadth of information literacy competencies to be mastered. Future assessment initiatives will investigate student and faculty citation activities, to gain deeper insight into how and how much of the library's collections is being used by students and faculty in instruction and learning settings.

Although full-time faculty recognize the value of the information literacy program and their roles building upon it, part-time faculty generally assume information literacy has been covered in full elsewhere in the program obviating their need to address the topic in their courses. Overcoming this mind-set is difficult, since face-to-face time with these faculty is so limited. They are usually not around on campus other than to teach and hold office hours. Reaching these practicing professionals will require creative solutions not yet devised.

Librarians could prepare and deliver mini-workshops or lectures for upper-level courses, in efforts to address assignment specific information literacy needs and to improve student success. Besides the difficulty of synchronizing schedules, some faculty believe that students need to learn on their own at this point in the program. Although this is largely true, certain assignments are challenging enough to cause traffic jams at the reference desk as groups of students seek assistance with research questions that require multistep research pathways and access to resources outside of Seneca Libraries. Obtaining face time with the class, often only requiring less than half a period, would minimize student and reference staff frustration.

CONCLUSION

Information literacy goals need not be limited to the parameters of the ACRL Information Literacy Competency Standards.[12] They can be used to meet library "bottom line" goals such as increasing collection usage. Academic libraries hold an iconic status in the culture of higher education. Accountability is a new concept to many administrators. The old "build it and they will come" paradigm has been discarded with the emergence of an environment of per capita funding declines and exponentially increasing numbers of information products. Defining success and proving it has been achieved, plays an increasing role in setting the funding of libraries. The role of libraries and librarians in student success and faculty success goes a long way to explaining the importance of libraries to the institutions that fund them.

The information literacy program has successfully increased collection usage, motivated students and faculty to acquire information literacy competencies, improved the learning experience of students, and increased student success in program coursework. The project serves as a model for sharing responsibility for teaching and learning information literacy skills among students, program faculty, and librarians. The "one-shot" information literacy class is routinely discredited by librarians as ineffective at meeting information literacy goals and objectives, but is better than nothing. This project demonstrates that a one-shot class can be successful, if limited in scope to basic research concepts contextualized to a specific discipline, and if students are given the opportunity to develop their own concepts of information literacy, through experience.

NOTES

1. *Corporate Communications Program.* Seneca College of Applied Arts & Technology, 2006. Available: <http://www.senecac.on.ca/fulltime/CCMC.html>. Accessed: February 13, 2006.

2. *Corporate Communications Collection Profile Year 1.* Seneca Libraries. Seneca College of Applied Arts & Technology, 2004. Available: <http://library .senecacollege.ca/Info_For_Faculty/Collection_Development/Collection_Profiles/ YorkCorpCommProfileYear1.pdf>. Accessed: February 13, 2006.

3. Grafstein, Ann. "A Discipline-Based Approach to Information Literacy." *Journal of Academic Librarianship* 28 (July 2002): 197-204.

4. Thomas, William J. "Department-Integrated Information Literacy: A Middle Ground." *Southeastern Librarian* 53 (Fall 2005): 38-42.

5. Small, Ruth V., Zakaria, Nasriah, and El-Figuigui, Houria. "Motivational Aspects of Information Literacy Skills Instruction in Community College Libraries." *College and Research Libraries* 65 (March 2004): 96-121.

6. Mackey, Thomas and Jacobson, Trudi. "Integrating Information Literacy in Lower and Upper-Level Courses: Developing Scalable Models for Higher Education." *Journal of General Education* 53 (Fall 2004): 201-224.

7. *Information Literacy Competency Standards for Higher Education.* Association of College & Research Libraries, 2000. Available: <http://www.ala.org/ala/

acrl/acrlstandards/informationliteracycompetency.htm#stan>. Accessed: February 13, 2006.

8. Kolb, David A. *Experiential Learning: Experience as a Source of Learning and Development*. Englewood Cliffs, NJ: Prentice Hall, 1983.

9. Fosmire, Michael and Macklin, Alexius. "Riding the Active Learning Wave: Problem-Based Learning as a Catalyst for Creating Faculty-Librarian Instruction Partnerships." *Issues in Science and Technology Librarianship* 34 (Spring 2002). Available: <http://www.istl.org/02-spring/article2.html>. Accessed: January 26, 2006.

10. Gresham, Keith. "Experiential Learning Theory, Library Instruction, and the Electronic Classroom." *Colorado Libraries* 25 (Spring 1999): 28-31.

11. Jamison, Kathleen. *Experiential Teaching and Learning: The 4-H Way of Educating Youth*. Microsoft PowerPoint presentation file. Available: <http://www.rce .rutgers.edu/learnbydoing/ExperLrngInservice2002.ppt>. Accessed: February 2006.

12. See note 5.

Chapter 3

Taking the Best of Both Worlds: Success and Challenges with the Hybrid Model of Library Instruction

Lucretia McCulley

INTRODUCTION

The University of Richmond (UR) is an independent, privately endowed institution, with a total student body of around 5,000 students. Undergraduate and graduate degrees are offered in the liberal arts, business, law, and leadership studies. Library instruction has been an integral part of the university libraries program since the 1970s, initiated by a five-year grant from the National Endowment for the Humanities College Library Program and the Council on Library Resources. During the past thirty years, the program has continued to grow and reinvent itself. Overall, the instructional services program can be described as a "hybrid library instruction model," emphasizing both course-related instruction throughout the curriculum as well as required Library 100 and Library 101 classes for first-year students. This case study will describe the process of planning and preparing for required classes, including the development of content and hands-on activities, technology components of instruction, instructor preparation, assessment of classes, administrative duties, future plans, and challenges. It will also describe how the Library 100/101 classes serve as a public relations tool and as a base for course-related instruction at the university.

SETTING

Approximately 125 course-related instruction sessions are offered each academic year in the humanities, social sciences, business, and science. At the current time, there is a heavy emphasis on instruction in the areas of sociology, psychology, political science, rhetoric, education, and gender studies. The number of course-related sessions has remained steady throughout the years under the strong liaison librarian program, but first-year student orientation and instruction have gone through several transformations since 1987, including the use of library skills workbooks, audiotape walking tours of the library, online tutorials with WebCT and Blackboard software, and virtual library tours on the library's Web site. Most of the methods were required orientation events for first-year students, but they were not a part of the university curriculum. Experiments with virtual instruction were successful to some degree, but librarians recognized the need for more personal interaction with students as well as giving students the experience of using the physical library. In addition, the UR community focuses on providing personal "high touch" service. As Van Scoyoc notes in an article about reducing library anxiety in first-year students, "a staff-led library instruction session can serve as a time for the students to meet and get to know the librarian as someone who can be a valuable resource in the future."[1]

With the popularity of Google, Yahoo, and other search engines, UR librarians found that increasing numbers of students have never used anything but the Internet to find information. Many students are unfamiliar with the concept of a library catalog and most students have no conception of scholarship and the role it plays in their education. Through focus groups and various library surveys, upper level students indicated that they would like to improve their knowledge of library resources and wish they had known more earlier in their academic careers. During the same time period, faculty also expressed concern about students' understanding of scholarly communication sources. Through the use of faculty focus groups, a faculty/librarian "Think Tank on Information Fluency" and numerous discussions and planning meetings between the outreach and instruction librarians and various groups of faculty, the entire university faculty voted affirmatively in spring 2003 to implement a graduation requirement for basic library research skills. All first-year students are required to attend two seventy-five-minute workshops, Library 100 in the fall semester and Library 101 in the spring semester, designed to develop essential library research skills. These introductory classes do not include information or instruction on library resources that are related to specific courses or majors at the university. Subject content continues to be covered by the liaison librarians in the various course-related sessions across the curriculum.

COURSE GOALS

The overall goal of Library 100 and 101 is to introduce students to basic library resources and services and to ensure that all students can identify and locate books, journals, and newspaper articles. These basic skills will help students identify material for first-year course-related research assignments and to help them recognize that the library's resources can answer many of the questions that arise as they prepare for and participate in classes. The UR Libraries Web page provides more detailed information on Library 100/101 goals, objectives and learning outcomes,[2] some of which are based on the Association of College & Research Libraries *(ACRL) Information Literacy Competency Standards for Higher Education.*[3]

Library 100 and 101 were launched at the beginning of the 2003/2004 academic year. Approximately forty-five sections of Library 100 were taught by eleven librarians during the fall of 2003. In spring 2004, five sections of Library 100 and forty-five sections of Library 101 were offered. This pattern of class sections has continued with both the 2004/2005 and 2005/2006 academic years. Close cooperation and communication with the University Registrar's Office have been extremely important in making the program work successfully. The registrar's office arranges the sections on the online registration system (BANNERWEB) as they would with any other class at the university. This means that students register for the sections during their appointed registration times and librarians manage class rosters, course communication, and grades through the computer registration system. To make the basic skills program relevant and effective, it is important for first-year students to complete the workshops during their first two semesters. The information provided is immediately helpful to them with their class assignments and serves as a foundation for further course-related instruction.

COURSE DEVELOPMENT

It might appear that designing two seventy-five-minute class sessions would not require a great amount of preparation time. However, with limited class time and the goal of making the sessions "hands on," interactive, and engaging, the outreach and instruction librarians spent several months developing the in-class exercises and instructional scripts so that all the materials could be covered appropriately. Small committees developed the details and then consulted with the teaching team of eleven librarians for feedback and suggestions. One challenge that the team wrestled with was how much information to convey in such a short class period and whether it was possible to incorporate hands-on activities within a limited time period. After much discussion, the instruction librarians decided to focus on three main components, knowing that students often respond well to short "chunks" of information within one class period. For the purposes of Library 100, the content focuses on the library's Web site, the library catalog, and one basic periodical database, Thomson-Gale's Expanded Academic Index. After the librarian provides a brief demonstration and explanation in class, the students complete an exercise of identifying specific sources and services on the library's Web site, so they will feel comfortable navigating the site on their own. Although it was forbidding at first, the teaching team decided to make the leap of incorporating a "book retrieval" search during class time. Students search for a book title in the catalog, identify subject headings and a call number, and then proceed to find the book in the stacks, returning to the classroom with book in hand. The third component of the class focuses on using Expanded Academic Index to complete a topic search and answer questions about the citations retrieved. Library 101 also employs this interactive approach with the exercise sheets. As of early 2006, the content focuses on using the librarian-created subject research guides on the library's Web site to find subject-specific databases, such as WilsonWeb databases (General Science Full-Text, Social Sciences Full-Text, etc.), how to interpret periodical holdings information in the catalog, how to cite sources, and how to effectively use LexisNexis to find newspaper articles. Students also go out into the periodicals stacks to retrieve a bound periodical, which they use to complete an exercise about citing a specific article.

In order to test the length of the class sessions and the amount of time that the exercises required, each member of the entire teaching team taught a practice session during summer 2003. Practice sessions were also videotaped so that instructors would have some immediate feedback on their performance. The "practice" audience consisted of other library staff members and student assistants. Using this audience had several benefits, such as obtaining comments and suggestions for the presentation of the course and educating all library staff about the new Library 100/101 program. The feedback received was extremely helpful with making adjustments with explanations, clarity, wording on the exercise sheets, and the general pacing of the class. This preparation paid off in the end, with the teaching staff feeling confident with the exercises and the technology used in the class sessions.

Technology is an important component of the Library 100/101 classes in that its presence enhances the presentation and adds important techniques for the teachers to use. An entertaining library news "tabloid" Web page was created to introduce the class sessions. Headlines on the tabloid include such phrases as "Confused students protest over cryptic LC! Just want to know where book is!" and "Tired of searching Google? Visit the UR Libraries Web site!"

NetOP[4] (classroom control software) was installed in the Boatwright Computer Classroom to restrain students from moving ahead, e-mailing, and instant messaging with friends during the class. This software works extremely well with the students and instructors are very pleased with its ease of use. Music, video, and PowerPoint interludes are used in both presentations to add energy and visuals to the classroom environment. For example, the parody song, "Read It in the Tabloids"[5] is used alongside the news tabloid Web page and serves as introductory music and visuals as the students arrive to Library 100. Various PowerPoint programs serve as in-class multiple choice quizzes and present additional facts about library services, similar to the film trivia screen presentations that are currently popular in movie theaters.

COURSE ASSESSMENT

How well do the students learn the material presented in Library 100 and 101? In *Evaluating Training Programs: The Four Levels,* Donald Kirkpatrick outlines four levels of assessment.[6] These levels include reaction (opinion), learning (skills), behavior (apply skills), and results (output improved). In terms of using these four levels of evaluation, the first two levels of assessment have been achieved: (1) What was the student's opinion of the experience, and (2) Did the student "learn" what you hoped they would learn? Both levels are assessed through the use of in-class exercises which are graded by each instructor and by the use of several evaluative wrap-up questions at the end of the exercises. It is important to note that each course is "Pass/Fail." If a student makes an effort in good faith to complete all the exercises, then he or she passes the course. Librarians do not deduct points for small mistakes on the exercise sheet. By assessing the answers to their questions on the evaluative sheets and by reviewing the students' mistakes or misunderstandings on the in-class exercises, librarians can make improvements and changes for the upcoming academic year. Appendix 3.1 provides a synopsis of answers to the wrap-up questions for both the 2003/2004 and 2004/2005 academic years and describes some of the adjustments made with course content and delivery.

Overall, Library 100/101 has been extremely successful in its first two years of implementation. Due to careful planning and excellent cooperation from the registrar's office, class schedules and various student scheduling issues have gone smoothly. To ensure that all students complete both sessions in their first year at the university, regular reminders are sent by e-mail to academic advisors and students, and holds can be placed on registration. As anticipated, there are problems with a small percentage of students forgetting to attend class, not understanding the requirement, or ignoring reminders about the program. Librarians make every effort possible to communicate with students in regard to the drop/add process, remind them about class meeting times, and schedule additional sections for those who missed class sessions earlier in the semester. At the end of each academic year, librarians are confident that efforts made in good faith have been made to accommodate the students' needs. Another goal is to avoid the scenario of disgruntled upperclassmen in a class full of first-year students. In an effort to enforce these requirements, the registrar's office has allowed the librarians to place registration holds on students' records if they have not completed the requirement by sophomore year. This process is administratively time consuming and at times frustrating, but it has resulted in the majority of students completing Library 100 and 101 in their first year at the university.

The data for both 2003/2004 and 2004/2005 indicate that the goal of raising student awareness of library resources was attained. Both class content and interactive class exercises are well received by the students and they seemed to appreciate the hands-on, practical learning approach to using appropriate library resources. Library 100 serves as an excellent opportunity to welcome students to the library environment at the UR and to emphasize the personal approach to library services, including reference/information services, personal research appointments, and assistance via e-mail or instant messaging. Outreach and instruction librarians also remind students of the "personal librarian" letter that is sent to each first-year student during the first week of the semester. This letter is from an individual librarian who offers each student to be his or her "personal librarian" and introduces the role of the academic librarian and describes the various library services that support student research.

The students' suggestion about offering Library 100 earlier in the first semester has been very successful and it has meant that students have been able to meet some of their early research needs related to their coursework. In addition, first-year students are fresh and eager in September and both instructors and students have benefited from "beginning of the year" enthusiasm. Evaluative comments about Library 101 enabled librarians to make some slight changes and improvements with the content of the class session.

Beginning in fall 2004, the liaison librarians created *Tip Sheet on Reinforcing Library 100/101 Skills,*[7] and distributed it to all faculty, along with a letter from the university librarian that explained the content and goals of Library 100/101. The tip sheet offers assignment suggestions on how students can continue to use the library catalog or find pertinent class information in *Expanded Academic Index.* Outreach and instruction librarians seek opportunities to meet with their liaison departments and to participate in other meetings with faculty to discuss how they can reinforce the basic skills presented in the two seventy-five-minute sessions. Other ideas on how to reach the faculty include workshops on how to specifically integrate basic library skills into course curricula or extension of invitations to faculty to observe a Library 100/101 session. When faculty approach librarians for higher-level, course-integrated instruction, liaison librarians also take that opportunity to remind them about what is covered in Library 100/101 and how further assignments and instruction can build upon that experience with upperclassmen. Librarians are encouraged that Library 100 and 101 have served as a base of knowledge for students so that course-related instruction can offer more time and focus on specific library sources and strategies.

CONCLUSION

Future opportunities for the first-year library research skills program include exploring further assessment strategies and the integration of library skills into first-year class assignments. As mentioned, the program was able to achieve the first two levels of assessment, but further work is needed to accomplish the next two levels, which include: (1) Did the student retain the learning?, and (2) Did the student apply the learning? These last two levels are difficult and expensive and to be truly successful, it would require extensive collaboration with faculty. Betsy Barefoot echoed this concern in a recent article in *The Chronicle of Higher Education* by stating that "even if students get an introduction to information literacy in a first-year seminar or a special course, they may not transfer what they learn to 'regular' courses across the disciplines."[8] Achieving continued course integration remains the biggest challenge with Library 100 and 101.

APPENDIX 3.1

Evaluative Questions for Library 100	**2003/2004 and 2004/2005**
1. What is the most interesting or useful thing you have learned today about using library resources?	The top two topics for both 2003/2004 and 2004/2005 were learning how to use *Expanded Academic Index* to find journal article citations and full-text articles and how to find books in the stacks by using the library catalog. These two

skills are probably the most important for students to know during their first semester and their answers confirmed the decision to focus on these elements.

2. Write down any question you may have.

For both years, about one-third of the students did not have any further questions, but the other two-thirds ranged from questions about checkout policies, printing credits, and interlibrary loan to "Does the library have a classics section?" Librarians added a personal touch with this question by responding to each student's question via e-mail. Answers to this question were also used to revise some of the course content for the upcoming academic year and to update the PowerPoint presentation on FAQs about library services.

3. What changes would make this workshop more effective?

In 2003/2004, students highly recommended offering the classes earlier in the semester, rather than mid-October. This advice was accepted and librarians worked with the registrar's office to start the Library 100 classes during the first week of September in Fall 2004. For the 2004/2005 academic year, 30% of students had no reply, 18% stated that the classes were very effective and the remaining answers varied across the spectrum. Some typical comments included "provide snacks," "more music," "make the session shorter," and "include a tour of the library."

Evaluative Questions for Library 101	2003/2004	2004/2005
1. What is the most interesting or useful thing you have learned today about using library resources?		
Learning the LexisNexis database	46%	33%
Finding journals in the stacks	20%	15%
How to cite sources	16%	21%
Using WilsonWeb	N/A	29%
2. Rate the overall value of your Library 100/101 class sessions		
Very useful	208 (26%)	201 (26%)
Somewhat useful	453 (58%)	442 (59%)
Not very useful	86 (11%)	65 (9%)
Not useful	36 (4%)	25 (3%)
3. How would you evaluate the effectiveness of the instructor?		
Very effective	564 (72%)	477 (63%)

Appendix 3.1 *(continued)*

Somewhat effective	198 (25%)	236 (31%)
Not very effective	15 (1%)	16 (2%)
Not effective	6 (less than 1%)	4 (less than 1%)
4. What change would make this workshop more useful and effective?		
"Nothing" or "Effective"	N/A	33%
No answer	N/A	23%
Shorter	N/A	8%
Earlier in year or combine with Library 100	N/A	5%

NOTES

1. Van Scoyoc, Anna M. "Reducing Library Anxiety in First-Year Students: The Impact of Computer-Assisted Instruction and Bibliographic Instruction." *Reference and User Service Quarterly* 42 (Summer 2003): 329-339.

2. University of Richmond Libraries. *Encouraging Student Inquiry: Library 100 and 101*. Richmond, Virginia: University of Richmond, 2006. Available: <http://library.richmond.edu/services/faculty/inquiry/libraryskills.htm>. Accessed: April 6, 2006.

3. Association of College and Research Libraries. *Information Literacy Standards for Higher Education*. Chicago: Association of College and Research Libraries, 2001.

4. NetOp School. Birkerod, Denmark: Danware Data A/S. Available: <http:www.netop.com>. Accessed: February 10, 2006.

5. Rivers, Bob. "Read It in the Tabloids." On *Best of Twisted Tunes*, vol. 2. Atlantic Records, 83045-2. p1997.

6. Kirkpatrick, Donald. *Evaluating Training Programs: The Four Levels*. San Francisco: Berrett-Koehler, 1994.

7. University of Richmond Libraries. *Tip Sheet on Reinforcing Library 100/101 Skills*. Richmond, Virginia: University of Richmond, 2006. Available: <http://library.richmond.edu/services/faculty/inquiry/tipsheetWeb.pdf>. Accessed: April 5, 2006.

8. Barefoot, Betsy. "Bridging the Chasm: First-Year Students and the Library." *The Chronicle of Higher Education,* January 20, 2006. Available: <http:chronicle.com/weekly/v52/i20/20b01601.htm>. Accessed: February 1, 2006.

Chapter 4

Who Wants to Be a Millionaire? Using Clickers to Enhance Learning in the Library

Janelle L. Wertzberger

INTRODUCTION

Gettysburg College's Musselman Library has an active and growing information literacy (IL) program based on faculty-librarian collaboration rather than institutional curriculum. While a few IL session sequences are taught within a specific course, the vast majority of instructional sessions are traditional "one-shots." As formal instruction time with students is limited, instruction librarians take care to include active learning and other participatory pedagogies to improve learning and increase the likelihood that students will return to the library, reference desk, and library Web site. Incorporating personal response devices or "clickers" into IL sessions is another technique for engaging students during a very short window of opportunity.

Clickers entered the U.S. and U.K. higher education markets around 2000; many of the earliest applications were in science, engineering, and mathematics courses, especially those with large enrollments. The devices have been used to support a range of objectives from taking attendance to assessing student understanding to administering quizzes.[1] Many authors cite the benefits of simultaneous feedback during a class session[2] and some also praise the technology's ability to spark discussion among students when their responses vary.[3] One economics professor concluded that using the new technology caused her to reflect on the amount of active learning in her classes.[4] Others point out that the clicker technology does not actively engage students on its own, but rather supports the instructor in engaging active learning objectives.[5]

Sometimes clickers are bundled with textbooks; a company called eInstruction has partnered with McGraw Hill.[6] Since there is no consolidation yet in the clicker market, students may be required to buy more than one clicker for different classes.[7] Student reception of the technology is generally positive, though some find constant "testing" to be stressful.[8]

SETTING

Gettysburg College is a residential, undergraduate, liberal arts college of about 2,500 students located in Gettysburg, Pennsylvania. Students choose from an array of liberal arts majors and minors as well as a management major; the college is also home to a conservatory of music. One central library serves the entire campus. The Reference & Instruction department of the library includes five librarians, though other librarians also contribute to the IL program. Most IL sessions taught by librarians (such as the ones discussed here) are delivered in Musselman Library's electronic classroom, which contains sixteen student computers and one instructor computer that projects to a screen. This classroom is the primary training space both for librarians and for instructional technology (IT) staff who work in the library building. Professors can schedule this room for occasional classes if it is available. Finally, it is used as a general lab when not reserved for teaching.

Librarians' use of the clicker system was encouraged by IT colleagues. Librarians attended a campus technology workshop in May 2005 that included a track on clickers. Many faculty and librarians were excited about the possibilities for enhancing teaching. IT installed the clicker system in the library's electronic classroom so that all interested parties would have access to it.

OBJECTIVES

The clicker-related learning objective is simple: Students will use clickers to engage actively during IL instruction sessions. Of course, other instructional objectives appropriate to the session also apply and these differ by course. During the first semester of clicker use, clickers were used in four courses: a first-year seminar about statistics in everyday life, a senior-level Health and Exercise Sciences (HES) seminar (IL instruction and clickers were used in three sessions for this course), an introductory management course (three sections), and a large introductory biology course with nine lab sections (which is considered a huge class by Gettysburg standards). In the HES and management classes, data taken from the clickers were recorded and became part of the student grade. In the other classes, clicker data were used only for in-class assessment and were not recorded.

METHODS

Gettysburg College's Information Technology department installed the TurningPoint group response system (produced by TurningTechnologies[9]) in the library's electronic classroom. The TurningPoint system was chosen from an array of similar systems because of its integration with the Microsoft Office Suite software with which all librarians and professors were already familiar.

The first step to using clickers was to prepare appropriate questions for class use. Questions should be integrated with class content and must be presented in multiple choice format (with only one correct answer). Librarians experimented with modifying items from Project SAILS[10] question bank (with permission) as well as writing original questions. Clicker questions are stored in a shared space on a network drive so that all librarians can draw from the growing pool of clicker questions.

Next, the questions must be inserted into TurningPoint PowerPoint slides. Once the TurningPoint software has been installed on the instructor's computer, a TurningPoint toolbar (see Figure 4.1) appears within PowerPoint. This toolbar allows the instructor to enter "interactive" questions within PowerPoint. In addition to typing in the question and multiple choice answers, the instructor designates the correct answer and chooses an output display. Gettysburg librarians also choose to insert a "response table" on the slides. This causes a numbered grid to appear at the bottom of the slide. Each numbered box corresponds to a student clicker. As the student responds, the

FIGURE 4.1. PowerPoint interface with TurningPoint toolbar.

corresponding box is highlighted. In this way, the instructor and the class can see when all students have "clicked in." The usual Power-Point design options are available so that the TurningPoint slides can be integrated seamlessly into an existing PowerPoint presentation.

Administering about ten questions is best for a typical sixty to seventy-five-minute instructional session. Questions should be divided into two or three groups so that student understanding about a topic is assessed as the content is presented, rather than saving all ten questions until the end of the session. Before the class, the clickers which are small devices about the size of a credit card (see Figure 4.2), need to be turned on and set up. Gettysburg librarians have chosen to set up the clickers before the students arrive. This process requires only a short series of clicks on the clicker buttons to ensure that the devices are communicating with the response system. The clickers are then placed by each computer keyboard in the classroom, or handed to students as they arrive.

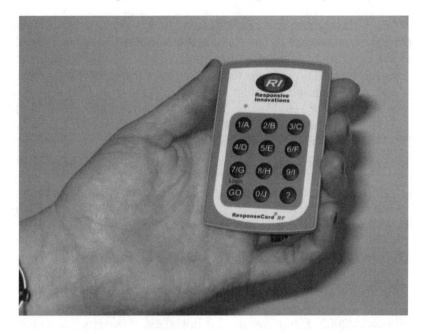

FIGURE 4.2. Personal response device or "clicker."

A few Gettysburg College professors require students to rent a clicker for the entire semester and bring it to class each day. The campus bookstore coordinates clicker rental. This approach works well when the instructor uses clickers many times throughout a semester-long course with the same students. It can also facilitate quiz administration and grading, as the clickers do the job of collecting and recording data. Librarians who teach for-credit courses may find this arrangement attractive.

During the class, the instructor simply runs the TurningPoint-enabled PowerPoint presentation. The presentation may or may not include content in addition to the TurningPoint interactive slides. Gettysburg librarians typically do not teach with PowerPoint and did not choose to create noninteractive slides for these classes. When the interactive slide appears, the system is ready to receive responses from the clickers. Students ring in. If the response table option has been incorporated into the slide, the instructor can easily see when all students have responded to the question.

When the instructor is ready to tally the answers, the PowerPoint presentation is advanced (by clicking the mouse button, using the right arrow key, or any of the usual methods). The next slide includes the question from the previous slide, as well as the response summary (displayed as a graph, pie chart, or other selected output display). The response summary enables the librarian and the professor to instantly gauge student comprehension and immediately address misperceptions. If 90 percent of the class selected the correct answer, then not much elaboration is required; certainly the multiple choice options that no one selected need to be discussed. If a lower percentage of students selected the correct answer, then the instructor has the opportunity to revisit a point immediately, perhaps by asking students to explain why they chose a particular answer.

RESULTS

The TurningPoint software was installed in the library classroom in August 2005. Librarians used it in sixteen IL sessions during the fall semester. The learning curve for librarians was relatively low, since TurningPoint integrates with PowerPoint, with which staff were already familiar. Composing the multiple-choice questions was more challenging than learning to use the TurningPoint software. Librarians were not accustomed to administering quizzes or other multiple-choice style assessments of student learning.

Not wanting to reinvent the wheel, instructors drew from existing questions rather than starting from scratch. Musselman Library administered Project SAILS in fall 2004 and librarians were familiar with many questions from that assessment. Permission to use and adapt SAILS questions for local assessment use was requested and received. The SAILS questions were transcribed and sorted by skill set. In order to help organize questions for easy retrieval, SAILS regroups outcomes and objectives from the Association of College & Research Libraries (ACRL) *Information Literacy Competency Standards for Higher Education*[11] into twelve skill sets.[12]

Using the SAILS questions came more naturally to some librarians than to others. As clicker assessments were administered several times during the IL session, questions that did not match the instructor's teaching style or presentation were obtrusive. Instructors sometimes wrote original questions that addressed a piece of content more directly than the SAILS questions. SAILS questions were also adapted so that the question content related directly to the course being taught. This made the assessment more relevant for students.

Clicker assessment was incorporated into IL sessions during the busiest time of the academic year, and instructors did not have a lot of time to formulate new questions, test them, revise them, and go through a lengthy adoption process. "Distractors" (the wrong answers) were selected to reflect misconceptions commonly held by students, based on years of experience with instruction and reference interactions. This "quick and dirty, in the trenches" approach works well at a small institution like Gettysburg. When time allows, though, librarians are interested in creating and revising questions in a more thoughtful way, perhaps consulting with social science research experts on campus.

The clicker pads proved to be completely intuitive for students to use. They perked up noticeably when asked to respond to clicker questions. They often began interacting with each other about the correct answer as the results were displayed. Students with a competitive nature often responded well to the clickers. Anecdotal data suggest that students found them fun to use.

The HES students completed an evaluation of their IL session several weeks after their final session. One question asked them to describe how clicker technology affected their learning during their time in the library. HES student feedback included the following insights:

- Clicker questions helped students review the material immediately and quickly correct any misperceptions about class content.
- Clicker questions helped reinforce content.
- Students who were not comfortable speaking up during class enjoyed the anonymity afforded by the clickers. They appreciated being able to learn from peers without putting themselves on the spot during class.
- Knowing that the session included clicker questions forced students to pay better attention during class.
- Some students did not enjoy using the clickers as a quiz device for material presented that day. Students felt that quizzes should only be graded when they had a chance to study outside class before taking the quiz.

The TurningPoint software allows instructors to record student answers individually or anonymously. Gettysburg librarians experimented with both approaches. Student answers were recorded individually and used as class quiz grades in the HES and management courses, while student answers were anonymous in the first-year seminar and biology classes. Gettysburg librarians prefer the anonymous data collection as they do not teach courses for credit and do not have the power to assign grades. Adding a quiz grade to the IL session changes the tenor of the class and, frankly, makes the students tense and less receptive to learning. Recording responses anonymously keeps the classroom atmosphere light and fun, while still allowing for reinforcement of learning concepts. In the HES and management classes where grades were given for clicker responses, students exhibited some unease at the idea of a librarian entering the grading relationship previously restricted to faculty and students. Obviously, this situation will differ from institution to institution. The TurningPoint software allows flexibility to use the approach that is best for local users.

CONCLUSION

Gettysburg librarians plan to continue using clickers during IL instruction sessions. Clickers will not necessarily be used in every session, but they constitute a new—and fun!—tool in an arsenal of active learning techniques. Students respond well to using the clickers, and lessons designed to take advantage of clicker technology encourage students to process and apply information during class. Gettysburg librarians might contact the campus bookstore to learn how many courses require students to purchase clickers, as outreach to these specific courses could be beneficial.

Use of the clickers to date has been *during* IL instruction sessions, assessing student comprehension only after content has been delivered by librarians. Clickers potentially could be used to quickly administer a pretest at the beginning of a session. The instant results of such a pretest could help librarians determine the overall literacy of the class and customize the level of instruction immediately. Librarians already do a certain amount of "reading" the audience in order to present material at the most appropriate level, but determining whether a group of students has beginning, intermediate, or advanced skills based on data would be more accurate than reading faces alone. Clickers do not automatically generate active learning, but the technology can prompt librarians to consider active learning strategies anew and help make class fun.

NOTES

1. "Clickers on Campus: Purdue Deploys Student Response System from eInstruction." *BizEd* 5, no. 1 (2005): 49.

2. Brewer, Carol A. "Near Real-Time Assessment of Student Learning and Understanding in Biology Courses." *Bioscience* 54, no. 11 (2004): 1034-1039.

3. Wood, William B. "Clickers: A Teaching Gimmick that Works." *Developmental Cell* 7, no. 6 (2004): 796-798.

4. Elliott, Caroline. "Using a Personal Response System in Economics Teaching." *International Review of Economics Education* 1, no. 1 (2003): 80-86. Available: <http://www.economicsnetwork.ac.uk/iree/i1/elliott.htm>. Accessed: April 27, 2006.

5. Nicol, David J. and Boyle, James T. "Peer Instruction Versus Class-wide Discussion in Large Classes: A Comparison of Two Interaction Methods in the Wired Classroom." *Studies in Higher Education* 28, no. 4 (2003): 457-473.

6. "Clickers on Campus."

7. Knudsen, Eric. "Students, Professors Debate Clicker Use in Classroom." *The Daily Campus* (February 20, 2006). Available: <http://www.dailycampus.com>. Accessed: April 27, 2006.

8. Carnevale, Dan. "Run a Class Like a Game Show: 'Clickers' Keep Students Involved." *Chronicle of Higher Education* 51, no. 42 (2005): B3-B3.

9. *TurningTechnologies*. Available: <http://www.turningtechnologies.com>. Accessed: April 27, 2006.

10. *Project SAILS: Standardized Assessment of Information Literacy Skills*. Kent, OH: Kent State University, 2005. Available: <https://www.projectsails.org>. Accessed: April 27, 2006.

11. *Information Literacy Competency Standards for Higher Education*. Chicago, IL: American Library Association, 2000. Available: <http://www.ala.org/ala/acrl/acrlstandards/standards.pdf>. Accessed: April 27, 2006.

12. *Project SAILS Skill Sets*. Kent, OH: Kent State University, 2005. Available: <https://www.projectsails.org/abouttest/skillsets.php?page=aboutTest>. Accessed: April 27, 2006.

PART B:
LIBRARY INSTRUCTION
IN UNIVERSITY LIBRARIES

Chapter 5

Interdisciplinary Inquiry Through Collaboration

Leslie Bussert
Suzan Parker
Mark Szarko

INTRODUCTION

At the University of Washington Bothell (UWB), a required foundation course, Interdisciplinary Inquiry, serves as an orientation to upper-division work while developing research skills for subsequent courses. This case study will focus on a successful model of collaboration between faculty and librarians and will describe information literacy assignments integrated into an interdisciplinary curriculum emphasizing problem-based learning.

SETTING

The Campus Library and Media Center, part of the University of Washington Libraries system, serves the UWB and Cascadia Community College (CCC) on a colocated campus. While CCC serves lower-division freshman and sophomore students, UWB serves primarily upper-division transfer and graduate students, many who transfer from Cascadia and other local community colleges. The majority of the UWB student population is over twenty-five years old and female. Most of these students attend classes part-time while holding jobs off-campus.[1]

An Introduction to Instructional Services in Academic Libraries

This case study focuses on the required foundation course for UWB's Interdisciplinary Arts and Sciences (IAS) program, Interdisciplinary Inquiry. The IAS program is geared toward helping working professionals, community college, and four-year institution transfer and adult returning students who have completed the first two years of study at the lower division. The program is "designed for students who . . . enjoy making unexpected connections across disciplines."[2] Information literacy is highly integrated into the curriculum, allowing for a developmental approach emphasizing collaboration, problem-based learning, and interdisciplinary research methods.

OBJECTIVES

A primary goal of Interdisciplinary Inquiry is to prepare UWB's transfer student population to begin work at the upper-division level, while developing research skills for subsequent courses. The course is typically taken during the first quarter of study, thus providing a common entry point for the approximately 500 students who transfer annually into the IAS program. The course serves as an orientation to upper-division work, as well as to several important academic services on campus, including the Campus Library and Media Center, Quantitative Skills Center, and the Writing Center. Interdisciplinary Inquiry creates cohesiveness among these students by providing a common language and set of experiences that build a foundation for students' further work in the program.

Course objectives for Interdisciplinary Inquiry are ambitious. Fundamentally, this course aims to explore what it means to do interdisciplinary work at the upper-division level, examining the assumptions and methods in doing interdisciplinary research. The course is designed to help students become better critical thinkers, researchers, writers, and speakers.

METHODS

The goals of Interdisciplinary Inquiry are met through the collaborative teaching efforts of faculty and librarians, along with academic services professionals representing the Writing and Quantitative Skills

Centers. These individuals collectively provide learner-centered, collaborative activities that build the foundation for upper-division work. This collective effort takes place over a ten-week period, with librarians typically cofacilitating four two-hour sessions. In addition, the directors of the Writing and Quantitative Skills Centers often teach one or two classes. This case study gives an overview of the information literacy sessions cofacilitated by librarians, as well as their role in the course as a whole. While librarians work with all sections of this course, there is variation across sections as to how and when librarians work with the students. This case study describes the most frequently utilized model.

The first library session typically involves the formation of research groups, or "clusters," comprising four to six students. Each research cluster then identifies a topic represented within the central course text, and develops this topic into a working research question that they will investigate, refine, and/or reformulate for the rest of the quarter. The second library session addresses the notions of scholarship and knowledge production across disciplines. Students learn how to search for and identify scholarly works, and locate at least one relevant scholarly article pertaining to their research cluster's question. The third and fourth visits with the librarian may vary depending on the instructor and section of the course. Typically the third session addresses qualitative research by locating information sources such as interviews or personal narratives. The final information literacy session demonstrates cultural artifacts, or primary sources, as evidence of knowledge and sources of information.

By the end of their tenth week in this course, students have been heavily exposed to library resources and librarians, as well as to the staff and services of the Writing and Quantitative Skills Centers. They will have engaged in the fundamental processes in research in an incremental fashion: identifying their information need by formulating a researchable question; locating and evaluating relevant online, print, and archival sources; and integrating those sources into the final course project, the "research proposal." This final research proposal is used to ask students to reflect on the paths taken in their scholarly investigations, and to lay a framework for how a fully developed research project might take shape. This progression of "scaffolded" research activities introduces students to understanding the *process* of research through collaborative, learner-centered activities emphasizing problem posing, and the varied ways that knowledge is produced.

RESULTS

Raspa and Ward define collaboration as a "special form of listening that comes from attending to the relationship behind the project."[3] One of the hallmarks of Interdisciplinary Inquiry is the high degree of collaboration among librarians, faculty, and other academic services staff, as well as among students in their research cluster activities. Participants enter into an ongoing and evolving pedagogical conversation to create a curriculum which best supports student learning.

Faculty and Librarian Collaboration

For each section of the course, it is not uncommon for librarians to teach or cofacilitate the class with faculty for eight or more hours per quarter. During these in-class teaching collaborations, librarians and faculty enter into dialogue with each other, breaking out of the model of individual experts teaching their own content, thus looking for intersections between their respective disciplines. This sometimes "messy" conversation between scholars mirrors what students experience in their research groups.

For collaboration between faculty and librarians to be successful at this level, broad departmental and institutional support is required. UWB's mission and goals statement explicitly mentions the need to "emphasize and develop critical thinking, writing, and information literacy, in order to graduate students with lifelong learning skills."[4] To achieve these institutional goals, faculty, librarians, and academic services professionals working with a particular course interact frequently before and throughout the quarter to assess if the learning goals are being met.

Student Collaboration

Students in the Interdisciplinary Inquiry classes learn to shape their thinking around research questions as they explore their own assumptions, perceptions, biases, or gaps in knowledge regarding these questions. This learning takes place through hands-on information literacy activities in their research clusters, as well as through small and large-group discussion (both in class and online), and group "facilitations" on a topic. Talking with their peers offers students opportunities to think critically about their questions and information in new ways, clarify their thoughts, and perhaps reconceptualize the context or lens through which research questions are considered.

During the first library session, students form research clusters around a topic of interest discovered within the assigned text for their section of the course. For example, several sections of the course have focused on the theme of tourism by reading Jamaica Kincaid's *A Small Place*. Together, students and their instructor identify several major themes within the work that could serve as a lens through which to understand the issues Kincaid raises about tourism in Antigua. A few previous examples have been post colonialism in the Caribbean, tourism industry, and environmental impacts of tourism. The interdisciplinary focus of these research topics allow students with different interests to bring their previous academic, professional, and life experiences to their group's research project. Lattuca, Voigt, and Fath suggest that an interdisciplinary pedagogy may accomplish more in such cases because students can establish connections between new knowledge they gain from the class with what they already know.[5]

After the students have chosen their research clusters, the librarian and instructor model for students how to move from a broad topic, such as "tourism in Antigua," to a narrower research question, such as "How have economic changes brought on by the tourism industry had an impact on poor and working-class Antiguans?" One successful strategy for helping students to develop a complex and rich research question has been the use of "concept maps" to show relationships between issues and ideas related to the theme. The librarian and course instructor model is for students how to develop a concept map for a sample topic on the white board (see Figure 5.1).

Students then work within their groups to generate concept maps for their research cluster's topic. After they have developed their maps, making connections between issues and raising questions, the librarian guides the groups in exploring their topics through the library's Web page of resources, introducing them to potential sources of information such as subject guides, online catalog, general/interdisciplinary

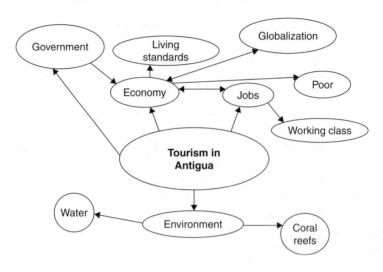

FIGURE 5.1. Concept map based on Jamaica Kincaid's *A Small Place.*

databases such as ProQuest, and other librarians and faculty with related subject expertise. Students also draw on skills and knowledge from their coursework at the lower division by working with sources that they may already have some confidence using. They are not expected to conduct extensive research at this point, but rather to get their toes in the water, familiarizing themselves with potential information resources, as well as with each other.

By the end of the first workshop, all research clusters develop a working research question that will guide them through the rest of the course. Subsequent workshops with the librarian involve investigating various ways in which knowledge is produced, such as through scholarly journal articles, narrative, qualitative, and quantitative research, and through visual, auditory, or tangible artifacts. Naturally, the groups' research questions change and evolve, sometimes quite dramatically, as they encounter these diverse information sources. These questions are also shaped by ongoing suggestions for refinement from librarians, teaching faculty, academic services staff, and other students.

Finally, the course culminates in a group research proposal drawing on all the sources they have encountered, and reflecting upon the iterative process of research. In contrast to a traditional research paper, the final research proposal addresses the value of the research question by asking students to reflect on the research process in terms of relevant information and knowledge sources to be consulted and research techniques to be employed.

Learner-Centered Pedagogies

As Ross-Gordon has noted, among students twenty-five years and older, learner-centered teaching strategies have been "associated with a greater sense of satisfaction and accomplishment."[6] Librarians teaching Interdisciplinary Inquiry incorporate learner-centered strategies such as problem-based and active learning pedagogies in order to engage students in authentic, meaningful research activities that are relevant to their interests. Research on learner-centered pedagogy suggests that students who engage in problem-based learning become self-directed learners, develop critical thinking skills, and build information-seeking strategies necessary for lifelong learning.

Problem-Based Learning

The pedagogical strategy of problem-based learning, sometimes called problem posing or inquiry learning, maps well to Interdisciplinary Inquiry's focus on the research question. This teaching strategy fosters critical thinking and lifelong learning by emphasizing the *process* of critical thinking rather than the end products of most undergraduate research, such as the term paper.[7] Common reading for many sections of the course is on Freire's "Banking Concept of Education," introduced in *Pedagogy of the Oppressed*. Freire proposes that learners and teachers take joint responsibility for the learning process.[8] This powerful essay provides students with a picture of themselves as active producers of knowledge, rather than just passive consumers or receptacles to be filled or "banked" with information. Providing a theoretical framework for how the rest of the course is conducted collaboratively, Freire's methods encourage students to take control of their own learning and to step into the teaching role. Rather than acting as the sole providers of knowledge, instructors and librarians of Interdisciplinary Inquiry function as facilitators, questioners, and listeners who guide students into higher-order thinking.

.

One way that students step into the teaching role is through group facilitation of the class discussions. In these facilitations, research clusters present on the ways in which their research question has been informed and re-formed through the various sources of information retrieved in their sessions with the librarian. Rather than a simple oral report or presentation, the group facilitations require students to engage their audience as active participants in the learning. In this way, student learning takes place through the act of teaching others, a key learner-centered strategy that also comes into play during their research cluster discussions with each other. It is hoped that this emphasis on dialogue rather than expert opinion also works to reduce student anxiety as they encounter the intellectual risks inherent in negotiating research questions. While some students may be comfortable navigating such risks independently, some express anxiety in being asked to move beyond their comfort zones of "report writing," illustrating the discomfort and possible frustration when students are asked to take ownership of their own learning and to become "producers of knowledge."

Blumberg's review of the literature on problem-based learning finds this pedagogical approach helps develop critical thinking and often produces students active in using libraries and librarians to seek out and effectively use a variety of information sources. Ultimately, these approaches may help students develop the self-directed learning skills necessary for lifelong learning.[9] Similar phenomena are often displayed by this course's students as the quarter progresses. By actively participating in their research cluster discussions and reflecting on their research through short writing assignments, students work on developing their higher-order thinking by identifying and addressing problems and questions in their thought processes. Early in the quarter, students receive structured practice selecting relevant sources and asking appropriate questions of information sources. By the third or fourth library session, students tend to display more confidence and self-direction in terms of analyzing and negotiating their research processes, and in selecting and evaluating information sources. By helping students to develop their critical thinking and information-seeking skills, it is hoped that this course cultivates and sets in motion self-directed and lifelong learning skills.

Active Learning

UWB librarians teaching this course use active learning techniques to developmentally guide students in finding, evaluating, and using information. Workshop activities are designed to allow students practice and time to build upon their research skills throughout the quarter with the goal of students better understanding not only the tools and mechanical procedures, but also the critical thinking processes necessary for inquiry-based (i.e., problem-posing) research.

One active learning exercise students undertake involves analyzing or "reading" a cultural artifact. Librarians and faculty guide the class through an evaluation and discussion of an artifact which is any primary source such as an image, document, or cultural object. A series of questions adapted from the document analysis worksheets from the National Archives helps students to structure their analysis of the object.[10] After practicing this evaluation process, students then consult print and online sources to find artifacts pertaining to their own research question: for example, still or moving images, diaries or interviews, musical pieces, travel souvenirs, car keys, electronic gadgets, or even the ubiquitous water bottle! Not only does this exercise offer an active learning opportunity, but it also requires students to think about their research questions from multiple perspectives and to think critically about the meaning and purpose of everyday cultural objects. This exercise also asks students to think broadly about varying kinds of information sources, applying an interdisciplinary methodology to their research.

Interdisciplinary Research Methods

All sections of Interdisciplinary Inquiry employ some kind of thematic foreground that allows an interdisciplinary approach to learning and scholarship. In addition to the section that focused on tourism that has already been discussed, other themes have included Malcolm X and the Civil Rights Movement, education, new media, and on a more local level for students from the Puget Sound region, the Cascadia bioregion. The interdisciplinary nature of the course allows students to explore knowledge production from multiple angles and methods of inquiry. Such a method fits with Barr and Tagg's notion of the Learning Paradigm, in which "knowledge is not seen as cumulative and linear, like a wall of bricks, but as a nesting and interacting of frameworks."[11]

The library sessions for the course often favor general full-text databases, as they readily demonstrate a cross-section of academic perspectives. Research clusters can be assigned activities in which they are asked to critically read articles in class, with both the faculty members and librarian on hand to assist. Search result screens often offer a snapshot of conversations across many disciplinary boundaries on a particular topic, placing sociologists in dialogue with film critics, for example. The results also frequently provide discussion prompts about the nature of scholarship itself, including the distinctions among peer-reviewed, scholarly, trade, and popular sources.

Such discussions also allow instructors to call attention to the signature features of scholarly articles and the process of scholarly communication itself. The directors of the Writing and Quantitative Skills Centers often participate in or lead these sessions, guiding students through strategies to help them read such material more effectively. Students are frequently asked to consider different kinds of evidence, such as the use of numbers or statistical data, interviews, or personal narratives. Such discussions also present scholarly communication as a series of ongoing conversations in the academic community, both within and across disciplinary lines. Students are then able to compare disciplinary interpretations of concepts like "refereed," "primary source," "research," and even "evidence" across a continuum rather than as static, fixed notions defined by or dedicated to a single discipline.

Lattuca, Voigt, and Fath point out that while further research is needed to document more explicitly whether interdisciplinarity promotes learning, a body of evidence is emerging to suggest that such an approach exhibits numerous advantages in helping students to grasp key concepts.[12] Librarians and faculty working with Interdisciplinary Inquiry have already noted many strengths of the curriculum, not the least of which is the more holistic approach to research that it promotes. In thinking from an interdisciplinary perspective, students may more easily develop the ability to tackle complex problems from multiple perspectives. Faculty teaching the course have noted that the research clusters tend to develop more interesting research questions, in turn generating greater student investment in their work. For instructors and librarians working with the course, interdisciplinarity creates more flexibility in terms of research activities and assigned readings for an individual section.

Assessment

Librarians and faculty use various methods to assess student learning and the efficacy of the library workshops. Formative assessment methods include faculty and librarian observations and frequent interactions with students and research clusters. Librarians and faculty actively review groups' research questions and the sources they choose. Other methods have included pre- and post-surveys on library or research skills; observation of research cluster class facilitations; review of short reflective writing assignments about the research process and sources; and review of the final research proposal. Future assessment plans include developing a uniform survey that will be administered to incoming juniors in all sections at the beginning and the end of the course.

Program-level assessment occurs on a quarterly and yearly basis. Faculty, librarians, and the directors of the Writing and Quantitative Skills Centers meet as a group every quarter to assess overall progress; report out on each section's activities; share syllabi; develop new curricula; and mentor faculty and academic staff new to teaching the course. This mentoring is critical if new instructors are not experienced in collaborative teaching. These conversations are capped off by a yearly large group meeting to review and revise course goals for the following year.

CONCLUSION

Interdisciplinary Inquiry introduces upper-division students to some of the resources and services they will need not only for the class, but also for their other courses in the IAS program. Owing to its focus on collaboration, problem-based learning, and interdisciplinarity, assignments such as the research proposal allow students to explore research questions in an environment that emphasizes critical thinking and process-oriented learning. The scaffolding in both the workshops and assignments allows students to achieve incremental, small successes over the span of several weeks, which is intended to engage them in key concepts without overwhelming them. The interdisciplinary approach to the course allows students to explore knowledge production from multiple angles and methods of inquiry, offering a more holistic way of conducting research and examining scholarship. Faculty and librarians teaching the course hope that this structure will help students to become better critical thinkers, researchers, writers, and speakers.

NOTES

1. University of Washington, Bothell. "2004-2005 Annual Report." Available: <http://www.uwb.edu/chancellor/uwbanuualreport_0405.pdf>. Accessed: February 14, 2006.

2. University of Washington, Bothell. "Interdisciplinary Arts and Sciences (IAS)." Available: <http://www.uwb.edu/IAS>. Accessed: February 2, 2006.

3. Raspa, Dick and Ward, Dane. "Listening for Collaboration: Faculty and Librarians Working Together." In *The Collaborative Imperative: Librarians and Faculty Working Together in the Information Universe,* edited by Dick Raspa and Dane Ward. Chicago: Association of College & Research Libraries, 2000, pp. 1-18.

4. University of Washington, Bothell. "Mission and Goals of the UWB." Available: <http://www.uwb.edu/about/mission.xhtml>. Accessed: February 14, 2006.

5. Lattuca, Lisa R., Voigt, Lois J., and Fath, Kimberly Q. "Does Interdisciplinarity Promote Learning? Theoretical Support and Researchable Questions." *Review of Higher Education* 28, no. 1 (2004): 23-48.

6. Ross-Gordon, Jovita M. "Adult Learners in the Classroom." *New Directions for Student Services* 102 (2003): 43-52.

7. *Encyclopedia of Education*, 2nd ed. "Instructional Strategies."

8. Freire, Paulo. *Pedagogy of the Oppressed.* New York: Continuum, 2000.

9. Blumberg, Phyllis. "Evaluating the Evidence that Problem-Based Learners are Self-Directed Learners: A Review of the Literature." In *Problem Based Learning: A Research Perspective on Learning Interactions,* edited by Dorothy H. Evensen and Cindy E. Hmelo. Mahwah, NJ: L. Erlbaum Associates, 2000, 199-226.

10. National Archives and Records Administration. "Document Analysis Worksheets." Available: <http://www.archives.gov/education/lessons/worksheets/>. Accessed: February 14, 2006.

11. Barr, Robert B. and Tagg, John, "From Teaching to Learning: A New Paradigm for Undergraduate Education." *Change* 27, no. 6 (1995): 12-25.

12. Lattuca, Voigt, and Fath. "Does Interdisciplinarity Promote Learning?"

Chapter 6

Immersion of Information Literacy and Technology into the Core Discovery Courses

Nancy J. Young
Diane Prorak
Beth Hill

INTRODUCTION

This chapter describes the development of an online information literacy tutorial, online research guides, and tailored class instruction for interdisciplinary freshman courses at the University of Idaho. Librarians, instructors, and information technologists collaborated to incorporate information literacy skills into these courses using a mix of online and face-to-face instructional methods.

SETTING

University of Idaho Library

In 2004, a group of Core Discovery instructors, librarians, and information technologists at the University of Idaho applied for, and were awarded, an Idaho State Board of Education (SBOE) grant for a project titled "Immersion of Information Literacy and Technology into the University of Idaho Core Discovery Courses."[1] The project brought together teams to design information literacy content and active learning components for the courses. Each team consisted of a librarian, Core Discovery instructor, and information technologist; working together, these teams developed instructional materials that were used in both online and face-to-face settings.

Traditionally, University of Idaho library faculty taught face-to-face library instruction sessions in English composition classes, with course content introducing the physical library, explaining how to find books and articles using the library's Web page, and reviewing the basics of evaluating Web sites. However, in 2000, after the University of Idaho began developing a new set of introductory courses for freshmen entitled Core Discovery, which included librarian involvement in the planning, it became apparent that this change in curriculum design warranted a change in library instruction approaches as well.

The Core Discovery courses were interdisciplinary, team-designed courses that examined topics of current cultural significance, and placed special emphasis on basic learning and communication skills, critical thinking, methods of inquiry, computer literacy, and diversity.[2] Librarian team members realized that information literacy was a set of essential skills that needed to be included.[3]

Other key components in teaching students to be active and critical users of information sources are the collaborative relationships that must exist among librarians, information technologists, and classroom instructors. At the University of Idaho, collaboration was a two-part effort, where partnership with Core Discovery instructors resulted in the development of additional information literacy components to incorporate in their courses and where collaboration with information technologists in the Center for Teaching Innovation (CTI) led to the development of an online information literacy tutorial.

Information Literacy in Academic Libraries

Academic libraries have responded to the educational challenge of creating information-literate students by enhancing the traditional face-to-face classroom session with interactive online tutorials and Web-based research guides. Tutorials allow students to learn at their own time and pace, achieve a sense of control over their learning, repeat sections, and assess their learning. Tutorials also aid librarians in teaching basic concepts with a consistent content and delivery to many students. In one 2002 survey, 78 percent of instruction librarians surveyed felt online tutorials were effective.[4] However, these same librarians overwhelmingly felt that the lecture/demonstration and the one-shot session were not obsolete, reinforcing the view that direct instruction by a librarian is still viewed as useful. The survey cites comments from librarians who believe that online tutorials should be accompanied by other library instruction.

Several studies have compared tutorial effectiveness to face-to-face instruction. Most have found no significant difference.[5,6] One study did find students learned more in the face-to-face class sessions and felt more confident about their library skills.[7] Though most studies show online tutorials can be effective for learning, some also found that some librarian involvement (face-to-face or direct feedback) was desirable. At SUNY-Oswego, students completed the tutorial in a classroom with the librarian present. The librarian provided help and sometimes supplemented the tutorial with a traditional worksheet because of resistance to completely eliminating the visit to the library and librarian involvement.[8] It was noted that the tutorial alone did not meet the needs of different learning styles. At the University of Arizona, librarians did not teach face-to-face but gave students e-mail feedback on the appropriateness of the articles they chose after completing the tutorial. This proved to be very helpful to students, but very time consuming for the librarian.[9] At Deakin University in Australia, the face-to-face session was able to provide an exercise relevant to the students' subject and that may have contributed to the higher scores compared to the online tutorial.[10] Thus, while the use of online tutorials has been increasing, there still appears to be a need for a mix of face-to-face and online when possible. This diversity of approaches supports various learning styles, but also presents a challenge in choosing the optimum mix of instructional methods to best meet teaching objectives.

The experiences of the University of Idaho librarians illuminated the inefficiency of conducting library tours and instruction sessions without relation to a specific assignment. Furthermore, generic tutorials can lack the specificity or flexibility to meet students' current information needs for a particular assignment.[11] Integrating information literacy into the curriculum by developing meaningful assignments through collaboration with course instructors leads to better learning outcomes.[12-14] It was hoped that through collaborative team-based efforts, information literacy components could be developed which would be incorporated into the Core Discovery courses.

By embedding information literacy instruction into the curriculum, the librarians sought to develop instruction that:

> result(ed) in assignments . . . where both the teacher's objectives and the librarian's objectives are not only achieved, but are mutually reinforcing—the teacher's objectives being those that help students attain a better understanding of the course's subject matter, and the librarian's objectives being those that enhance the students' ability to find and evaluate information.[15]

OBJECTIVES

One of the primary goals of the grant project was to provide the necessary skills and concepts for students to manage information in a complex, technological environment, an essential prerequisite for critical thinking, conducting research, and for functioning as informed citizens. To effectuate that grant program goal, the following practical objectives for the project were developed: (1) integrating information literacy and technology into the curriculum of interdisciplinary freshman Core Discovery classes; and (2) enhancing collaboration among faculty, librarians, and information technologists.

METHODS

The intention was to design the information literacy tutorial collaboratively and to immerse its components into the Core Discovery curriculum. Collaborative relationships would result in the increased use of librarians as consultants in the instruction process. The librarians were closely involved in the grant-writing process from the very beginning and proposed the following two-pronged approach:

1. Enhance the collaboration with Core Discovery instructors by developing the information literacy components. Other forms of collaboration might include being consultants in the course design stage, resource consultants for faculty, and research consultants for students, as well as teaching in the classroom.
2. Develop an online information literacy tutorial in partnership with information technologists. This would be made available to

college and university educators, K-12 teachers, students, librarians, information technologists, and members of the general public throughout the state.

Collaborating with Core Discovery Instructors

Consulting with Core Discovery instructors at the course design stage gave librarians an opportunity to suggest assignments that highlighted the research process and promoted information literacy skills. For example, during planning sessions, instructors for the "Race, Ethnicity, and Identity" course shared the course project objectives with the librarian. The librarian suggested changes to both the timing of the library sessions and the "Required Sources" section of the assignment. Originally, the library session had been scheduled two months before the assignment was due. The students would have had no idea about what was being covered in the library session and why it was important. Changing the timing of the instruction to coincide with an actual assignment serves to make the instruction much more meaningful for students. More importantly, the planning session gave the instructors and librarian a chance to talk together about the project and ensure that all were "on the same page." In another course, the librarian met with the instructor when the syllabus was being developed and determined dates she would meet with the class and what she would cover. The students' assignment was to create an oral history project about local gays and lesbians, so they first would need background on oral histories, and then they would need to research gay/lesbian issues that related to their interviewee. The course instructor and librarian determined that the first session would be a typical lecture demonstration, but by the next session the students would have established their groups, would know their interviewee and the issues to research. Thus, the second session was planned as a way for the librarian to consult with each group.

Acting as resource consultants, librarians gathered materials for the Core Discovery instructors to use in their classes. Rather than the traditional "show and tell" of resources in a class session or supplying students with a printed bibliography, online library research guides were created to describe the sources.[16] A template (see Figure 6.1) was used for consistent design, making it easy for different librarians to change sections specific to each class. The goal of these online

Core 101 ◆ **Race, Ethnicity, and Identity**

research guide

Librarian: Karen Hertel
E-mail: karenh@uidaho.edu

UI Library Website: www.lib.uidaho.edu

If you need additional help with your research, try:

- Ask a Librarian (email reference)
- Research Assistance Program (RAP)
- Visit the Information Desk on the 1st floor of the Library or call 208-885-6584

The first guide became the template for others.

Reference Works

The reference section can be the best place to start your research.

...ore...   ...or Ref H......

Arrival in the United States	
Passenger and Immigration Lists Index: a Guide to Published Arrival Records of About 500,000 Passengers Who Came to the United States and Canada in the Seventeenth, Eighteenth, and Nineteenth Centuries	Ref CS68.P3

Articles

Articles are found in periodicals. Examples of periodicals are magazines, journals, and newspapers. Scholarly (also called peer-reviewed or refereed) journals are one of the primary means of disseminating ideas in academic scholarship.

If you are unsure how to differentiate between a scholarly journal and a popular magazine, two helpful websites are:

- http://www.skidmore.edu/library/reference/scholarlypop1.htm
- http://www2.cumberlandcollege.edu/library/Li/svpj.htm

How To Find Articles

Articles are located by searching for your topic in an article database (sometimes called an article index). First, select an appropriate database from the Library Find Articles page. The **info** next to the database title gives information about the coverage of the database.

After selecting a database to search, type in search terms. Articles are generally more specific than books and may require a narrower search. For more help see the How to Find Periodical (Magazine) Articles.

Selected Article Indexes for *Race, Ethnicity and Identity*

Title/Description
America: History and Life: No full-text of articles, abstracts only. Many of the articles will need to be requested through Interlibrary Loan. The best database for finding regional historical materials. Only one user at a time so try later if you can't access the database.
Project Muse: Contains the full-text of articles. Articles are all from peer-reviewed, scholarly journals.
JSTOR: Contains the full-text of articles. Articles are all from peer-reviewed, scholarly journals. Must select a "discipline" from the list before clicking the "Search) button.

FIGURE 6.1. Research guide template.

pathfinders was not just to supply a list of resources, but also to teach information literacy skills by:

- describing unique characteristics of different types of resources (i.e., books, scholarly/popular articles, government documents, reference works, Web sites, secondary/primary sources);
- suggesting specific article databases;
- showing examples of search strategies; and
- providing links to more in-depth research help.

In some cases, these guides were developed and used in a class session. Other guides were developed in close consultation with the faculty member to meet the needs of an assignment <http://www.lib. uidaho.edu/instruction/CoreDiscovery/>. In several classes, the Web page was used as the home page for the class session demonstrations and activities. Students in the "Race, Ethnicity and Identity" course were given a printed version of the guide, which was used as an outline for the session, and as a place to take notes.

Examples were brought into the classroom of each type of source (reference books, government documents, periodicals) and the librarian discussed how each source could be used. The librarian also devised a linked example page from her research guide, which in essence was an example of how the class assignment could be approached, and of decisions made regarding possible references to use (see Figure 6.2).

In several "Sex and Culture" Core Discovery classes, links to oral history sites provided visual descriptions as well as sound files (see Figure 6.3). The class listened to a song by a former slave from the Library of Congress American Memory site, saw pictures, and printed interviews of gay and lesbian activists. The links to library databases were also used to demonstrate searching in the session and to show how the guide could be a one-stop research source for their class projects.

In another Core Discovery class, the Web page listed library holdings of old magazines. These print issues were used in a class activity that analyzed how the concept of body image has changed through the decades of the twentieth century. Students browsed magazine issues and referred to the holdings list after the class session.

In gathering resources for the multidisciplinary Core Discovery classes, librarians sometimes found gaps in the collection. In one case

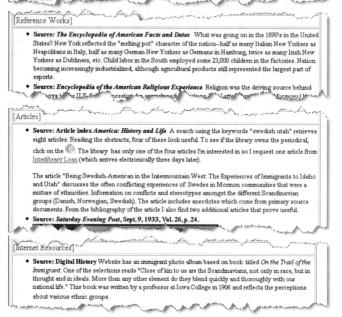

FIGURE 6.2. Examples of approaching the assignment.

(the jazz-based course titled "Feel the Groove"), librarian consultation with the faculty before the classroom sessions led to just-in-time purchase of two book series covering American popular culture decade by decade that were placed on reserve in time for the final project.

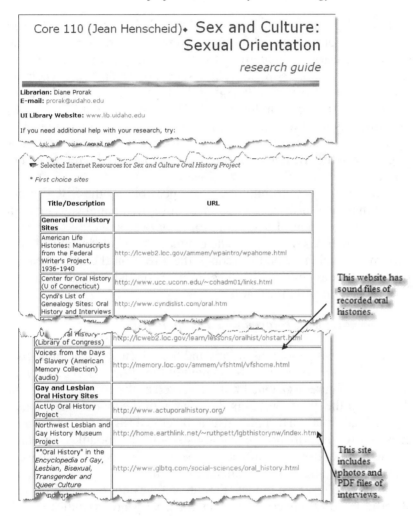

FIGURE 6.3. Research guide with sound files, interviews, and other sources.

In addition to classroom instruction and online research guides, librarians acted as research consultants for students needing extra assistance. Students were encouraged to take advantage of RAP (Research Assistance Program)[17] which gave students the opportunity to meet one-on-one with a librarian. Some librarians set up appointments with small groups of students. For example, one librarian showed groups of students how to find and interpret demographic information on their ancestor's ethnic group by using immigration data found in *U.S. Congressional Serial Set* volumes. In another class, when helping small groups with the "Work, Aging and University of Idaho History" assignment, the librarian located old University of Idaho yearbooks that students used to find information and pictures for a project in which they interviewed university retirees and researched issues of gender in the workplace during the time periods the retirees were active.

Some of the new technology made possible by the SBOE grant meant that face-to-face, in-class instruction was not always done in the library classroom. The sessions for the jazz class were set up by the instructor with his own laptop and equipment already installed in the classroom, which helped to reduce the stress on the often heavily scheduled library classroom and eliminate confusion for the students about where to meet for that day.

Collaborating with Information Technologists

Collaboration among librarians and the information technologists at the CTI focused on the development of the information literacy tutorial (see Figure 6.4). One librarian served as the co-coordinator for this part of the grant, outlining the content of the modules and meeting with information technologists to discuss design and technical issues. As the information technologists built the modules, she then met with other librarians to get comments and revisions, which were relayed to the information technology team.

Unlike the research guides, the tutorial was not designed for one specific Core Discovery class, but for a very broad audience—all Idaho citizens, as specified in the SBOE grant. There was an inherent dilemma in trying to develop a tutorial to meet the needs of two specific audiences: the students in the subject-oriented Core Discovery classes and anyone in the state of Idaho who needed to hone information literacy skills. Working with the CTI, technologists and designers helped to bridge this gap. The technologists were neither instructors nor librarians, and so could serve as a more neutral audience to determine whether various versions of the tutorial were useful and understandable. They also gave valuable advice about the best

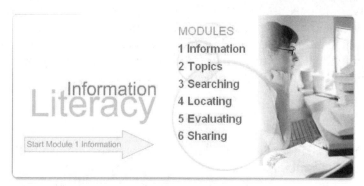

WHAT IS INFORMATION LITERACY?

Information Literacy is the ability to identify what information is needed, understand how the information is organized, identify the best sources of information for a given need, locate those sources, evaluate the sources critically, and share that information. It is the knowledge of commonly used research techniques.

WHY IS INFORMATION LITERACY IMPORTANT?

Information literacy is critically important because we are surrounded by a growing ocean of information in all formats. Not all information is created equal: some is authoritative, current, reliable, but some is biased, out of date, misleading, false. The amount of information available is going to keep increasing. The types of technology used to access, manipulate, and create information will likewise expand.

HOW WILL I USE INFORMATION LITERACY SKILLS?

Information literacy skills are used for academic purposes, such as research papers and group presentations. They're used on the job—the ability to find, evaluate, use and share information is an essential skill. Consumer decisions, such as which car or vacuum cleaner to purchase, are critical. You'll also use these skills by participating fully in a democratic society as an informed citizen by understanding issues and voting.

Modules: 1 Information | 2 Topics | 3 Searching | 4 Locating | 5 Evaluating | 6 Sharing

©2006 All rights reserved.
University of Idaho
Information Literacy Portal
UI Core Curriculum
Credits

FIGURE 6.4. Information literacy tutorial home page.

ways to convey information via graphics, use of interactive exercises, and comprehensibility of library terms.

Other challenges inherent in working with the requirement that the tutorial be available to everyone in Idaho meant that WebCT course software could not be used, despite the recommendations of the CTI. Instead, the tutorial was done with Flash Player and other commonly available downloadable software. Likewise, some of the assessment tools commonly used in WebCT-based courses (such as automatically graded and randomly generated quiz questions) were not available for use in the tutorial. Such tools could have been used to evaluate student learning, and to motivate them to participate by assigning points for completion of all or part of the online tutorial.

RESULTS

In the collaboration with Core Discovery instructors, initially only selected instructors worked with librarians to incorporate information literacy skills into their classes. However, by fall 2005, librarians partnered with four additional Core Discovery classes, using online research guides, face-to-face sessions, and e-mail assistance. This pilot project has demonstrated its success by these additional requests from instructors who heard about these resources and services.

Findings regarding the methods of information literacy instruction mirror the studies cited earlier, showing a need for a mix of online and face-to-face. The results of a questionnaire sent to the Core Discovery instructors, as shown in the comments below, indicate that most of these instructors want a variety of teaching methods to be used. One instructor was very pleased with the Web research guide created, but soundly rejected the thought of using an online tutorial instead of face-to-face sessions with the librarian. She felt strongly that the human interaction was important. Another instructor, whose class came for face-to-face sessions, said:

> Although I believe that similar information could be provided on-line, the face-to-face interaction worked particularly well for freshman, who are relegated to online sources most of their time. The face-to-face nature of the workshop made the information stick longer and made it more important to receive the information in the first place. Also, the students could start working in

small groups as part of this workshop, rather than scheduling a follow-up meeting with their group members.[18]

Another instructor, due to time constraints, opted to use only a Web page guide to assist students in evaluating sources and finding book reviews. He later commented that he thought more students would have used the Web-based research guides if the librarian had introduced the pages and concepts in person. However, another instructor, who had a face-to-face session, felt that appropriately sequenced tutorials would have adequately replaced the session with the librarian.

The Web-based research guides were used in a variety of settings. One instructor commented that students found the research guides very helpful in identifying appropriate source material. In addition, the guides helped reference desk staff find materials for students in the classes. In another class, the instructor was very enthusiastic about the research guide, but when the librarian attended the final project presentations, and looked at students' sources, it did not appear the guide had been used as much as hoped. The instructor commented that a greater emphasis on quality sources in the final product would be made in the future. Another instructor confronted this issue saying, "I am expecting students to use the resources developed for them in the project they're completing now. I will insist that they consult the resources and calibrate their grade accordingly."[19]

The collaboration with CTI technologists resulted in the completion of six modules of the tutorial.[20] Core Discovery instructors and the Core program director have reviewed the tutorial. In the future, there will be an increased focus on marketing the tutorial, with suggestions for how instructors might use parts of the tutorial with graded assignments. Future plans also include developing more modules tailored to the use of the University of Idaho Library's online catalog and article databases, development of tools for assessing the tutorial's effectiveness, and consequently, updating the tutorials with revisions as needed.

CONCLUSION

The purpose of these collaborative efforts was to incorporate information literacy skills into the Core Discovery classes in line with the

Core program's stated objectives. Instructional focus consisted of using a mix of online and face-to-face instructional methods, which met the approval of the collaborating instructors. A strong foundation has been established in terms of resources and collaborative relationships. This teamwork approach has led to more interaction with the director of the Core Discovery program and more visibility for the library. Using this additional contact with the director, heightened institutional support to implement more use and assessment of the tutorial can be expected, with greater participation from more of the Core Discovery instructors.

NOTES

1. Hill, Elizabeth, Schlater, David, and Young, Nancy. *Immersion of Information Literacy and Technology into Freshman Core Courses.* Available: <http://www.educause.edu/librarydetailpage/666&id=WRC0544>. Accessed: February 8, 2006.

2. *Core Discovery Courses. Numbers and Descriptions.* Available: <http://www.students.uidaho.edu/default.aspx?pid=99667>. Accessed: January 31, 2006.

3. *Core Discovery: General Course Objectives.* University of Idaho. Available: <http://www.students.uidaho.edu/default.aspx?pid=92805>. Accessed: January 31, 2006.

4. Hollister, Christopher and Coe, Jonathan. "Current Trends vs. Traditional Models: Librarians' Views on the Methods of Library Instruction." *College & Undergraduate Libraries* 10, no. 2 (2003): 49-63.

5. Germain, Carol Anne and Bobish, Gregory. "Virtual Teaching: Library Instruction Via the Web." *Reference Librarian* 77 (2002): 69-86.

6. Nichols, James, Shaffer, Barbara, and Shockey, Karen. "Changing the Face of Instruction: Is Online or In-Class More Effective?" *College & Research Libraries* 64 (September 2003): 378-388.

7. Churkovich, Marion and Oughtred, Christine. "Can an Online Tutorial Pass the Test of Library Instruction?" *Australian Academic and Research Libraries* 33 (March 2002): 25-35.

8. See note 6.

9. Bracke, Paul J. and Dickstein, Ruth. "Web Tutorials and Scalable Instruction: Testing the Waters." *Reference Services Review* 30, no. 4 (2002): 330-337.

10. See note 7.

11. Ferguson, K. Stuart and Ferguson, Alice. "The Remote Library and Point-of-Need User Education: An Australian Academic Library Perspective." *Journal of Interlibrary Loan, Document Delivery & Electronic Reserve* 15 no. 3 (2005): 43-60.

12. D'Angelo, Barbara J. and Maid, Barry M. "Moving Beyond Definitions: Implementing Information Literacy Across the Curriculum." *Journal of Academic Librarianship* 30, no. 3 (2004): 212-217.

13. Hine, Alison et al. "Embedding Information Literacy in a University Subject Through Collaborative Partnerships." *Psychology Learning and Teaching* 2, no. 2 (2002): 102-107.

14. Noe, Nancy W. and Bishop, Barbara A. "Assessing Auburn University Library's Tiger Information Literacy Tutorial (TILT)." *Reference Services Review* 33, no. 2 (2005): 173-187.

15. Farber, Evan. "Faculty-Librarian Cooperation: A Personal Retrospective." *Reference Services Review* 27, no. 3 (1999): 229-234.

16. *Core Discovery Research Guides.* University of Idaho. Available: <http://www.lib.uidaho.edu/instruction/CoreDiscovery>. Accessed: February 1, 2006.

17. *Research Assistance Program.* University of Idaho. Available: <http://www.lib.uidaho.edu/reference/rapform.html>. Accessed: February 1, 2006.

18. Sandra Reineke, e-mail message to authors, August 20, 2005.

19. Gary Williams, e-mail message to authors, April 13, 2005.

20. Core Information Literacy Tutorial. University of Idaho. Available: <http://www.webs.uidaho.edu/info_literacy>. Accessed: February 1, 2006.

Chapter 7

PUC 101: A Collaborative Effort for Freshman Orientation

Tammy S. Guerrero
Kristin M. Harkin

INTRODUCTION/SETTING

Purdue University Calumet is located in Hammond, Indiana, which is about thirty miles east of Chicago. This area is home to a diverse ethnic population. Three-fourths of Purdue Calumet students are first-generation college students and more than one-third are minority students. Over 90 percent are Indiana residents. More than half of Purdue Calumet students are enrolled on a part-time basis. Enrollment for the spring 2005 semester was around 9,200 students. Purdue Calumet offers associate's degrees in twenty different fields, bachelor's degrees in 112 fields, and master's degrees in fourteen different fields of study.

The library's collection includes over 200,000 volumes, over 2,500 current journal subscriptions, including electronic journals. The library is open seventy-five hours per week, including evenings and weekends. The library is staffed by a director, assistant director, six professional librarians, two paraprofessionals, seven full-time and three part-time clerical staff, and numerous student assistants. Purdue Calumet librarians are held to the same standards as the classroom faculty. They publish in scholarly journals in their field and hold offices in and sit on university and library committees. They continuously conduct research in their field; contribute to librarianship by reviewing books and journal articles, and presenting papers at national and international conferences. Participating in these activities enables the librarians to draw and learn from the experiences of peers, and deliver the best possible reference services to their patrons.

The Purdue University Calumet Orientation Office is housed in The Center for Career and Leadership Development, an office that offers student life and activities, leadership programming, student employment, and career services in addition to the office of orientation. The office of orientation includes several different types of orientation programming, each geared for different populations including, first-year students, transfer students, nontraditional students, and international students. In order to effectively implement these programs, the orientation office hires twenty student orientation leaders to assist with programming, in addition to a small staff consisting of an assistant director, graduate aide, and support staff.

In order to ensure that incoming freshmen and transfer students feel comfortable at, want to attend, and want to graduate from Purdue University Calumet, a multifaceted orientation program called PUC 101 was created. This program is a collaboration of the Center for Career Development which houses the Office of Orientation, nearly every other academic office on campus, especially the library.

The following case study is a model for an innovative and effective program set up to meet the needs of a very diverse, multiage, multicultural population that Purdue Calumet serves in Northwest Indiana and the surrounding Chicagoland area. The PUC 101 program reaches a very diverse population, with exciting and innovative ways of bringing the information to a vastly different group of people.

OBJECTIVES

The objective is to present incoming students with an opportunity to become familiar with the campus, meet other new students and get acquainted with the many services and programs needed to become a successful student. Accomplishing these objectives leaves a student feeling more "connected" to the university and positively increases student retention.

It is important to note, that having a goal to increase student retention is not enough. It requires a focus on improving student success foremost, with retention following. "Retention efforts that do not put students first will not work."[1] Studies show that fostering success in the first year is the most significant intervention an institution can make toward student persistence. In fact, a student's first two to six weeks of college comprise the critical transition period when the student begins to decide whether to return for the second year.[2]

With these goals in mind, PUC 101, a new student orientation program, was created. The intention was to develop a program that eased a new student's transition to college, and have a little fun along the way. As this program progressed, several other efforts have been developed as offshoots of the original PUC 101, to target different special populations including transfer, international, and nontraditional students.

The traditional orientation program, designed for first-year students transitioning from high school, is a day-long program which includes various enrollment steps such as placement testing, academic advising, and registration. The day also includes essential components such as a campus tour with stops at Computer Services, Library, Financial Aid, and the Information Desk, where student identification cards are issued. Academic overviews, student life scenarios, and small group exercises are conducted with the intent of helping students get acquainted. The program also includes a session for parents and family members, which runs concurrently (but separately) with the programs for incoming students.

Parents and family members are a vital part of students' learning. With this in mind, PUC 101 offers the half-day session for parents and family members designed to help strengthen the three-way partnership that the student, parent/family member, and Purdue University Calumet will share during a student's college years. Although it is important for students to be independent, they also need support from their family members, which will help them handle many changes and transitions that will occur during the college experience. The Purdue Calumet Parent and Family Member Program offers opportunities to:

- meet faculty and staff from a son/daughter's academic department;
- understand the level of commitment a PUC student is making;
- get important information on how to best support a PUC student;
- learn about parental rights related to academic information; and

- learn to identify the key changes and adjustments a student will make while attending college.

Nontraditional and Transfer Students

As mentioned, additional specialized programs have been developed to address the unique and specific needs of nontraditional, transfer, and international students. The first of these programs is called, "Get Set Saturday," a program designed for nontraditional and transfer students. A nontraditional student is defined as an adult beginning college for the first time or returning to school after years in the work force. Many students are trying to put their lives back together, starting with their education. These student populations have concerns that are much different from that of the traditional eighteen-year-old student, and the PUC 101 program addresses their needs and helps build their confidence.

This conference-style program is much different than the PUC 101 program for traditional students. Nontraditional and transfer students can select sessions, listen to panel discussions, and talk one-on-one with faculty and staff. The panel discussion, a favorite for students as well as faculty and staff, consists of past and current nontraditional students who have completed college degrees or are in the process of obtaining a college degree. These discussions have proven to be a great help to incoming nontraditional students. The program is very touching, and always reveals stories of a life transition. Students rave that this program has eased their anxiety and quelled their trepidation. Many have told us that "Get Set Saturday" gave them the confidence to stay in school and graduate.

International Students

Another example of a special PUC 101 is an orientation program called "Passport" which is designed to meet the needs of international students. This program is customized to include topics such as finding out where to shop, opening a checking account, immigration requirements, obtaining an on-campus job, and adjusting culturally to campus life. Many of these students are away from their home countries for the first time and do not have friends or relatives in the area.

Language barriers, differing cultural expectations and norms, communication styles, and attitudes regarding gender roles may make the transition more difficult for international students both socially and academically.[3] "Passport" provides the opportunity to meet new people, including other international students and American students. This program also includes a social component that introduces typical "American" activities, such as playing pool and eating pizza. Meeting new people through "Passport" helps international students become adjusted which has a strong impact on their success as American students.

The decision to target these unique students and conduct their orientation programs separately has proven to be very helpful and has made those "special" students feel more comfortable when they go to class. Many of the nontraditional students stated that they feared being the "old lady" or "old man" in the class, but were pleasantly surprised to find that there were, in fact, others in the class their age or older. On that same note, several "traditional" age students have commented that they enjoy being in class with older students. They have shared many stories about how much an older student has to offer to class discussions because they have simply lived longer, and are more experienced than the so-called traditional student.

The Library's Involvement

The library has been involved with PUC 101 since its onset. The library is an important lifeline to the university, and this is stressed from the beginning. Library and orientation leaders collaborate to combine programs which introduce incoming first-year students to the library's physical facility as well as the services offered. Participation from the library, as well as all campus resources, is essential to having a "seamless" orientation approach. "Seamless learning" is a concept first introduced by G. D. Kuh as a way of integrating educationally purposeful activities and eliminating boundaries between academic and student affairs.[4]

The seamless orientation approach also suggests that orientation is not a single, static event, but rather a dynamic process that begins when a student expresses interest in a college or university and continues through the formal orientation/advising/registration, program, and welcome week activities.[5] Seen in this way, orientation becomes a campus-wide responsibility shared by faculty, student leaders, and student services staff. All "stakeholders" need to know, support, and convey key institutional values in an effort to welcome new members of the campus community. Coordination of efforts among university departments is needed to ensure that new students receive consistent messages about the values and expectations held for them.

METHODS

The methodology used in PUC 101 is threefold. The librarians and director of orientation decided that since some people comprehend and retain concepts differently from others, that three different types of programs should be offered, with the intention of reaching a maximum number of students, in the fashion that they adapt to best. In other words, some students respond to a large, auditorium-type presentation, some prefer smaller, one-on-one interaction, while others benefit from a combination of both. PUC 101 and the other instructional/orientation programs have followed this three-pronged approach, and found it to be very successful.

Addressing the Entire Group

In order to give the incoming students and parents in attendance a clear understanding of what the university offers, a formal auditorium-based presentation is given to the entire group. Using a PowerPoint slide show, representatives from various university divisions (including the library) speak about the services offered by each office. In addition, students are provided with packets of information including brochures and handouts from each department. This is a very "formal" way to greet everyone, and since this approach can be overwhelming to certain students, other methods have been found to be more successful.

Working with Smaller Groups

Another effective way to familiarize students and their parents with the university is to divide them into smaller groups, with an orientation leader assigned to approximately ten students. Each group takes a walking tour of the university, stopping at the various offices, including the library, for a closer look at the services offered. A representative from each office gives the group a short speech, followed by a quiz question related to the information that was given. When the correct answer is supplied, the orientation leader is a particular puzzle piece. After all the offices have been visited, a completed puzzle is the group's ticket to lunch. This is a great opportunity for the groups to mingle, get to know each other, and hopefully, feel even more comfortable with the university.

Offering Instructional Literacy Class Sessions

After freshmen have been introduced to the library, their experience is supplemented with library instructional sessions, which take place during the regular semester. Professors from Freshman Experience courses, as well as English Composition, General Studies, Behavioral Sciences, Communication, and some Science courses, devote one of their class periods to library instruction. The students meet in the library's electronic classroom for a three-part session which consists of a lecture, library tour, and one-on-one assistance from the social sciences librarian. These instructional sessions introduce students to the library's electronic card catalogue, electronic databases and journals, and the physical layout of the library via a walking tour. Students are encouraged to work on the computers in the classroom after the lecture is concluded. The social sciences librarian canvasses the room for people in need of help, and conducts one-on-one instruction. Students are introduced to Boolean operators, wild card characters, and truncated searches, and learn how to differentiate among scholarly, consumer, and trade publications. Many times, a library scavenger hunt is given, which challenges the student to search for specific titles, types of material, and electronic entries. This exercise familiarizes the students with the library and teaches them how to use databases and electronic card catalog. Many times the instructor will use these scavenger hunts as a graded exercise. Some will offer it as extra credit. These sessions have proven to be very effective in making the incoming students feel more familiar with the library and the surrounding campus community.

RESULTS

PUC 101 has proven to be very successful in accomplishing its goals. The programs have been very well received by students, parents, and family members, and have received positive benchmarks for student attendees related to retention, completion rates, and impact on Grade Point Average (GPA). Student attendees have enjoyed PUC 101 programs overall and found them to be beneficial. Survey results show that:

- 98 percent of students have a better understanding of what educational resources (tutoring center, library, writing center, and other student services) are available to them;
- 88 percent of students found it easy to network and meet new people at PUC 101;
- 76 percent of students now feel more confident about starting classes at Purdue University Calumet.

In addition, parents and family members found the day to be valuable and wrote many comments thanking the staff for providing the program. Survey results for parents and family members attending PUC 101 show:

- 99 percent of parents/family members have a better understanding of available educational resources (tutoring, writing center, and other student services);
- 99 percent of parents/family members have a better understanding of their parental rights and how they can better support their student throughout college;
- 99 percent of parents/family members found the materials distributed were relevant and helpful;
- 99 percent of parents/family members enjoyed the day.

The Orientation Office has started to benchmark student success as it relates to first-year students. At this point, data have been collected from 2002 to 2004 (see Table 7.1).

By using the first-year students of 2002 as a control group, the benchmark study shows that students who attended PUC 101 and completed a Freshman Experience Course had an 8 to 9 percent higher retention

TABLE 7.1. One year (fall to fall) retention outcomes.

	N	Students retained	Retention rate (%)
Fall 2002	1,051	620	59
Fall 2003 (limited PUC 101)	171	117	68
Fall 2004 (both PUC 101 and Freshman Year Experience [FYE])	530	354	67

rate than those students who did not. University and library staff will continue to track the success of first-year students, and use it to improve orientation and freshman experience programs. Another effective way to measure the collaborative efforts of PUC 101 is to conduct a library survey. During library instructional sessions, the social sciences librarian distributes evaluation forms using a program called Flashlight. This form asks the student ten questions concerning the instructional session that has just taken place. See Figure 7.1 for session results for fall 2005 semester.

The library director, assistant director, and social sciences librarian review and discuss these numbers, and adjust or redesign the instructional sessions accordingly. This is the same evaluation program that the "in class" faculty uses. The Purdue Calumet Library is in the process of redesigning this evaluation process to better serve the needs of students. For the spring 2006 semester, the social sciences librarian had designed a different type of evaluation process that could give a better indication of the librarian's teaching skills. First, a pretest is given to the students prior to attending the library instructional session. The ten questions relate to content that will be covered in the instructional session such as library holdings, Boolean operators, and determining whether a journal is scholarly or not. After the instructional session, the librarian administers exactly same questions as a posttest. The goal is to improve scores from the pretest to the posttest, demonstrating that the students leave the session with a great deal more knowledge about the library. This testing process is in its infancy, but early results show that students scored an average of 38 percent correct on the pretest, and an average of 81 percent correct on the posttest. These early data prove that the students are learning from the instructional lectures. Purdue Calumet librarians feel that this is a better method

Core Questions:

1. Librarian creates an atmosphere highly conducive to learning.
2. Librarian's explanations are especially clear.
3. Assignments are relevant, interesting, and well-integrated.
4. Librarian has stimulated my thinking.
5. Librarian seems well prepared for class.
6. Librarian stimulated interest in the Library.
7. Overall, I feel I have learned a great deal in this workshop.
8. I would enjoy taking another workshop from this instructor.
9. Librarian made me less apprehensive about doing research.
10. Librarian made me feel comfortable with the Library.

	a. Strongly Agree	b. Agree	c. Neutral	d. Disagree	e. Strongly Disagree	No. of Students	Weighted Mean
Q1	156	193	57	6	27	439	4.01
Q2	123	201	44	18	24	410	3.93
Q3	66	164	129	24	28	411	3.53
Q4	95	141	121	46	22	425	3.57
Q5	189	175	36	8	24	432	4.15
Q6	103	137	81	36	13	370	3.76
Q7	118	169	98	20	25	430	3.78
Q8	81	154	73	33	29	370	3.61
Q9	96	142	107	26	27	398	3.64
Q10	121	149	68	10	16	364	3.96

FIGURE 7.1. Fall 2005 session results.

of measuring student learning outcomes. Figure 7.2 illustrates the success of PUC 101.

CONCLUSION

PUC 101 is an innovative and effective way to introduce students to the library as well as other important areas on campus. By focusing on student success first, it is possible to make a positive impact on students and their families. This is a great way to get students involved and acclimated to the library from the time they first set foot on campus. The methods used by PUC 101 directors, faculty, staff members, and orientation leaders are successful at calming student fears, giving them confidence, and supporting the university's strategic plan overall by increasing enrollment and retaining students. Although PUC 101

#	Question	Strongly Agree	Agree	Disagree	Strongly Disagree
1	The info. mailed to me was clear and helpful.	27%	69%	4%	0%
2	I now have a better understanding of what educational resources (tutoring, writing center, and other student services) are available to me.	42%	56%	1%	0%
3	It was easy to meet new people at PUC 101.	19%	69%	9%	0%
4	All of my questions were answered today.	23%	67%	9%	0%
5	I feel confident about being a new student at PUC.	36%	40%	4%	0%
6	Orientation has made me less anxious about attending PUC this semester.	18%	49%	27%	5%
7	The PUC 101 staff and orientation leaders were knowledgeable and friendly.	59%	38%	1%	0%
14	I felt comfortable in the testing environment during the math placement test.	34%	53%	4%	0%

#	Question	Excellent	Good	Fair	Poor	N/A
8	The orientation Web site	27%	59%	11%	0%	2%
9	The check-in process	40%	51%	8%	0%	--
10	The orientation leader skits	47%	40%	9%	2%	--
11	The resources presentations	33%	57%	8%	0%	--
12	The campus tour	30%	47%	17%	3%	--
13	The computer lab session	29%	55%	14%	1%	--
15	Your overall PUC 101 experience	37%	55%	6%	0%	--

FIGURE 7.2. PUC 101 feedback.

is in its infancy, it has already proven to be a very effective program that benefits everyone involved, most importantly, Purdue Calumet students. Improvements will be made to the PUC 101 program and new ideas will be brought to life as Purdue University Calumet continues to carry on Purdue pride, reaching one student at a time and leaving no one behind.

NOTES

1. Levitz, Randi and Noel, Lee. "Connecting Students to Institutions: Keys to Retention and Success." In *The Freshman Year Experience,* edited by M. L. Upcraft and J. N. Gardner. San Francisco: Jossey-Bass Inc., 1989, pp. 65-81.

2. Rode, Dennis. "The Role of Orientation in Institutional Retention." In *National Orientation Directors Association Orientation Planning Manual* (2000): 1-7.

3. Cawthorn, Tony W. and Miller, Michael. "Today's Students and Their Impact on Orientation and First-Year Programs." In *Designing Successful Transitions: A Guide for Orienting Students to College,* edited by J. A. Ward-Roof and C. Hatch.

Columbia, SC: University of South Carolina, National Resource Center for The First-Year Experience and Students in Transition, 2003, pp. 1-14.

4. Kuh, George D. "Guiding Principles for Creating Seamless Learning Environments for Undergraduates." *Journal of College Student Development* 37 (February 1996): 135-148.

5. Rode, Dennis. "The Role of Orientation in Institutional Retention." In *National Orientation Directors Association Orientation Planning Manual* (2000): 1-7.

Chapter 8

Making the Case for Enhanced Learning: Using Case Studies in a Credit-Bearing Library Course

Christopher V. Hollister

INTRODUCTION

The case study teaching method has been adopted by an increasingly broad community of academic disciplines. Current pedagogical literature is replete with evidence of this trend. The author will demonstrate how the method is effectively employed to teach information literacy skills in a credit-bearing library course. The sample case described in this chapter is broken down into its core elements, including classroom management techniques and assessment of learning outcomes. The chapter author also provides working definitions of the case method and related concepts, recommendations for developing a case, and a discussion of the method's history and its effectiveness.

SETTING

The University of Buffalo's Arts and Sciences Libraries offers the stand-alone, credit-bearing library course, ULC-257: Library Research Methods. The course is an increasingly popular and effective way for instruction librarians to integrate themselves into educational curricula, and to continue the advancement of information literacy on campus. Librarians who teach this course have the opportunity to use more creative, effective, and research-proven instructional methods than they are accustomed to using for traditional one-shot library instruction sessions. Using case studies is one such method that has been shown to facilitate enhanced student learning. The author will demonstrate how case studies are used to teach a module of ULC-257 on evaluating information.

OBJECTIVES

The course objectives for students enrolled in the ULC-257 course include (1) becoming effective and efficient researchers and library users; (2) honing abilities to analyze and critically evaluate information; and (3) developing the skills necessary for becoming information savvy and lifelong learners. Strong emphasis is given to the second of these objectives. Case studies help students to better understand complex information literacy issues and interrelated processes through application. Students develop and refine their critical thinking skills as they learn to apply information literacy concepts to relevant, real-world scenarios. The case method also stimulates a more lively and engaging classroom, and a more active learning environment.

The sample case discussed in this chapter was developed to help students examine reasons for and influences on news stories. The goal is for students to develop specific criteria for evaluating those stories. Cases are also used for coursework on other real-world information-related issues such as censorship, disinformation, information overload, intellectual freedom, media bias, plagiarism, and privacy. Standardized course evaluations, students' written responses, and comparisons of test scores and final grades all suggest the usefulness and effectiveness of applying case studies to teach information literacy skills.

CASE STUDY METHOD

History

Evidence of teaching with case studies dates back to 1870 at Harvard Law School.[1] The method was subsequently adopted by other prominent American law schools, and then by the Harvard Graduate School of Business Administration in 1908.[2] These professional schools were the staging grounds for using case studies. With the exception of medicine, there is little evidence to show that the method was used significantly to teach in other academic disciplines until the 1980s when many areas of study became more professionally oriented. In 1986, Lee Shulman proposed the use of case studies for developing teachers in the field of professional education and, more universally, in the liberal arts.[3] Later, the American Association for Higher Education investigated the potential of using case studies to develop the teaching skills of college and university faculty.[4] In 1994, Clyde Herreid put forth the method as a novel approach to improving science education.[5]

During the past two decades, the body of case study literature has grown significantly, and the practice has spread to widely disparate disciplines within the arts and humanities, social sciences, and sciences. In 1999, the National Center for Case Studies Teaching in Science <http://ublib.buffalo.edu/libraries/projects/cases/case.html> was established to "promote the development and dissemination of innovative materials and sound educational practices for case teaching."[6] The Center provides opportunities for faculty to receive training in the method, and its Web site provides access to an ever-expanding database of peer-reviewed cases.

What Is Case Study Teaching?

As with any form of instruction, there is room for variation when using case studies. There are, however, basic principles of the method that must be present: the case itself, case questions, small group work, and case debriefing.[7] The most obvious feature is the case itself. A case is an instructional instrument that appears in the form of a narrative that includes information and/or data that is relevant and directly applicable to course subject matter, and is presented as a real-world scenario. Typically, cases are presented as complex issues or problems that require in-depth examination, discussion, and debate. As Paul Lawrence writes, "A good case is the vehicle by which a chunk of reality is brought into the classroom to be worked over by the class and the instructor. A good case keeps the class discussion grounded upon some of the stubborn facts that must be faced up to in real-life situations."[8]

Study questions follow at the end of a case. Instructors will sometimes employ the interrupted case method,[9] which also allows for questions to be addressed in the middle of the case. These questions, like the case itself, are designed with specific learning objectives in mind that require students to deeply examine the concepts, consequences, and issues of the case at hand.

Students work in small groups to examine, discuss, and report on case study questions. The chapter author typically uses the think/pair/share[10] technique for small group work. For this method, students are broken up into pairs. They are instructed to think individually about their responses to case questions, and then to discuss responses with their group members. Groups must decide how best to respond to the questions, and then report to the rest of the class during case debriefing.

Debriefing is the feature of case study teaching that binds the experience together. The traditional and most common models of classroom instruction are teacher-dominated, typically involving lecture that is interspersed with sporadic student input. With the case method, instructors become facilitators, and students provide most of the analysis and classroom discussion and debate. It is the instructor's job to keep groups on task, prod students into deeper examinations of the case, ask probing or open-ended questions, imbue students with confidence to express themselves, and encourage open, fair, and honest debate. Instructors must be neutral on the issues of a case and, at times, they must play the devil's advocate. The method is a balancing act that requires instructors to think quickly, be flexible, and give up a measure of classroom control.

Why Use Case Studies?

The ultimate reason for using the case method is to improve learning outcomes by moving beyond routine memorization to an actual understanding of course subject matter. However, cases must be developed with specific learning objectives in mind. As noted, having students hone their abilities to analyze and critically evaluate information is a primary objective for the library course that the author teaches. As Clyde Herreid writes, "If reading, arguing, and challenging are hallmarks of critical thinking, then case studies are the poster children for the process."[11] According to Kunselman and Johnson, "Integrating case studies will provide well-rounded, critical thinkers, which, in turn, will result in students becoming better informed."[12]

There is no shortage of pedagogical literature touting the benefits of active learning techniques in the classroom, and case study teaching is one such technique. The theory behind active learning is that students will internalize subject matter better when they are more directly involved in their own learning. Active learning techniques create a classroom environment of cooperative learning where students learn not only from their instructor, but also from one another.[13] Learning outcomes for students engaged in active learning activities include their "ability to think critically, to engage in problem solving and to improve communication skills."[14]

Until recently, there was very little empirical research in the literature to demonstrate the effectiveness of case method teaching. Published evidence, although universally positive, was primarily anecdotal or theoretical in nature. Recognizing this, Olorunnisola, Ramasubramanian, Russill, and Dumas developed an instrument to assess the use of case studies in a general education course.[15] About the study's results, the authors write, "Our use of the case study method enhanced students' learning of course material."[16] Another benefit of using the case method is the rethinking of course materials and of the actual teaching process by classroom instructors. Kunselman and Johnson report that, "Using case studies could serve to renew instructors' interest in course material, thereby creating a higher level of enthusiasm that hopefully will come across to students. Thus, both students and instructors can benefit."[17]

Developing a Case

Instructors must have very specific learning objectives in mind when developing a case. They must also have a clear idea of how to teach the case, what questions to ask, and how to steer case debriefing. Cases can be actual, unedited, preexisting accounts, such as news stories, or stories that are modified to target specific learning objectives. Clyde Herreid, Director of the National Center for Case Studies Teaching in Science, writes about cases derived from preexisting materials such as advertisements, cartoons, magazines, motion pictures, newspapers, novels, and television dramas.[18] Cases can also be, and often are, complete works of the imagination, though they must be based on relevant, real-world scenarios. In short, cases may come from any number of sources that, in ways that are authentic and recognizable, tell a story. For the case discussed in this chapter, the author wrote a narrative that compares, contrasts, and questions how two newspapers provided significantly different coverage of the same news story.

THE LIBRARY COURSE

The ULC-257: Library Research Methods course taught by the chapter author is an undergraduate level, general education offering. The course attracts students from their freshman through their senior years, and from widely diverse academic disciplines. As noted earlier, one of the primary goals for the course is for students to hone their abilities to analyze and critically evaluate information. Using cases that involve current and/or controversial issues generates enhanced student interest and enthusiasm, as well as lively classroom discussions and debates.

The case is introduced to students when they have completed several modules on information literacy concepts and issues as a matter of their regular coursework. Students learn about different types of information, the organization of information, and advanced methods for finding information. The case discussed below is used to teach a course module that focuses on analyzing and critically evaluating information. It is also noteworthy that students quickly become accustomed to the case study method for learning course material. By the third or fourth week of the semester, they are working in established small groups for classroom activities, and they are aware of their responsibilities within their groups.

SAMPLE CASE STUDY

"Rising Temperatures, Differing Viewpoints: A Case Study on the Politics of Information" was developed from two articles published in the *The New York Times* (NYT) and *Wall Street Journal* (WSJ) about the release of a 2003 Environmental Protection Agency (EPA) report on the state of the environment.[19] The NYT article features White House editing of the report, which eliminated several references to the causes and dangers of global warming. The WSJ article, conversely, highlights the EPA report's evidence of recent environmental improvements. The case study author uses indicative portions from each article to construct the case. The primary learning objective for the case is for students to develop specific criteria for evaluating news stories.

The first half of "Rising Temperatures, Differing Viewpoints" discusses the NYT article, and the second half reviews the WSJ article. This is an interrupted case, which allows for questions to follow each section, and for those sections to be considered independently before the case is examined and debriefed on the whole. The author employs the think/pair/share technique to review case questions. In addition, the author strategically steers debriefing by progressively disclosing supplemental information that is relevant to the case. Progressive disclosure follows study questions that have been reviewed and reported on, and it segues into the succeeding questions.

Classroom Management

The case is taught in one fifty-minute class. Students begin by pairing up with their study partners. Arrangements are made for the inevitability of absent or tardy partners. The author distributes copies of the case. Valuable time could be gained by having students read the case before class. However, not all students will comply, and those that do may forget useful details of the case. Before work begins, students are instructed to focus their attention on the case's informational aspects, and to avoid debating political ideologies. Students are also informed that they may supplement their answers, discussions, and reports with prior knowledge of the subject matter, but only if it is factual.[20]

Work on the case begins. Students are instructed to stop reading after the first half of the case, to consider what overriding message is being communicated by the NYT article, and to report to the class on their findings. Students then read the second half of the case, and likewise, consider and report on the overriding message being communicated by the WSJ article. During case deliberations, the instructor moves from group to group to ensure that discussions do not go astray

from the learning objectives, and that they do not become overtly political. The author facilitates group reporting to the class, and reporting duties alternate from student to student within the groups.

An additional set of study questions require students to examine
the case on the whole. Student groups are instructed to review and report on each question one or two at a time. After each question is debriefed, the instructor discloses supplemental information pertinent
to the case for students to weigh as they consider the next question.
Progressive disclosure includes quotes from interviews with the
authors of both articles that are featured in the case, and quotes from
the publishers of both newspapers that seem to suggest editorial preferences. The instructor also reads from an article published in a peer-
reviewed journal about the elevated level of mistrust between the
White House and the scientific community. In addition, students are
reminded to consider economic, political, practical, and pragmatic
issues: the pending presidential campaign, the current President's ties
with the energy industry, the actual sources of information, and the
bottom line need for newspapers to sell to target audiences.

After case questions are debriefed, groups are asked to report the
criteria used to evaluate news stories. The author facilitates discussion, and a student volunteer is asked to write group answers on the
whiteboard or blackboard. Following their reports, the instructor sum-
marizes group answers based on specific learning objectives, and may
modify group answers or add to them, because students will be tested
on the material at a later date. Test questions will not be related to the
subject matter of the case or the newspaper articles cited therein. Instead, students will be asked to list specific criteria for critically evaluating news articles. Acceptable answers include accuracy, authority,
consistency, coverage, currency, instinct, objectivity, and source.

RESULTS

The chapter author compared the final grades of students in his
sections of the ULC-257 course for those that were taught by instructors who do not use the case method. In all, there were six sections of
the course sampled: three taught by the author, and three by other instructors. The final grades for both groups of students were translated
into cumulative grade point averages. The cumulative ULC-257 grade

point average for students in the author's sections of the course was 3.3/4.0. The cumulative average for students in the other sections of the course was 3.0/4.0.

The author also compared students' scores on identical tests given to two separate groups of students: those who learned specific course material through the case method, and those who learned it through lecture and course readings. Both groups were taught by the author, but during different academic semesters. The average test scores for students who learned course material through lecture and course readings was 7.5/10. The average test scores for students who learned the same material through case studies was 8.5/10.

The University at Buffalo's standardized course evaluations were also reviewed to gauge the instructional preferences of students. The evaluations compared sections of the ULC-257 course taught by the author with sections of the course taught by other instructors. They also compared the author with all other university faculty, and the author's sections ULC-257 to all other university courses. The scale of evaluation scores, or ratings, for all of the above ran from 0 at the lowest to 5.0 at the highest.

For the purpose of this chapter, there are three student-rated items addressed on course evaluations:

1. This course improved my analytical thinking, creativity, technical skills, or competence.
2. I would recommend this course to other students.
3. I would recommend this instructor to other students.

For item 1, the author's sections of the ULC-257 course received a ranking of 4.6/5.0, compared with 4.1/5.0 with other sections of ULC-257, and compared with 3.9/5.0 for all other university courses. For item 2, the author's sections of the ULC-257 course received a ranking of 4.7/5.0, compared with 4.2/5.0 with other sections of ULC-257, and compared with 3.9/5.0 for all other university courses. For item 3, the author's sections of the ULC-257 course received a ranking of 4.8/5.0, compared with 4.4/5.0 with other sections of ULC-257, and compared with 4.0/5.0 for all other university courses.

Written responses on course evaluations completed by students also provided some insight into their attitudes toward the chapter author's approach of teaching ULC-257. Of particular note were responses such as, "[the author/instructor] has very creative methods of making students understand the content and made the class really fun," and, "[the course] went into depth on information literacy, which can be applied everywhere in life."

The relationship between the positive outcomes described here and the use of case study teaching is correlative, not causal. There are numerous variables not discussed, and the results of these analyses may be attributed to many factors. Still, the positive results are parallel to those that are voluminously described in the literature. As such, the author is encouraged to continue using the case method for teaching the ULC-257 course.

CONCLUSION

Although the analyses described above are not conclusive, they certainly suggest that there is a positive relationship between the use of case studies, desired learning outcomes, and an enhanced learning environment for a credit-bearing library course. More empirical research is needed to prove or disprove the usefulness and effectiveness of the method. The chapter author's experience with case-method teaching is that it greatly enhances all aspects of the learning environment. Students perform better when measured against desired leaning outcomes, and their participation in learning activities is notably enhanced. In addition, the author's interest in course subject matter and in the teaching process is reinvigorated.

NOTES

1. Merseth, Katherine K. "The Early History of Case-Based Instruction: Insights for Teacher Education Today." *Journal of Teacher Education* 42 (September/October 1991): 243-249.

2. Ibid.

3. Shulman, Lee S. "Those Who Understand: Knowledge Growth in Teaching." *Educational Researcher* 15 (February 1986): 4-14.

4. Hutchings, Pat. *Using Cases to Improve College Teaching: A Guide to More Reflective Practice.* Washington, DC: American Association for Higher Education, 1993.

5. Herreid, Clyde F. "Case Studies in Science: A Novel Method of Science Education." *Journal of College Science Teaching* 23 (February 1994): 221-229.

6. *National Center for Case Studies Teaching in Science.* Available: <http://ublib.buffalo.edu/libraries/projects/cases/case.html>. Accessed: December 30, 2005.

7. Wassermann, Selma. *Introduction to Case Method Teaching: A Guide to the Galaxy.* New York: Teachers College, Columbia University, 1994.

8. Lawrence, Paul R. "The Preparation of Case Material." In *The Case Method of Teaching Human Relations and Administration,* edited by Kenneth R. Andrews. Cambridge: Harvard University Press, 1953, pp. 215-224.

9. Herreid, Clyde F. "Mom Always Liked You Best: Examining the Hypothesis of Parental Favoritism." *Journal of College Science Teaching* 35 (October 2005): 10-14.

10. Lyman, Frank T. "The Responsive Classroom Discussion: The Inclusion of All Students." In *Mainstreaming Digest: A Collection of Faculty and Student Papers,* edited by A. Anderson. College Park: University of Maryland Press, 1981, pp. 109-113.

11. Herreid, Clyde F. "Can Case Studies Be Used to Teach Critical Thinking?" *Journal of College Science Teaching* 33 (May 2004): 12-14.

12. Kunselman, Julie C. and Johnson, Kathrine A. "Using the Case Method to Facilitate Learning." *College Teaching* 52 (Summer 2004): 87-92.

13. Kunselman and Johnson, "Using the Case Method."

14. Lumb, Richard C. and Blowers, Anita. "Teaching Criminal Justice Through the Social Inquiry Method." *Journal of Criminal Justice Education* 9 (March 1998): 103-118.

15. Olorunnisola, Anthony A., et al. "Case Study Effectiveness in a Team-Teaching and General Education Environment." *Journal of General Education* 52 (July 2003): 175-198.

16. Olorunnisola, Ramasubramanian, Russill, and Dumas, "Case Study Effectiveness."

17. Kunselman and Johnson, "Using the Case Method."

18. Herreid, "Case Studies in Science."

19. Hollister, Christopher. *Rising Temperatures, Differing Viewpoints: A Case Study on the Politics of Information.* National Center for Case Study Teaching in Science, 2005. Available: <http://www.sciencecases.org/rising_temps/rising_temps.asp>. Accessed: December 30, 2005.

20. Hollister, Christopher. *Case Teaching Notes for Rising Temperatures, Differing Viewpoints: A Case Study on the Politics of Information.* National Center for Case Study Teaching in Science, 2005. Available: <http://www.sciencecases.org/rising_temps/rising_temps_notes.asp>. Accessed: December 30, 2005.

Chapter 9

Using Problem-Based Learning
to Teach Information Literacy Skills
in a Freshman Seminar

Emily Johnson
Cristine Prucha
Petra M. Roter

INTRODUCTION

Information literacy skills are crucial to academic achievement and professional and personal success in today's information-rich world. Academic librarians struggle to find appropriate strategies to teach information literacy skills to college freshmen who typically expect instant gratification of their information needs,[1] and while experienced with technology, they may lack the ability to articulate research questions, analyze sources, and think critically about the research process. When students do not find the information they seek, they tend to assume the resource is inadequate rather than critically examine their own search strategies.[2] One of the challenges of effective information literacy instruction is crafting a learning experience that engages students and leads them to critically examine their own research process.

This chapter focuses on the use of problem-based learning (PBL) to help freshman-seminar students learn library research skills. The first year of college is an important time to introduce information literacy since the freshman year is when most students establish habits and strategies for college success [3] and when the largest gains in critical thinking seem to occur.[4] PBL and information literacy instruction share the goal of helping students become critical thinkers and "continual learners" who are able to locate, evaluate, and utilize appropriate information.[5]

The Transition to College

The readiness of high school seniors for the rigors of college has received considerable attention over the past several years. It is not uncommon to find disparaging reports in higher education publications as well as the popular press about the academic skills and socioemotional readiness of the traditionally aged college freshmen. College and university officials find that even well-prepared students do not always develop the study habits, time management skills, or other strategies needed for academic success. First-year students are often unprepared for the more stringent grading patterns, course load, reading requirements, and often depersonalized classroom environment.[6]

The first year of college also brings about a major life transition in which students must assume new roles and responsibilities for themselves as young adults. Kidwell refers to this transition as the "purgatorial zone of the first-year college experience." He suggests that students who survive the first year have learned to take responsibility for their own education. One of the challenges facing both first-year students and instructors is moving students away from a perception of learning as a passive activity to helping them see themselves as integral and active players in the construction of their own knowledge.[7]

Cognitive and Intellectual Development

Constructivist learning theory holds that understanding is self-created, "puzzlement" is the stimulus and organizer for learning,[8] and knowledge evolves in a social environment in which understanding can be tested and examined. Social constructivist theorists such as Vygotsky argue that intellectual skills develop when individuals actively interact with their social, cultural, and physical environments.[9] Two additional elements in Vygotsky's theory include the view of the teacher as a "facilitator of learning" and the zone of proximal development. As the student is at the center of the learning process, the teacher does not deliver knowledge. Rather, the teacher provides learning episodes that stimulate emerging abilities or those that are just beyond the learner's current level of understanding or independent problem-solving ability. Working within this zone of proximal development, the facilitator observes, asks questions, provides suggestions, or in other ways supports the learner's attempts to understand.[10]

Theories of intellectual and ethical development also shed light on the challenges faced by students caught in the purgatorial first-year experience.[11] The work of Perry[12] and Belenky et al.[13] suggest that most college freshmen come in as dualistic or nonreflective thinkers. They tend to hold firm beliefs of right and wrong, good or bad, which are informed by beliefs in the power of authority figures. Many students enter college without the skills or confidence to examine other perspectives, acknowledge the possibility of multiple problem-solving strategies, challenge authorities (e.g., textbooks or professors), or examine the evidence supporting a point of view.

First-Year Seminars

The first year of college is a watershed year that not only predicts retention and persistence,[14] but also one in which students develop the strategies and habits that enhance or impede academic success.[15] As colleges and universities now recognize the unique needs of first-year students, first-year seminars have proliferated. Although the content, structure, and goals of these seminars vary, an overarching goal is to help students develop the necessary knowledge, skills, and dispositions for college success. Zlotkowski goes further to suggest that first-year programs must prepare students to "understand both the challenges and opportunities of higher education" in the twenty-first century and to "appropriate for themselves the identity of a truly educated person."[16]

Information literacy is an area that educators feel is essential, not only for academic success but for lifelong learning and responsible citizenship. Yet students do not always understand the value of information literacy skills or recognize the campus library as a rich and valuable resource. Barefoot argues that first-year students are afraid of the library, see it as a relic of the past, and avoid entering the campus library doors or make use of its resources.[17] Mellon was one of the first librarians to study "library anxiety," or college students' unease in using the campus library.[18] This unease, or anxiety, stems from feelings of inadequacy in library skills, embarrassment about perceived lack of proficiency, and fear of asking questions that may demonstrate inadequacies. Given the importance of establishing both library and college success skills early, first-year seminars and other required first-year courses provide ideal opportunities to introduce and integrate information literacy instruction.

Problem-Based Learning

Problem-based learning is an instructional model based on constructivist learning theory and derived from the principles of inquiry-based learning. It originated in medical education and is now used in a variety of undergraduate and graduate programs as well as K-12 education.[19] In accordance with constructivist theory and inquiry-based learning, students are actively engaged in the learning process, while instructors serve as mentors, facilitators, or mediators for learning.[20]

According to Harold Barrows, one of the pioneers of PBL, the core characteristics of PBL include student-centered learning, small group interaction, and teachers as facilitators.[21] In addition, problems rather than specific disciplines serve as a stimulus and focus for learning, and require that students use critical or analytical reasoning skills. These authentic, real-life problems also serve as a means to develop problem-solving skills and allow for self-directed learning as a means for acquiring new information. Students work collaboratively to formulate a hypothesis and conduct research to find evidence that supports the solution they propose.[22] By design, students are not given all the information they need. Instead they must work together to identify needed information and resources, and to determine whether the information retrieved is credible and useful in resolving the problem.[23] In this way, students, individually and as a group, assume the responsibility for their own learning.[24] The instructor must provide a problem that, while novel, allows students some level of familiarity or activates existing knowledge, thereby creating a zone of proximal development.

Students involved in PBL learn to communicate effectively, think critically as they analyze and solve complex problems, apply information to real-life situations, and develop skills necessary for lifelong learning.[25] Realistic problems discussed in small groups more readily engage the learner in the problem-solving processes, and increase the likelihood that information gleaned from the problem will be better understood and remembered. PBL provides a motivational context in which to connect prior knowledge with new knowledge, which in turn, has the potential for deeper understanding and more purposeful learning.[26] PBL can be an effective instructional strategy for introducing freshmen to information literacy skills as it actively engages students in library research, makes the content more relevant, and helps students distinguish between Internet searching and research.[27] PBL provides a supported learning environment that challenges students to construct knowledge as they examine various points of view and evaluate evidence.

SETTING AND OBJECTIVES

The University of Wisconsin-La Crosse is a medium-sized campus with an enrollment of approximately 8,500 students. The first-year student seminar is a one-credit elective course in the General Education Program. The course introduces students to the art of inquiry, the meaning and purpose of a liberal education, and campus resources. The major aim of the first-year student seminar at the University of Wisconsin-La Crosse is to help "students make a transition to the rigors and responsibilities of intellectual work and the challenges of university life." This goal is addressed as students grapple with the question, "What does it mean to be an educated person?" An introduction to library research is a required element of the course. This unit provides an active learning experience designed to ensure that students become familiar with the use of the library Web site and the library, and that students learn how to use core library databases, evaluate information, and distinguish between primary and secondary sources.

METHODS

Faculty members teaching the First-Year Seminar at the University of Wisconsin-La Crosse have had encouraging experiences using PBL to teach information literacy skills. The director of general education, dean of students, and information literacy librarian collaborated over a four-year period to develop three problems for the information literacy segment of the seminar, in a partnership that was beneficial to all involved. Each problem required two fifty-five-minute class periods in the library's specially designed computer classroom where students worked in groups. A presentation was required of all students for the three problems. It was anticipated that PBL would have the added advantage of shifting the emphasis in the library instructional sessions from the ability to access information to evaluating the information effectively.[28]

The three problems developed to date include *A Fair and Balanced Report: Does the Islamic Religion Advocate Terrorism?*, *Free Speech Zone*, and *The Right to an Education*. Each explores a different controversial issue such as the relationship between the Islamic religion and terrorism, whether Pell grants should be used to fund college courses for prisoners, and offensive speech on campus. The faculty felt that the controversies presented in these problems would readily engage students, a crucial aspect for setting the stage for active learning.

The *Free Speech Zone* problem was the most successful of these efforts. The scenario relates an incident in which a street preacher visits campus and upsets some students with name calling and loud sermonizing on the issues of premarital sex and abortion. As the story goes, some students respond by forming a task force to propose banning offensive speech on campus and establishing a free speech zone area for public speakers and protesters away from high traffic areas on campus. The conflict in the problem takes place when the campus newspaper holds a forum in which each of three groups (task force, student senators, and street preachers) must present their views with supporting evidence on three issues: the return of the street preacher to campus, establishment of a free speech zone, and a campus speech code. The newspaper reporters are responsible for asking questions based on their own investigative research. During the forum, students must support their viewpoints with at least two pieces of evidence, and submit documentation at the end of the assignment. Sources must be cited properly and labeled as primary or secondary.

In order to facilitate PBL during the instructional library sessions, the librarian served as a coach or facilitator rather than lecturer. Mini-lectures were used sparingly to present essential information. Key to the process was the librarian and classroom instructor interaction with each group of learners. In keeping with PBL pedagogy, the focus was on listening rather than speaking, and on asking key questions rather than providing answers.[29]

RESULTS

Lessons Learned

As an initial assessment of PBL's impact on the ability of students to learn research strategies, the student evaluation form was used to compare fifty-seven freshmen experiencing the PBL instruction with sixty freshmen receiving a more Traditional Instructional Session (TIS). The traditional session is lecture-based and features some hands-on computer lab time to research topics of interest.

By a margin of nearly two to one, TIS students commented on learning about the library, while PBL student comments reflected a broader scope of knowledge gained. Nearly 100 percent of the TIS student comments related to various aspects of the library research session, such as "I learned about the different databases," or "I learned about library research." Their responses could be categorized as "surface level" in that they represented a list of topics covered during the instructional session. Although almost all of the TIS students recognized that they had learned about library research and resources, their comments suggested a lack of understanding about specific strategies to be used if given a paper topic or project as a future assignment.

Comments from PBL students, on the other hand, included a much broader range of responses that suggested a better understanding of information research strategies. Even though many of the PBL student comments included surface level statements such as, "I learned to use the databases," they were more likely to make insights such as, "The words used really matter in the quality of items found," "Primary sources are golden," or "It is important to have accurate information that supports your topic." The credibility or reliability of sources was specifically mentioned twelve times by PBL students and only once by TIS students. Although several TIS students alluded to techniques for establishing credibility (e.g., "how to accurately find data"), PBL students applied credibility to the problem and their personal lives. Credibility for students participating in the PBL was not just about sources but rather about what they themselves claimed to be true (e.g., "Even if you feel your point of view is right, there may be no law to back you up—What's morally right and what the law is are not always the same," "more than one side has valid points," or "that it's important to know what you are talking about"). These comments also suggest that these instructional experiences may challenge dualistic or nonreflective belief systems held by students.

Overall, PBL student comments reflected the fact that PBL allowed students to develop a multiplicity of skills in addition to basic library research skills. Students reported learning about the benefits and drawbacks of teamwork, citizenship, complexity of "rights," and the need to examine and consider different points of view. Moreover, their comments suggested more engagement or investment in the experience.

However, only about 50 percent of PBL students commented that the most important thing they learned was how to do library research. Since the students were so focused on the problem at hand, they may not have understood that the evaluative component of PBL was a component of the research process. Furthermore, students may not have understood that searching electronic databases as well as "googled" Internet sources are both components of library research. Several students remarked that they "didn't learn anything about library research." It is certainly possible that they were already well informed about library research strategies, but it is more likely that they did not consider that library research included identifying appropriate keywords, selecting appropriate databases, or evaluating the information and its source. For many students, library research means walking the floors of the physical library, searching for physical objects (books, bound or unbound journals, newspapers, etc.) that pertain to topics. The electronic age of library resources may not be salient for them.

CONCLUSION

The University of Wisconsin-LaCrosse faculty experience with PBL supports using it as an effective pedagogical tool to teach information literacy to first-year students. Its attraction is intensified given its ability to simultaneously address several other academic goals. PBL provides students with the opportunity to not only learn about available library tools but also strategies for finding and evaluating resources pertaining to a particular topic. Students also are introduced to particular topics, or add to existing knowledge. PBL creates opportunities to engage students in analytical and critical thinking that may serve to nudge them away from dualistic, nonreflective thinking, and to develop the ability to work effectively in groups. PBL's multiplicity of learning opportunities makes it an attractive pedagogical tool.

However, these results also suggest that students do not always recognize that they are engaged in library research when focusing intently on a particular problem. Some aspects of the traditional library instruction may need to be brought into the learning episodes to make various components of information literacy or library research significant to students. Furthermore, PBL requires considerable planning and when first introduced as a concept, requires very carefully constructed problems. Collaboration between the library instructor and course instructor is essential, with the course instructor willing to provide the classroom time necessary for full engagement in the problem. Disadvantages of PBL include the time that it takes to use the case method as opposed to lecture, and the fact that not as much content can be presented in the learning session. Furthermore, students entrenched in dualistic thinking may be frustrated with the uncertainty of PBL, lack of "correct" answers, and need to work in groups.[30]

Although designing a problem-based information literacy instruction unit is time intensive and requires increased communication and a concerted collaborative effort between librarian and course instructor, these efforts are worthwhile. The librarian can expect to develop a better understanding of the course and its students, as well as gain insight into the adequacy of library resources, and the types of search strategies that are especially useful or crucial.[31] The course instructor can expect to develop a better understanding of library resources including recent changes in collections and search engines. Another important factor in the success of PBL is a well-designed library computer classroom that is flexible enough to encourage both small-group interaction and individual research.[32]

Future Plans

Based on these findings, future instructional sessions must include strategies that ensure student understanding and that they are using library resources and not the Internet when they search databases and explore links from the library Web site. Student comments that they did not learn to use the library may actually suggest that the library is thought of as a physical place with physical materials. PBL instructional sessions may need to be complemented with a library tour or scavenger hunts. Conversely, the instruction must also include elements which facilitate student understanding of the virtual library concept as distinct from the Internet, and that the use of electronic subscription resources provided by the library is not equivalent to freely available Internet resources. Students must understand that technology is as much a part of the library today as are the physical materials. However, elements need to be built in that make the learning apparent for students, such as asking them to keep a research log with explanations of the rationale behind decision points.

Future assessment of PBL's efficacy for teaching information literacy will focus on long-term impact. One question to be addressed is whether students engaged in TIS will differ from students who experienced PBL in their ability to use library resources efficiently and effectively at later points in time. Student self-reports of what they learned do not directly assess their ability to apply the knowledge in an independent assignment. A future hypothesis to be tested, emerging from constructivist theory, would explore whether providing a context for the learning episode as with PBL would lead to deeper understanding and increase the likelihood of successful independent problem solving.

NOTES

1. Atlas, Michel C. "Library Anxiety in the Electronic Era, or Why Won't Anybody Talk to Me Anymore? One Librarian's Rant." *Reference & User Services Quarterly* 44 (Summer 2005): 314-319.

2. Pelikan, Michael. "Problem-Based Learning in the Library: Evolving a Realistic Approach." *Portal: Libraries and the Academy* 4, no. 4 (2004): 509-520.

3. Barefoot, Betsy. "Bridging the Chasm: First-Year Students and the Library." *Chronicle of Higher Education* 52, no. 20 (2006): B16.

4. Pascarella, Ernest T. and Terenzini, Patrick T. *How College Affects Students.* San Francisco: Jossey-Bass, 1991.

5. Duch, Barbara J., Groh, Susan E., and Allen, Deborah E. "Why Problem-Based Learning? A Case Study of Institutional Change in Undergraduate Education." In *The Power of Problem-Based-Learning,* edited by Barbara J. Duch, Susan E. Groh, and Deborah E. Allen. Sterling, VA: Stylus Publishing, 2001, 3-12.

6. Furco, Andrew. "High School Service-Learning and the Preparation of Students for College: An Overview of Research." In *Service-Learning and the First-Year Experience: Preparing Students for Personal Success and Civic Responsibility,* edited by Edward Zlotkowski. Columbia: University of South Carolina, National Resource Center for the First-Year Experience and Students in Transition, 2002, pp. 3-14.

7. Kidwell, Kirk S. and Reising, Bob. "Understanding the College First-year Experience." *Clearing House* 78, no. 6 (2005): 253-255.

8. Savery, John R. and Duffy, Thomas M. "Problem Based Learning: An Instructional Model and Its Constructivist Framework." *Educational Technology* 35 (September/October 1995): 31-38.

9. Vygotsky, L. S. *Mind in Society: The Development of Higher Mental Processes.* Cambridge, MA: Harvard University Press, 1978.

10. Ibid.

11. Kidwell, 254.

12. Perry, William G. *Forms of Intellectual and Ethical Development in the College Years: A Scheme.* New York: Holt, Rinehart, & Winston, 1970.

13. Belenky, Mary Field, et al. *Women's Ways of Knowing: The Development of Self, Voice and Mind.* New York: Basic Books, 1986.

14. Tinto, V. "Dropping Out and Other Forms of Withdrawal from College." In *Increasing Student Retention,* edited by E. Noel, R. Levitz, and D. Saluri. San Francisco: Jossey-Bass, 1985, 28-43.

15. See note 3.

16. Zlotkowski, Edward, ed. *Service-Learning and the First-Year Experience: Preparing Students for Personal Success and Civic Responsibility.* Columbia, SC: University of South Carolina, National Resource Center for the First-Year Experience and Students in Transition, 2002.

17. See note 3.

18. Mellon, Constance A. "Library Anxiety: A Grounded Theory and Its Development." *College & Research Libraries* 47 (March 1986): 160-165.

19. Savery, 31-34.

20. Frank, Moti, Lavy, Ilana, and Elata, David. "Implementing the Project-Based Learning Approach in an Academic Engineering Course." *International Journal of Technology and Design Education* 13, no. 3 (2003): 273-288.

21. Barrows, Howard S. "Problem-Based Learning in Medicine and Beyond: A Brief Overview." In *Bringing Problem-Based Learning to Higher Education: Theory and Practice,* edited by LuAnn Wilkerson and Wim H. Gijselaers. San Francisco: Jossey-Bass, 1996, pp. 3-12.

22. Macklin, Alexius Smith. "Integrating Information Literacy Using Problem-Based Learning." *Reference Services Review* 29, no. 4 (2001): 306-313.

23. Mierson, Sheella and Parikh, Anuj A. "Stories from the Field: Problem-Based Learning from a Teacher's and a Student's Perspective." *Change* 32, no. 1 (2000): 20-27.

24. Tanner, C. Kenneth and Keedy, John L. "Problem-based Learning: Relating the 'Real World' to Principalship Preparation." *Clearing House* 68, no. 3 (1995): 154-158.

25. Enger, Kathy Brock, et al. "Problem-based Learning: Evolving Strategies and Conversations for Library Instruction." *Reference Services Review* 30, no. 4 (2002): 355-358.

26. See note 24.

27. See note 20.

28. Pelikan, 516.

29. Ibid., 514-516.

30. Ertmer, Peggy A. and Russell, James D. "Using Case Studies to Enhance Instructional Design Education." *Educational Technology* 35, no. 4 (1995): 26-27.

31. Cheney, Deborah. "Problem-Based Learning: Librarians as Collaborators and Consultants." *Portal: Libraries and the Academy* 4, no. 4 (2004): 495-508.

32. Smith, Stefan A. "Designing Collaborative Learning Experiences for Library Computer Classrooms." *College & Undergraduate Libraries* 11, no. 2 (2004): 65-82.

Chapter 10

Introducing Primary Documents to Undergraduates

Shelley Arlen
Chelsea Dinsmore
Merrie Davidson

INTRODUCTION

In the past decade or so, the primary document (eyewitness account, letter, diary, or similar document) has been recognized as an excellent means of generating a new enthusiasm for studies among younger students. High school history classes, in particular, gained a reputation for being dull and irrelevant to students' lives, but teachers found that primary resources can be used to bring social studies to life. By reading accounts of participants caught up in historical events, students begin to see people of the past as human beings with motives and feelings much like their own. With original documents, history is personalized.

Similarly, recent pedagogical emphasis on "active learning" has stimulated interest in using primary documents at the undergraduate level in universities and colleges.[1] Although graduate students are expected to use original records for their research, most undergraduate assignments have, until recently, required only secondary sources like scholarly articles or critical analyses of events and historical processes. Faculty and students discover the pleasure and benefits of working with original materials, and using contemporary documents gives new life to college course work.

Primary documents can be defined as "any documents, written materials, or artifacts that were created contemporaneous to the events they describe."[2] The more frequent call for original materials in class assignments has been facilitated by the increased access to primary documents via Internet sites and Web-based databases. Three such electronic collections of historical materials include *Early English Books Online* (EEBO), *Eighteenth Century Collection Online* (ECCO), and *Early American Imprints, Series I: Evans, 1639-1800* (Evans).[3] Beginning in the 1930s, these collections were originally compiled as part of microfilming projects to preserve rare books and other printed material. EEBO, ECCO, and Evans now provide digitized facsimile images of historical documents that display original fonts, images, and spelling variations. These databases are available by purchase or subscription, but many other authoritative document collections, such as the Library of Congress American Memory resource, are available free on the Web. As students and professors seek out historical data, librarians are on the front line, not simply helping them search the databases to find primary materials, but also acting as guides in the use and interpretation of the documents. In an effort to increase instructor and student awareness of these online collections, three librarians at the UF Libraries developed a one-session bibliographic instruction course titled, "Primary Sources Online." In this course, students are taught how to search databases of primary sources, and are given some basic critical thinking tools to begin the process of evaluating these documents; students then search other databases such as *America: History & Life* for secondary sources that have used specific documents.

SETTING

The UF Smathers Libraries has two computer lab classrooms, each with twenty-four computers that are used for bibliographic instruction. The computers are Internet-enabled, so students can follow the keyboard actions of the instructor as they are projected from the podium. The Primary Sources Online class was advertised several ways, including a notice posted on the library Web site. An e-mail message was sent to departments, specifically to the faculty of History and English and graduate students (many of whom direct small discussion sections for undergraduates). Flyers showing an illustration of a hanging were posted across campus in classroom buildings and branch libraries.[4] Five sessions were offered at staggered times and on different days to accommodate the different schedules of interested students. When these sessions ended, an anthropology instructor requested a library orientation for his class. With the professor's permission, the session included a version of the Primary Sources Online class, custom-designed to appeal to anthropology students.

ONLINE COLLECTIONS OF PRIMARY DOCUMENTS

EEBO

Early English Books Online (EEBO) is a digital collection of practically all known printed works published in England and its colonies during the period 1475-1700; as such, EEBO includes works printed in Scotland, Wales, and Colonial America, primarily in English but also in many other languages, including Algonquin, Arabic, and Aramaic. The collection surveys a wide array of early modern English life, from sociocultural, political, and economic aspects to popular songs and ballads, plays and poems. Based on Pollard and Redgrave's *Short Title Catalogue (1475-1640)* and Wing's *Short-Title Catalogue (1641-1700)*, EEBO also includes the Thomason Tracts (1640-1661), which feature controversial literature of the English Civil War period—and the Early English Books Tract Supplement which are mostly broadsides and pamphlets collected in topical scrapbooks. EEBO is an ongoing digitization project that currently consists of about 98,000 facsimile documents; almost 10,000 of these have also been transcribed into word searchable text.

Searches may include keyword, author, title, and subject. An advanced search may be limited by language, date, date range, type of illustration (portrait, coat of arms, etc.), and owning library. As English spelling lacked consistency during this time period, the searching mechanism allows for typographical variants. Documents can be viewed as a record (full citation including title, author, imprint, date, subject headings), facsimile images of the complete work; illustrations in the book, and in some cases, transcribed text.

ECCO

When completed, ECCO will consist of digital images of over 150,000 English-language titles and editions, published between 1701 and 1800. All are British and American materials referenced in *The English Short Title Catalogue* (ESTC), a union list of British Library holdings, as well as catalogs from university, private, and public libraries worldwide. Genres and formats include broadsheets, books, directories, Bibles, sheet music, sermons, and advertisements. Topics in the database are not restricted to British ones; there is quite a bit of material on the American Revolution and the Atlantic slave trade which allows for in-depth analysis of the British viewpoint on world events. ECCO provides fuzzy searching capabilities to account for different spellings. Brief records provide links to the tables of contents and to illustrations. The texts are word-searchable.

Evans

Early American Imprints, Series I: Evans, 1639-1800 (Evans) is based on the *American Bibliography* by Charles Evans, enhanced by Roger Bristol's *Supplement to Evans' American Bibliography,* and originally compiled in cooperation with the American Antiquarian Society. Evans is considered the definitive resource for information about every aspect of life in seventeenth- and eighteenth-century America, from agriculture and auctions through foreign affairs, diplomacy, literature, music, religion, Revolutionary War, temperance, witchcraft, and just about any other topic imaginable. An additional 1,000 documents have been cataloged and digitized since the inception of the project.

Evans provides comprehensive searching as a result of optical character recognition (OCR) scanning and excellent indexing. While Evans provides a helpful discussion of alternate spelling as well as an excellent explanation of the long "s" character (which looks similar to a lower case "f" and is taken as such by the OCR software), it does not provide fuzzy searching. A chart of common spellings is provided in addition to examples for using wildcard searches to lessen the impact of nonstandard spelling on search results. Of the three databases, Evans provides the most comprehensive and useful subject headings. It is also perhaps the most user-friendly, since it was more recently digitized and has the advanced functionality of a more updated interface.

OBJECTIVES

Five public sessions were taught as a pilot project to analyze and integrate hands-on instruction with class discussion. For instance, a fifty-minute session does not allow time for students to read and comprehend a book or even a pamphlet during the session. Instead, the instructors chose to focus on the bibliographic information found in the citations and on illustrations in the documents. After examining many citations, it was determined that the front matter can often offer pertinent clues to a document's purpose and perspective. The objectives of the "Primary Sources Online" classes offered at the UF Smathers Libraries included:

- publicizing online primary document collections available through the library;
- introducing students to these collections and giving instruction on effective search methods; and
- encouraging use of the databases and primary sources by offering insights into interpreting and using documents for research purposes by giving examples from secondary sources such as published articles.

Sensitive to possible faculty "territorial" issues, the librarians planned the sessions to supplement classroom instruction, not to replace a faculty member's instruction on using primary documents. Faculty and librarians can collaborate to ensure student understanding of the research process. As Fister says:

> Leaving students to flounder on their own—or simply teaching the skills required to find materials for a single library-related assignment—is not doing justice to our students or to the educational aims of our institutions. Furthermore, it doesn't make sense to teach disparate library skills without putting them in the context of the research process. The students in our classrooms want to see some pattern behind the skills, want to see how the pieces fit together.[5]

By focusing first on the primary document and then on the secondary literature, one can show students the different ways that researchers have used the same or similar kinds of documents as evidence for their theses. In this way, students are exposed to the research process and can "participate."

LITERATURE REVIEW

There is abundant literature about teaching with primary sources. Not surprisingly, most articles are written with the elementary or secondary school teacher in mind, with some directed to the school media specialist. There is also a growing literature designed for teaching college-level students. Articles in *The History Teacher, Social Studies,* and *Social Education* are particularly useful.[6-11] However, only a handful of articles deal to any extent with post-secondary *library* instruction using primary materials.[12-14] Even the recent American Library Association (ALA) publication on teaching with primary documents is directed specifically to school teachers and school media specialists.[15] Nevertheless, taking into account the varying sophistication and ages of the students, the basic procedures offered in the literature are applicable to all ages. Some Web sites are also helpful. The History Section of the Reference and User Services Association (RUSA), a division of the American Library Association, offers an excellent site, "Using Primary Sources on the Web"[16] that is useful for any age level. The site discusses the definition of a primary source, how to find them, and how to evaluate those Web sites for authority, purpose, and reliability based on document format (e.g., facsimile or transcribed).

A number of articles discuss how to interpret primary sources and pose questions that elicit meaningful information.[17-21] For the UF Libraries sessions, additional questions were considered. These questions were compiled in a handout for students (see Appendix 10.1). Amid all the buzz and excitement of interpreting primary sources, however, it is important not to mislead students about the nature of historical documents or to perpetuate false assumptions. As one cautionary article explains, a number of myths about primary documents exist.[22] It is not true that all primary sources are accurate testimony about the past, are more reliable than secondary sources, or that all are inherently interesting. Each document must be considered individually.

METHODS

Five pilot sessions of "Primary Sources Online" gave the librarians an opportunity to practice and refine their presentations. They also afforded more realistic expectations of how much could be covered in a single class period, so when the opportunity arose to provide bibliographic instruction for an anthropology class, the librarians were better able to integrate the primary source material into the session.

The class on Native Americans of the Southeast, was a good complement to the primary document collections. The databases contain numerous works on the travel and exploration of the New World by Captain John Smith, Sir Walter Raleigh, and others. Many of these focus on the people and resources of a large territory vaguely defined as Virginia and Florida.

The instruction session was scheduled in a library classroom during the regular class time. Twenty-three undergraduates and their instructor attended the fifty-minute session. As the students entered the classroom and found seats, projected PowerPoint slides depicted some of the more interesting illustrations and extracts from the digitized documents. Thus, interest was immediately captured. As requested by the professor, approximately twenty minutes was spent on a general introduction to the library. As most students indicated a familiarity with the online catalog, instruction focused on the "Anthropology Subject Guide" to databases, created by UF librarians, that links to AnthroSource, JSTOR, eHRAF, and others. The students were then shown how to access EEBO from both the online catalog and Database Locator, the library's Web guide. In the pilot sessions, each of the three librarians had taken responsibility for one of the databases. For this class, two librarians each focused on EEBO and ECCO, while the third worked with the class in searching the databases for their own topics, then encouraging preliminary analysis of their findings.

The students were given a general description of EEBO and the types of documents and subjects covered. To pique interest, special mention was made of topics undergraduates might be interested in, including recreational, sensational, or controversial subjects such as archery and fencing manuals, guides for midwives, conduct and prayer books, religious heresy trials, crimes, and execution accounts.

Search Strategy

Using the basic search screen, a strategy was analyzed to access illustrated works on Indians in Virginia. The search results included a book by Thomas Hariot that relates his travels in the New World.[23] The full citation and its parts were examined, including the detailed title, illustrations by Theodore de Bry, and subject headings (see Appendix 10.2). The librarian encouraged discussion about how much information can be gleaned from the citation, especially from the title. The citation was also examined for keywords that might be useful in searching for similar documents. Students were alerted to the fact that EEBO subject headings are fairly broad in scope and, while their use in subsequent searches would lead to some similar works, a subject keyword search might be even more productive. The icons representing available formats were explained: citation, facsimile document images, illustrations, and transcribed text. Hariot's work included an illustration of two chiefs.

Author Viewpoint

Class discussion followed on the nature of the highly detailed illustration and characteristics of the men. The etching shows two dignified Native Americans in poses similar to those of Greek statues—in other words, an idealized rendering. Glancing back at the citation, it appeared that the title itself sounded very positive about America. The instructor offered hypothesis on the "bias," or perspective of the writer and illustrator. Did they present the New World in an optimistic, rich light to encourage people to come and settle there? As food for thought, the instructor also commented that other EEBO documents seemed to contradict Hariot's view of America. For example, other explorers wrote of the land as full of ignorant savages and unused resources, a place full of possibilities for the entrepreneur to exploit. The students were left to ponder the question of why these accounts were so different.

Secondary Sources

Finally, secondary sources (articles in scholarly journals) that cited Hariot's account were sought. America: History and Life database was chosen for this process of discovery. Not only is it the major online guide to the secondary literature in American history, it also includes abstracts that are keyword searchable. Using the advanced search screen, the keyword "Hariot" resulted in a number of hits. Titles of several articles appeared to be relevant and, by expanding the records to display abstracts, the class could read the summaries to make decisions about which articles were most significant to the topic. An SFX link from one relevant record located the full-text article.

A similar kind of exploration on the topic of Native Americans was made in ECCO, resulting in the examination of James Adair's 1775 work describing the customs of the indigenous people.[24] Of particular interest to the students was Adair's argument that the Americans were the lost tribe of Israel and thus related to the Jews. A discussion of Adair's logic ensued. At the end of the session, the students were asked to fill out a brief evaluation form (see Appendix 10.3).

RESULTS

During the class, students appeared unusually engaged, compared to the librarians' observations of similar classroom situations. Measures used were "number of students checking e-mail" and "number of students asleep or nodding off" with a lower number indicating higher engagement. In this case, during the fifty-minute period, no students were observed using e-mail and only one student appeared to nod off. That student was quickly reengaged by simply asking whether the student had found anything interesting. Yes, she actually had found an article of interest.

Class Discussion

The students actively engaged in searching for primary documents and, in the discussion period after an initial shyness, they responded to questions. There was lively discussion on the origins of the authors' beliefs regarding Native Americans and the New World. In response to questions about what they might specifically learn from inspecting the citations, students noted the publication date and author fields. The instructor pointed out that the place of publication and publishing house might prove useful in considering historical context and that the keywords and subject headings could be very helpful in better defining a search.

In response to the questions about bias or author perspective in Adair's book, which argued that Indians were descended from the Jews, students observed that the author was writing about Native Americans as if they were all from the same tribe. The class also was able to discern the author's logic:

- Indians do X
- Jews do X
- Therefore, Indians = Jews

Adair's correlation of Passover with a Native American spring festival elicited the comment from one student, "Like everyone in the world doesn't have a spring festival!"

Evaluation

At the end of class, seventeen evaluations were received from the twenty-three students. The results of the evaluations indicated that all respondents expected to be able to search the databases at a later time and most of them thought they would use the databases again. Almost three-fourths responded they would specifically use the online collections for personal interest (see Tables 10.1 and 10.2).

CONCLUSION

Working with primary documents is a powerful way to engage with history. It makes the general specific, brings historical events to life, and enables students to view people of the past as humans with the same emotions and problems. The historical record can be contradictory, as the example of Hariot and other EEBO documents shows.

TABLE 10.1. Students' intended future use of the primary source databases.

	Yes	No
Do you think you'll be able to search these databases on your own?	17	0
Do you think you'll want to use this database again?		
For class?	16	1
For personal interest?	12	4

TABLE 10.2. Student responses to evaluation questions.

What did you feel you learned from this session?	
There are a large # of UF resources	3
There is more on Internet than just Google	1
How to access/use databases at UF	6
New UF resources, esp. for anthropology	5
What else do you wish we had covered?	
More direct anthropological research	1
How to find primary sources cited by secondary sources	1
More help searching databases	1
More questions will come to me later	2

However, one of the most fascinating and rewarding aspects of research is to reconcile such differences and determine why accounts differ. The inquiry in these sessions went beyond the process of "sourcing," which is, the process of discovering bias, that is frequently promoted in the literature and just as often criticized.[25] The question is not to determine whether a document is biased, but to determine what bias is apparent in the document. As Kobrin explains, bias and prejudice are not the same thing. "To be biased means to have a perspective, a frame of reference, a particular point of view . . . to be human is to be, well, biased." As he points out, every historian has a bias. "[They] must make choices. A point of view guides, and limits, the selection of sources as well as the analysis of sources."[26]

The librarians set out to develop a library session that would not only teach how to use a resource tool (databases of primary documents) but also help students understand how such documents might be interpreted and used in research. Although it was not verbalized at the time the sessions were planned, the project was initiated as much for the librarians as for the students. This enriching experience was enjoyable to plan and enjoyable to teach. Brief analyses of primary documents—even if only of citations and illustrations—not only introduced students to thinking critically, but also showed that primary documents need not be dry legalese, but are fascinating encounters with history, and provide glimpses of the attitudes and beliefs of people and their time period. Library sessions on primary documents can be independent of class assignments and still be quite useful. By encouraging students to search for topics of personal interest, library instruction on original sources can provide impetus for lifelong learning.

Future Plans

Library instruction succeeds best when students learn not just how to search databases, but also how to begin thinking about the materials they find. In the future, each session will be limited to the examination of a single database, allowing time for students to learn the technical aspects of searching and to focus more fully on developing critical thinking skills by analyzing primary sources.

The pilot sessions were occasionally attended by students whose research interest or historical time period was different from what was offered in EEBO, ECCO, or Evans. However, the students quickly became so engrossed in the databases that they remained for the entire session and searched the databases on their own. Furthermore, as stated before, students in the anthropology class remained attentive and interested throughout their library session. These open sessions will continue, and future classes can be directed toward students and faculty in a broader range of academic disciplines such as history of chemistry, especially alchemy; botanical herbs; and Greek and Latin texts and translations.

Electronic databases of primary sources are underutilized, especially in relation to their cost and to the interest expressed by library and teaching faculty in their acquisition. Therefore, librarians, in collaboration with teaching faculty, should promote, demonstrate, teach, and integrate use of these online collections into library and classroom instruction and assignments. The librarians hope to generate more awareness of, and enthusiasm for, EEBO, ECCO, and Evans by setting up booths at college orientations, meetings, and festivals—even at local Medieval and Renaissance Fairs, where students interested in period details might be enticed by examples of illustrations, ballads, and diaries of the day. Additional open sessions will be planned for the beginning of each semester. Library orientations for classes requested by faculty should include at least one example of searching for and using primary documents. Since the three databases cover every aspect of past times from 1470 to 1800, the librarians will encourage their colleagues to incorporate at least one primary document in the classes they teach.

APPENDIX 10.1. USING PRIMARY SOURCES

Definition: Firsthand evidence of historical periods and events, eyewitness accounts created near the time of an event.

Types: Illustration, letter, diary, newspaper account, sermon, etc.

- Whenever possible, select documents that cover topics you are interested in.
- Primary sources can reveal a great deal about the document's creator and his or her society—the political/economic situation, customs, ideas, biases, fears, etc.
- Attitudes toward other social groups, nations, religion, ethnic groups, sexes.

Things to consider: Who, what, when, where, why; Purpose of the document; Why was it created? Who was the intended audience?

Other questions:

- What else was happening around that same time period?
- A period of political/social/economic upheaval or stability?
- What words are used that might indicate attitude/bias?
- What is the tone of the work (fire-breathing, impassioned, calm, reasonable)?
- What other questions does it raise?
- What other information do you wish you had?
- What are some similar sources?
- How could you use this document?
- What kinds of research topics could the evidence in this document lead to?
- Can you find other primary sources that would confirm or refute your thesis? Which documents give the strongest evidence?
- What could account for contradictory evidence found in another document?
- What have others said about this document (primary or secondary sources), or the topic or issues that it raises? How have others used this evidence?

APPENDIX 10.2. EEBO CITATION OF WORK BY THOMAS HARIOT

Title: A briefe and true report of the new found land of Virginia of the commodities and of the nature and manners of the naturall inhabitants.

Discouered by the English colon there seated by Sir Richard Greinuile Knight in the eere 1585. Which remained vnder the gouernement of twelue monethes, at the speciall charge and direction of the Honourable Sir Walter Raleigh Knight lord Warden of the stanneries who therein hath beene fauoured and authorised by her Maiestie: and her letters patents: This fore booke is made in English by Thomas Hariot seruant to the abouenamed Sir Walter, a member of the Colon, and there imploed in discouering Cum gratia et priuilegio Caes. Matis Speciali

Additional Titles: America.

Author: Hariot, Thomas, 1560-1621.

Other Authors: Bry, Theodor de, 1528-1598; White, John, fl. 1585-1593; Hakluyt, Richard, 1552?-1616; Veen, Gijsbert van, 1558-1630.

Imprint: Francoforti ad Moenum: Typis Ioannis Wecheli, sumtibus vero Theodori de Bry anno M D XC. Venales reperiuntur in officina Sigismundi Feirabendii.

Date: 1590

Bib Name/Number: STC (2nd ed.)/12786

Pages: 33, [11]; [84] p., folded map:

Notes: Also published in French, Latin, and German, and forming part 1 of de Bry's "America" series in the latter two languages.

The title page is engraved; the roman numeral date is made with turned C's.

Signatures: a4 b6 c4 d; A6 B-C D6 E F6.

"The true pictures and fashions of the people in that parte of America novv called Virginia .. Translated out of Latin into English by Richard Hackluit. Diligentlye collected and draowne by Ihon White .. now cutt in copper and first published by [H] Theodore de Bry att his wone [sic] chardges" has separate divisional title on d3r. "Som picture, of the Pictes which in the olde tyme dyd habite one part of the great Bretainne" has separate divisional title on E1r. These illustrated sections are newly added in this edition.

Includes index.

With a final colophon leaf followed by a blank leaf.

Several plates are signed by G. Veen.

Reproduction of the original in the Henry E. Huntington Library and Art Gallery.

Copy from: Henry E. Huntington Library and Art Gallery

UMI Collection/reel number: STC/246:03

Subject: Raleigh's Roanoke colonies, 1584-1590–Early works to 1800; Indians of North America–Virginia–Pictorial works; Virginia–History–Colonial period, ca. 1600-1775–Early works to 1800.

APPENDIX 10.3.
PRIMARY SOURCE SESSION EVALUATION

1. Do you think you will be able to search these databases later on your own?
Yes _____ No _____
2. Do you think you will want to use this database again:
For class?   Yes _____ No _____
For personal interest? Yes _____ No _____
3. What do you feel you learned from this session?
4. What else do you wish we had covered?

NOTES

1. Booth, Alan. *Teaching History at University: Enhancing Learning and Understanding.* London: Routledge, 2003.

2. Kobrin, David. *Beyond the Textbook: Teaching History Using Documents and Primary Sources.* Portsmouth, NH: Heinemann, 1996, p. 13.

3. Fister, Barbara. "The Research Processes of Undergraduate Students." *Journal of Academic Librarianship* 18 (July 1992): 163-169.

4. Drake, Frederick D. and Brown, Sarah Drake. "A Systematic Approach to Improve Students' Historical Thinking." *The History Teacher* 36 (August 2003): 465-489.

5. See note 3.

6. See note 4.

7. Gustafson, W. Norman. "Content Analysis in the History Class." *Social Studies* 89 (January/February 1998): 39-44.

8. Potter, Lee Ann. "Connecting with the Past: Uncovering Clues in Primary Source Documents (What are They?)" *Social Education* 67 (November/December 2003): 372-375.

9. Rulli, Daniel F. "Big and Famous Is Not Always Best: Guidelines for Selecting Teachable Documents (What Are They?)." *Social Education* 67 (November/December 2003): 378-380.

10. Singleton, Laurel R. and Gliese, James R. "Using Online Primary Sources with Students." *Social Studies* 90 (July/August 1999): 148-151.

11. Thorp, Daniel B. "Historical Methods and the Little Bighorn." *The History Teacher* 26 (August 1993): 439-447.

12. Chen, Eva, Fales, Corinna, and Thompson, Julie. "Digitized Primary Source Documents from the Library of Congress in History and Social Studies Curriculum." *Library Trends* 45 (Spring 1997): 664-675.

13. Lightman, Harriet and Reingold, Ruth N. "A Collaborative Model for Teaching E-Resources: Northwestern University's Graduate Training Day." *Portal: Libraries and the Academy* 5 (January 2005): 23-32.

14. Yakel, Elizabeth. "Information Literacy for Primary Sources: Creating a New Paradigm for Archival Researcher Education." *OCLC Systems & Services* 20 (June 2004): 61-64.

15. Veccia, Susan H. *Uncovering Our History: Teaching with Primary Sources.* Chicago: American Library Association, 2004.

16. History Section, Reference & User Services Association, American Library Association. "Using Primary Sources on the Web." Available: <http://www.lib .washington.edu/subject/History/RUSA/>. Accessed: January 12, 2006.

17. "Document Analysis Worksheets: Teaching Students to Successfully Analyze Primary Sources Begins with Teaching them to Ask (and Answer) Good Questions. The Following Worksheets, Developed by the Education Staff of the National Archives, Are Intended to Guide Student Analysis (How Do I Use Them?)" *Social Education* 67 (November/December 2003): 417-428.

18. Northrup, Mary. "Up Close: Looking at Primary Sources." *Library Media Connection* 21 (March 2003): 43.

19. Robyns, Marcus C. "The Archivist as Educator: Integrating Critical Thinking Skills into Historical Research Methods Instruction." *American Archivist* 64 (Fall/Winter 2001): 363-384.

20. Seidman, Rachel Filene. "Making Historical Connections: A Historian Shows How Documents Can Be Used to Teach Critical Inquiry." *School Library Journal* 48 (July 2002): 36-37.

21. Strickland, Susan Cary. "History Students as Detectives." *College Teaching* 38 (Fall 1990): 146-147.

22. Barton, Keith C. "Primary Sources in History: Breaking Through the Myths." *Phi Delta Kappan* 86 (June 2005): 745-753.

23. Hariot, Thomas. "A Briefe and True Report of the New Found Land of Virginia. 1590." Original in Henry E. Huntington Library and Art Gallery. Early English Books Online. ProQuest. Available: <http://gateway. proquest.com/openurl? ctx_ver=Z39.88-2003&res_id=xri:eebo&rft_id=xri:eebo:citation:99842143>. Accessed: February 15, 2006.

24. Adair, James. "The History of the American Indians." 1775. Original in the British Library. Eighteenth Century Collections Online. Gale Group. Available: <http://galenet.galegroup.com/servlet/ECCO?c=1&stp=Author&ste=11&af=BN& ae=T086841&tiPG=1&dd=0&dc=flc&docNum=CW103118189&vrsn=1.0&srchtp= a&d4=0.33&n=10&SU=0LRH&locID=gain40375>. Accessed: February 15, 2006.

25. Barton, p. 747.

26. Kobrin, pp. 90-91.

Chapter 11

A Tale of Two Syllabi: Program-Integrated Information Literacy Instruction in Chemistry and Journalism

Margy MacMillan

INTRODUCTION

Program-integrated information literacy (IL) instruction offers librarians a chance to think beyond the stand-alone fifty-minute class typical of much academic instruction. Working with entire instructional departments to build IL incrementally throughout a program of studies is rewarding for librarians, department faculty, and most importantly, students, who develop increasingly sophisticated research skills in tandem with a growing knowledge of their chosen disciplines. Librarians and department faculty benefit from the enhanced communication demanded by the planning process and the time to develop and deliver workshops and assignments that take advantage of the myriad resources beyond the catalog and basic databases. The case studies in this chapter examine the process of creating and implementing instruction plans for two quite different programs, key requirements for success, and feedback from students indicating that program-integrated instruction is well worth the extra time required for planning and coordination. To avoid confusion between the academic programs and the IL programs, the term "syllabus" will be used to denote the content and sequence of program-integrated IL sessions.

An Introduction to Instructional Services in Academic Libraries

SETTING

Mount Royal College in Calgary, Alberta, Canada, is an undergraduate institution offering diplomas, applied degrees, university transfer programs and brokered bachelors degrees to some 13,000 students. The college has a long-standing commitment to IL as part of its mandate to promote student success and satisfaction. In the 2004/2005 academic year, library personnel delivered course-integrated IL instruction in more than 650 classes in all disciplines at the college.

Information literacy instruction at Mount Royal incorporates several success factors noted in the literature.[1,2] The focus on course-integrated instruction ensures that each IL session is tailored to the individual needs of particular courses and assignments. Most sessions for first-year students follow a pattern of demonstration and assisted practice to incorporate scaffolding,[3] which supports learners as they develop new skills. Sessions for more senior students incorporate more exploration to encourage students to apply what they already know to new resources and research methods. This makes use of the "curiosity gap" principle, developed by Lowenstein[4] and applied to IL instruction by Borowske.[5] Under this principle, the learner is engaged by striking the right balance between boredom and panic; material must be new enough to stimulate curiosity, but not appear so challenging as to induce anxiety. Instruction at Mount Royal is also informed by Chickering's seven principles for good practice in undergraduate education, particularly in the emphasis on active learning, time-on-task, communication between faculty and students, and respect for multiple learning styles. In most sessions, visual learners are engaged through demonstration, auditory learners through lecture, and kinesthetic learners through hands-on practice.[6] In developing the program-integrated syllabi in this case study, other critical factors were that each program has a well-defined sequence of courses and that in both chemistry and journalism, the professional requirements for IL are clear.

In accordance with the literature on IL in higher education, the most significant factor in the development of Mount Royal's program-integrated IL syllabi has been the collaborative relationship between the librarians and other faculty. These relationships have been maintained, despite changes in personnel on both sides, due to a well-established culture of collaboration. Librarians are true partners in the educational process. In 1997, Mount Royal established six College-Wide Outcomes,[7] one of which was "Information Retrieval and Evaluation." This indicated strong institutional support for IL instruction that matched the individual support that librarians receive from other faculty. The current membership of the Information Retrieval and Evaluation Outcome Team includes the chair of journalism and the chemistry coordinator, both of whom have been key partners in developing the IL syllabi.

This collaborative relationship was even more critical in the evolution from course-integrated to program-integrated instruction. Partnerships with individuals had to be extended to integrating the work of departments. D'Angelo and Maid[8] noted the challenge of working in courses with multiple instructors. Orr et al.,[9] Grafstein,[10] and Mackey and Jacobson[11] all describe the importance of working with faculty to extend IL beyond the confines of IL sessions and into the fabric of courses and programs. The need to build long-term relationships is underlined by Christensen[12] who describes the organic process of weaving IL into a discipline's curriculum as a "slow process, often taking years if not decades to accomplish." The process as experienced at Mount Royal has proven the value of faculty-librarian partnerships. The trust, mutual respect, and development of common values led to the success of program-integrated IL instruction.

OBJECTIVES

The underlying rationale for developing program-integrated syllabi was to deepen student understanding of information resources in specific disciplines through closer ties to curriculum and assignments. Despite significant differences in process, the development of IL plans for chemistry and journalism shared a common set of objectives:

- Ensure comprehensiveness—that key skills and resources identified by the department and library faculty are incorporated in the syllabi.
- Build on students' prior knowledge by incorporating some repetition.
- Ensure that new information is included in each class and develop variations in activities and assignments to sustain student interest.

- Introduce more complex information resources to higher-level students.
- Ensure IL instruction matches discipline/course curriculum, that is, that resources are useful in the course, not just for the library assignment.

CASE STUDY 1

Chemistry at Mount Royal

Chemistry as a discipline has been a long-time supporter of IL, and there are numerous current resources to assist librarians in developing programs.[13-15] The Committee on Professional Training of the American Chemical Society notes that "a student who intends to be a practicing chemist . . . should know how to use the chemical literature effectively and efficiently."[16] The chemistry faculty at Mount Royal teach two high-school equivalent courses, the first two years of university chemistry courses, and a chemical engineering course for the environmental technology program. The IL syllabus for chemistry began in 1989, with the development of a session for one first-year chemistry class that led students through a number of reference tools, online catalog, and Wilson's *General Science Index*. This was later supplemented by a similar session for students in a high-school equivalent course. While the sessions were course integrated and introduced students to a broad range of resources, many of the chemistry-specific tools were too advanced for first-year students, and there was no follow-up IL instruction in senior courses where more complex resources were more appropriate.

Methods

Developing the Chemistry IL Syllabus and Assignments

In 2001, instruction librarians and chemistry faculty met to plan an expansion of IL into more chemistry courses. The firm, shared belief that chemists should know how to find out if what they were working with could kill them provided the basis for a rich discussion. Librarians and chemists established key skills and sources, developed ideas for assignments and a plan that matched elements of the IL syllabus with each course's curriculum. The librarians extended excellent relations with two chemistry faculty, chemistry coordinator, and senior lab instructor, to include the entire department, achieving much wider understanding of the importance of IL to chemists. In discussing course curricula with each other, chemistry instructors developed a greater awareness of their expectations of students' knowledge at each stage of the chemistry program and were able to effectively map IL content to developing knowledge of chemistry. The chemistry faculty also saw the IL sessions as a way to connect chemistry in the laboratory with chemistry in daily life, which informed the development of several of the assignments.

This fruitful meeting and the discussion with individual faculty that followed resulted in expanding the IL syllabus for chemistry from two courses to seven, stretching from a junior high-school-equivalent course to a chemical engineering course for the environmental technology program. This led to a considerable increase in the resources and skills incorporated into the chemistry IL syllabus and a commensurate increase in demands on the library. The chemistry librarian was responsible for developing the syllabus, activities, and assignments, teaching all senior courses, and maintaining the program through liaison with the chemistry department (because each chemistry course has several sections, all instruction librarians teach in the high school equivalency and first-year courses).

A complicating factor in developing the program was the recognition that each course (CHEM 0115, CHEM 0130, or CHEM 2201) might be the last chemistry course a student takes, as these are prerequisites for other science specialties. The group decided to keep the content of these sessions and assignments relatively general and transferable, and to focus on chemistry-specific resources from CHEM 2203 onward. Also, as most students in CHEM 2201 have not previously taken CHEM 0115 or 0130 at the college, reducing duplication between those sessions was not a major factor in developing the syllabus. Students in CHEM 3357, the engineering course, typically have no prior library instruction in chemistry and require significant instruction in the use of many resources needed to accomplish the major course project. The preliminary syllabus that arose from the meeting described what each course would include. Students would be expected to demonstrate an increasing familiarity with information resources as they progressed through the program, not only in their library assignments, but also in their lab reports, and would be graded accordingly. Appendix 11.1 includes the current IL syllabus for chemistry, and examples of the assignments and handouts found on the chapter author's Web page <http://www2.mtroyal.ca/~mmacmillan/pubs/t2s/index.htm>.

The nature of Mount Royal's chemistry program and that of the information needs and resources of the discipline have combined to make the chemistry IL syllabus remarkably stable. As students do not pursue significant chemical research in their first two years, the emphasis has been on developing their familiarity with key print and electronic chemistry reference resources, and their skills in researching various environmental, social, medical, and industrial aspects of chemistry using the catalog, general news and journal databases (e.g., ProQuest Research Library, Wilson OmniFile), and the Internet. IL sessions and course assignments also incorporate evaluation of sources, and correct citation and documentation of information.

Although there have been some changes in the past ten years, the IL assignments and activities continue to serve the students well. In 2002, faculty requested that basic patent searching be added to the senior courses, to reflect the growing recognition of the importance of patent literature. In December 2005, the chemistry faculty met again with the chemistry librarian to check on the status of the IL syllabus. The meeting provided an opportunity for the faculty to discuss other broad curricular goals, and the only significant change to the IL program requested was a greater emphasis on citation and documentation.

The exception to the stability of the syllabus has been Chemistry 2201, the introductory credit course which has seen several changes in lead instructor and corresponding changes to the activities and assignments. The large number of sections of this course, taught by several different lab instructors is a separate challenge to maintaining a consistent level of support for the library sessions. Librarians wishing to implement program-integrated instruction will need to maintain close ties with individual instructors to ensure the continued viability and usefulness of the IL sessions, and with the department as a whole to monitor and adjust the syllabus to accommodate changes in curriculum.

Results

Although there is no formal review of the chemistry IL syllabus, the recent meeting with instructors demonstrates that it continues to serve the needs of the department and to meet the objectives outlined earlier in this chapter. Of all of those objectives, the one that students most appreciate is that each class in the core program (2201, 2203, 3350 and 3351) is significantly different in content, assignment, and activities. Students have remarked that they benefit from the brief review, but always learn something new from the library sessions. In 2005, students in second-year courses were asked to fill out an I-SKILLS résumé[17] before a library session. A review of what they included as skills showed considerable retention of knowledge from previous classes.

CASE STUDY 2

Journalism at Mount Royal

The development of the IL syllabus for journalism has taken quite a different path, reflecting both the rapid change in information skills required by the profession, and major expansion of the journalism department. In contrast to the stability of the chemistry department's courses, much of the journalism curriculum remains under development and the content and sequence of courses are still evolving to meet changing needs in the profession. Like the chemistry faculty, the journalism instructors strongly support information retrieval and evaluation as key skills in their discipline; journalism students are also readily convinced of the relevance of IL instruction to their professional aspirations. As in chemistry, there is also strong support for IL in the professional associations. In their *Standards for Accreditation,* the Accrediting Council on Education in Journalism and Mass Communications lists the ability to "conduct research and evaluate information by methods appropriate to the communications professions in which they work," as one of the Professional Values and Competencies journalism graduates should have.[18] Also similar to chemistry is the range of literature available on teaching various aspects of research to journalism students.[19-22]

Methods

The Evolution of the Journalism IL Syllabus

The IL syllabus for journalism began with one class and one very supportive instructor, and has grown to the point where there is some formal IL instruction in almost every journalism course throughout the three years of the program. A strong initial syllabus developed in 2001 lapsed as curriculum and instructors changed, but a meeting with the instructors in 2004 served to recommit everyone to integrating IL skills more thoroughly with the program. A key factor in this turning point was that the instructor who worked most closely with the librarian, and who was a member of the Information Retrieval and Evaluation Outcome Team, became Chair of the Journalism Department. This enabled closer links between the department and the library, greater sharing of information, and a much more active role for the librarian in developing curriculum. The librarian attended several planning meetings in the department and continues to meet frequently with individual instructors to develop new assignments and activities. The current IL syllabus for journalism is included in Appendix 11.2 and interested readers can trace its development through several iterations on the chapter author's Web page.

The overriding concern of the librarian and the department faculty has been to develop student knowledge of both professional and academic information environments, which includes not only the use of specific tools but also an understanding of how information is generated, used, misused, and communicated. Students in the program research and write both news stories and academic papers, and their ability to locate, evaluate, analyze, and synthesize information is crucial to their success. Library assignments tend to focus on specific types of information (e.g., government, legal, theoretical) or information-gathering activities (e.g., Web evaluation, fact-checking, finding human sources for stories) to highlight particular skills or resources. In more senior courses, students assess their own skills for gaps and library sessions are often built around the needs they identify. Classes at all levels include discussion of the broader aspects of information from the views of both consumers and producers, generally led by the journalism faculty, but often in collaboration with the librarian.

Results

The journalism IL syllabus has grown from three classes for one senior course to its current state of fourteen classes for eleven courses spread throughout the program. This is an indication both of the value journalism faculty place on IL and of their commitment to developing an integrated syllabus. As new instructors have joined the department they have also become active collaborators in creating relevant learning experiences. In meeting the objectives for developing program-integrated IL syllabi listed at the beginning of this case study, the librarian and journalism faculty have created a dynamic suite of instruction sessions. Journalism students are encouraged to evaluate and track their developing information skills through using the same I-SKILLS résumé the senior chemistry students wrote, but in a much more deliberate way. Each student writes a résumé in their first semester and submits it to the librarian who returns it in the second and third year for updating. These résumés allow the students to reflect on their understanding of the information environment, and provide excellent information about what students are learning. The range and diversity of skills reported and the depth of articulation of those skills in the résumés indicate that the students are developing IL over the course of their program and that they value the skills and knowledge gained through the program-integrated instruction sessions.

CONCLUSION

The IL syllabi for chemistry and journalism both benefit from strong faculty and library support. The needs of the students in the programs, and the nature of information in the disciplines have profoundly affected the development of each program. In both disciplines there is a clear value to both academic and professional careers in learning how to locate, evaluate, and use information. The single most important factor in the success of both programs is the open, collaborative partnership between the librarians and the journalism and chemistry faculty who have invested the time to plan and coordinate IL instruction with the curriculum; a process that required significant trust among the partners. Teaching is an autonomous and oddly solitary pursuit, and integrating information skills throughout a program requires that faculty open their classes to others, and negotiate space, time, and power both within the department and with the librarians. Some are more comfortable with this process than others, but the leadership of the Chair of journalism and the coordinator of chemistry has ensured the continued strength of collaborations with the librarians.

For those who wish to create program-integrated syllabi, the first step is to cultivate and maintain excellent partnerships with the teaching faculty. The IL syllabus can be tended like a garden, by paying constant attention to the changes in the environment, resources, curricula, and most importantly, student needs. Weed and prune material relentlessly as needs change, and be alert to additions that may enrich and diversify plans. Allow for cross-fertilization and transplanting; move ideas, activities, and assignments around to suit a discipline's curriculum. Accept that parts of the syllabus will change, grow, or even disappear as faculty come and go and institutional priorities shift. Most importantly, give it time. The development of program-integrated instruction requires patience, and may take years to establish. The benefits to librarians, faculty, and students are worth the effort.

Students benefit from program-integrated IL instruction by developing their skills over time within the context of their curriculum, in sessions that enhance retention through some repetition, and sustain interest and motivation through innovative and diverse activities. Thorough integration of IL with the curriculum encourages students to see these skills as essential, academic, and professional abilities, and to value them accordingly. Spreading IL classes throughout a program allows for a greater diversity of content and learning experiences, which in turn allows the discipline faculty to diversify their research assignments. Faculty also benefit from the process of developing program-integrated IL by examining the courses they teach in the larger context of the department. The greatest benefits, however, accrue to the librarians. The increased involvement in curriculum planning has encouraged the development of more innovative and effective instruction sessions and delivery modes, improved collection development through greater knowledge of the discipline, and has facilitated richer, more rewarding relationships with both faculty and students.

APPENDIX 11.1. Research and Information Retrieval Syllabus for Chemistry (2005/2006)

Course	Lectures/Activities	Outcome Desired	Resources	Supporting Assignment
CHEM 0115 *Basic Chemistry I*	Familiarize with library, catalog, books, and videos	Learn location of key resources in the library (chemistry videos and books)	Library catalog	
CHEM 0130 *Basic Chemistry II*	Demonstration/work with reference tools, articles, and Google	Learn to use basic resources to find info Limiting Google searches to .gov or .edu info Practice proper citation	Print and online reference tools (Access Science) Article databases (Research Library, Wilson Web) Google and selected Web sources	Group presentation on a chemical
CHEM 2201 *General Chemistry I*	Introduction/review of 0130 material, hands-on work with CCOHS, focus on environmental info	Learn how to use CCOHS, where to get news info and chemical info and the difference between them	As for 0130, plus CCOHS database. Chemical examples are those used in the labs	Group presentation on a chemical
CHEM 2203 *General Chemistry II*	Intensive session with print reference sources	Learn how to use standard chemical tools, learn about CAS, LD50, and other chemistry information lingo	*CRC Handbook, Merck Index* *Sax's Dangerous Properties,* *Patty's Industrial Hygiene,* and other reference tools	In-class assignment—determine which was the fatal chemical and who might have killed the victim and why

APPENDIX 11.1 *(continued)*

Course	Lectures/Activities	Outcome Desired	Resources	Supporting Assignment
CHEM 3350 *Organic Chemistry I*	Review of prior knowledge, work with print and electronic sources	Learn how to search for historical information, pharmaceutical information, processing information Practice proper citation	*Ullman's Encyclopedia of Industrial Chemistry* *Kirk-Othmer Encyclopedia of Chemical Technology* *Dictionary of Scientific Biography,* MRC and University of Calgary Catalogues, Access Science Research Library/ WilsonWeb	1. Group poster on chemical instrument or technique 2. Group assignment on chemistry of painkillers
CHEM 3351 *Organic Chemistry II*	Review of prior knowledge, introduction to patents	Learn how to do basic patent search, understand relationship between academic and industry information	As above, and CCINFO U.S. Patents	Group assignment on a chemical—manufacture through environmental effects
CHEM 3357 *Industrial Organic Chemistry*	Introduction to chemical information	Learn how to locate, evaluate and use chemical information	As for 3351, but as students have generally had no prior instruction in chemical information, more review of book and article information is necessary	Group assignment on establishing a chemical manufacturing plant in Alberta, requiring information on production, uses, legal, and environmental aspects

APPENDIX 11.2. Research and Information Retrieval Syllabus for Journalism Program

Course	Lectures/Activities	Outcome Desired	Resources	Supporting Assignment
Semester One				
ACOM 2207 News Agenda I	Searching for News	Understand different sources for different purposes, underlying systems	Google, Google News, Rocket news, Canadian Newsstand, Deep Web, searching CBC and other news sites Blogs	Build their own news service, with e-mail feeds, RSS feeds from news sites etc.
	Focus on professional information environment Assessing sources	See broader picture of info environment— different types of information	Information continuum Canadian Business and Current Affairs Reference Collection	Finding other articles relating to one of the assigned readings in databases or reference sources
	Introduce I-SKILLS résumé	Reflect on skills/room for growth		I-SKILLS résumé
ACOM 2211 News Reporting I	Web site evaluation/credibility of sources, discussion, criteria generation	Critical thinking/ investigation/evaluation of information	WebGuardian Google Groups Internetarchive.org	Determine of WG is good site, investigate roots. Develop criteria for assessing information Ask—how do the tools/ criteria help you as a journalist
	Finding People Business research	Use a variety of sources to find people Locate and understand business info	Print/Online Directories/ reverse directories, CBCA SEDAR/EDGAR	Track down a variety of sources from a list, profile a company/organization
ACOM 2231 Introduction to Communication	Focus on academic information environment	Academic information environment; scholarly information/versus	Databases: Communications and Mass Media,	Locate and cite material for annotated bibliography about

APPENDIX 11.2 (continued)

Course	Lectures/Activities	Outcome Desired	Resources	Supporting Assignment
		nonscholarly; citations	Muse/JSTOR Books (including academic reference works) Chicago-style citations	a theorist communications
Semester Two				
ACOM 2217 News Agenda II	Statistical sources	Govt., association, and research data—who collects what, how to get it	Stats Can/ Alberta/City of Calgary Associations (e.g., brewers.ca) Article search review	Explore three sources, generate two story ideas from each
ACOM 2221 Newswriting and Reporting II	Political sources Fact checking	Use Hansards to find quotations from members of parliament	Hansards More advanced searching, evaluation	Develop story ideas from an members of parliament's speeches in the house, fact-check and correct a number of statements
Semester Three				
ACOM 3327 Newsroom I	Searching civic sites for stories and sources; using backfiles of news to follow an issue	Learn where to look for what, how to use deep Web sites	Calgary city site, other civic sites related to "beats"—police, school board, etc.	Stories on city beat
ACOM 3345 Journalists Workplace I	Meet with student re I-SKILLS résumé	Students reflect on and articulate information skills		I-SKILLS résumé

Semester Four

ACOM 3335 Journalism and the Law	Class with PBL— What do journalists need to know about the law?	Students explore legal/journalism information to determine useful sources for future work	CanLII, ACJNet Ref sources for law Review of databases	Follow up in discussion list on sources/questions, add to workbooks
ACOM 3337 Newsroom II	Class with hands-on searching for specific type of news (e.g., local sources, disaster reporting)	Familiar with deep searching of news/ government sites, using databases, using news search tools		Tie into stories students are writing

Semester Six

ACOM 4407 Web Journalism I	Finding technical information	Learn how to use ACM database, Web resources	ACM databases Blogs on New Media paradigms	Find applicable articles on HCI; interface design, current trends in online news
ACOM 4425 Journalist's Workplace II	Session on seeking sources	Students learn advanced location techniques	Review print/ online directories, news databases, search techniques	Advanced sources assignment I-SKILLS résumé
	Meet with students re I-SKILLS résumé	Students reflect on and articulate information skills	Anything students say they need a review of	

NOTES

1. Rockman, Ilene F. "Successful Strategies for Integrating Information Literacy into the Curriculum." In *Integrating Information Literacy into the Higher Education Curriculum: Practical Models for Transformation,* edited by Ilene F. Rockman. San Francisco: Jossey-Bass, 2004, p. 66.

2. Information Literacy Instruction in Higher Education: Trends and Issues. ERIC Digest ED 465375. 2002. Available: <http://searcheric.org/digests/ed465375.html>. Accessed: January 29, 2006.

3. Bordonaro, Karen and Richardson, Gillian. "Scaffolding and Reflection in Course-Integrated Library Instruction." *Journal of Academic Librarianship* 30 (September 2004): 391-401.

4. Lowenstein, George. "The Psychology of Curiosity: A Review and Reinterpretation." *Psychological Bulletin* 116 (1994): 75-98.

5. Borowske, Kate. "Curiosity and Motivation-to-learn." ACRL 12th National Conference. Available: <http://www.ala.org/ala/acrl/acrlevents/borowske05.pdf>. Accessed: January 29, 2006.

6. Chickering, Arthur W. and Ehrmann, Stephen C. *Implementing the Seven Principles: Technology as Lever.* Available: <http://www.tltgroup.org/programs/seven.html>. Accessed: January 29, 2006.

7. *Curriculum Renewal.* Calgary, AB: The Academic Development Centre, Mount Royal College, 2003. Available: <http://www.mtroyal.ca/cr/>. Accessed: January 29, 2006.

8. D'Angelo, Barbara J. and Maid, Barry M. "Moving Beyond the Definitions: Implementing Information Literacy Across the Curriculum." *Journal of Academic Librarianship* 30 (May 2004): 212-216.

9. Orr, Debbie, Appleton, Margaret, and Wallin, Margie. "Information Literacy and Flexible Delivery: Creating a Conceptual Framework and Model." *Journal of Academic Librarianship* 27 (November 2001): 457-463.

10. Grafstein, Ann. "A Discipline-Based Approach to Information Literacy." *Journal of Academic Librarianship* 28 (July 2002): 197-204.

11. Mackey, Thomas P. and Jacobson, Trudi. "Information Literacy: A Collaborative Endeavor." *College Teaching* 53 (Fall 2005): 140-144.

12. Christensen, Beth. "Warp, Weft and Waffle: Weaving Information Literacy into an Undergraduate Music Curriculum." *Notes* 60 (March 2004): 616-631.

13. Böhme, Uwe and Tesch, Silke. *Teaching Chemistry in the Information Age: Internet, Online and In-House Databases.* Available: <http://www.chem.tu-freiberg.de/~boehme/lehre/cheminfo/cej/publ_cej.html>. Accessed: January 29, 2006.

14. "About The Chemical Information Instructor." *Journal of Chemical Education.* Available: <http://jchemed.chem.wisc.edu/AboutJCE/Features/CII/>. Accessed: January 29, 2006.

15. *Undergraduate Professional Education in Chemistry: Guidelines and Evaluation Procedures.* Committee on Professional Training, American Chemical Society, 2003. Available: <http://www.chemistry.org/portal/resources/ACS/ACSContent/education/cpt/guidelines_spring2003.pdf>. Accessed: January 29, 2006.

16. *Chemical Information Retrieval.* Committee on Professional Training, American Chemical Society, 2003. Available: <http://www.chemistry.org/portal/a/c/s/1/acsdisplay.html?DOC=education\cpt\ts_cheminfo.html>. Accessed: January 29, 2006.

17. MacMillan, Margy. "Open Résumé: Magic Words for Assessment." *College & Research Library News* 66 (July/August 2005): 516-520.

18. ACEJMC Committee on Standards and Assessment. "Curriculum and Instruction—Professional Values and Competencies." *Standards for Accreditation.* The Accrediting Council on Education in Journalism and Mass Communications (ACEJMC), 2004. Available: <http://www.ku.edu/~acejmc/BREAKING/New_standards_9-03.pdf>. Accessed: January 29, 2006.

19. Drueke, Jeanette and Streckfuss, Richard. "Research Skills for Journalism Students: From Basics to Computer-Assisted Reporting." *Research Strategies* 15 (Spring 1997): 60-67.

20. Bolding, Julie. "Research Skills Instruction in Undergraduate Programs." *Journalism & Mass Communication Educator* 51 (Spring 1996): 15-22.

21. Cohen, Jeremy. "Connecting the Dots Between Journalism Practice and Communication Scholarship." *Journalism & Mass Communication Educator* 59 (Winter 2005): 335-338.

22. Singh, Annmarie B. "A Report on Faculty Perceptions of Students' Information Literacy Competencies in Journalism and Mass Communication Programs: The ACEJMC Survey." *College and Research Libraries* 66 (July 2005): 294-310.

Chapter 12

Teaching Information Literacy to ESL Students

Iona R. Malanchuk

INTRODUCTION

Anyone who has had the experience of living and studying in a foreign country will understand the multiple adjustments made by foreign students who are enrolled in an American college or university. English as a Second Language (ESL) students try to cope with language and cultural changes that are exciting and exhausting. Add to that effort the need to develop an understanding of the organization and use of a complex, modern academic research library (ARL) one can appreciate how essential a program of information literacy is to this special category of students. This chapter describes one successful program of information literacy developed by librarians at the University of Florida (UF) for a unique and talented group of foreign students enrolled in the university's English Language Institute (ELI).

SETTING

Collaboration between the ELI and the Education Library at UF began in 2002 and continues to this day. ELI administrative and teaching teams in conjunction with the Education Library staff developed a program in response to a mutual recognition of the crucial role that

An Introduction to Instructional Services in Academic Libraries

information literacy plays in the success of foreign-born students in higher education today. They knew how those "feelings of isolation and alienation can interfere with college success."[1] In addition to helping ELI students avoid those pitfalls, they wanted the students to gain the "long term transfer value of research skills."[2]

Established in 1955, ELI is one of the oldest intensive English-language programs in the United States. The enrollment statistics for the 2004/2005 semesters reveal the annual global reach of this successful program with over 275 ELI students coming to UF from five continents. Females comprised 55 percent of the enrolled students and males comprised 45 percent during the 2004/2005 academic year. Among the thirty-one countries of origin were eighty-seven students from South Korea, twenty-five from Venezuela, twenty-three from Taiwan, and nine from Brazil. The remaining 131 students came from the Cote d'Ivoire, Poland, Switzerland, Germany, Colombia, Thailand, Italy, Russia, etc. That same year, 3 percent of the students were already enrolled as UF graduate students and an additional 5 percent, after completing the ELI program, enrolled in one of UF's many graduate programs, 8 percent planned on enrolling in UF's undergraduate program, and 10 percent went on to undergraduate or graduate programs at other universities. Of the remaining students who planned to return to their own countries, half were employed professionals and half were university students. Consequently, many ELI students are mature and professionally established people sent to the UF by their company or university. Some are professional educators, doctors, scientists, and business people enrolled for the expressed purpose of learning English in a successful language immersion program.

How did this ongoing comprehensive, information literacy program originate in the Education Library and not the main library at UF? Due to the Education Library's close proximity to their classes, these ESL students were already frequent visitors. ELI is administered by the Department of Continuing Education with academic ties to the Department of Linguistics. The preparation of students for academic study in higher education is part of ELI's mission. ELI classrooms and administrative offices are located within the UF's large Norman Hall complex, which houses the nationally ranked UF College of Education. Their proximity to the two-story, attractive, and inviting Education Library resulted in their frequent use of that library. Their unique needs became obvious to Education Library staff, and as a result, a comprehensive proposal for library instruction was presented to the five members of the ELI administrative team. They responded quickly and with gratitude. The ELI reading/writing coordinator and the head of the education library began to meet regularly to work out the details. It is imperative that librarians "reach out to faculty members to develop cooperative and collaborative partnerships through course-integrated or course-related instructional opportunities."[3] Consequently, they continue to collaborate on this year-round program of information literacy for ELI students. Since spring 2002 when the program first began, there have been three revisions in three years resulting from a continuous evaluation process and cooperation between the two university departments.

OBJECTIVES

It was apparent that part of the success of integrating so many diverse foreign students and scholars within a large, public, American university is having direct access to the ARL system, one of the most important university resources. "Research in an unfamiliar library can be intimidating for international students, particularly while they are struggling to overcome language barriers."[4] A viable program of bibliographic instruction/information literacy is crucial to the successful navigation of a large and complex ARL, as found at the UF. There are nine different libraries on the UF campus that serve over 49,000 students. In order to prepare ELI students both linguistically and academically for the two semesters that fall within each single semester of the university's classes, there had to be a systematic introduction to the library system, its multiple resources, and the development of skills to successfully navigate the maze of electronic databases. Successful implementation of such a program requires continued close cooperation and communication among library staff and ELI administrative and teaching teams.

ELI students have library borrowing privileges, clearance for electronic searching, and therefore, total access to the many research collections and specialized databases available to all of UF's affiliates. UF Libraries contain more than 4 million volumes, thousands of journals, government documents, full-text databases, and electronic book collections. There is an overwhelming array of vast holdings, multiple formats, and complex electronic systems that the majority of foreign students have had little or no similar experience with prior to their enrollment at the UF.

Several ELI instructors questioned whether their students actually knew how to use a major academic library. They doubted if their students did indeed comprehend the variety of resources available to them and if they were able to access and navigate what they needed electronically. Both departments separately recognized the need for a collaborative teaching effort. Since it was obvious that the students were already using the comfortable, safe, and accessible Education Library, the library staff contacted ELI administration and initiated a cooperative effort between the two university departments. The goal was to incorporate basic search strategy skills with the use of a variety of information resources that would cover both the general and specific subject interests of the vast majority of ELI students. The focus had to be on the students' need for multiple learning opportunities but in a low-anxiety setting. The knowledgeable and service-minded library staff met the academic and support needs of these foreign students who also had multiple cultural issues to contend with as they coped with adjustment to unfamiliar surroundings.

METHODS

All formal instruction took place within the Education Library due to its ease of access. The ELI program has a rigorous schedule. Classes run five days a week typically from 8:30 a.m. to 5:00 p.m. and include special evening and weekend ventures that take the students to other areas on and off the large 2,000-acre campus as well as to places of interest throughout the state. There are six semesters of classes throughout the year. The two-hour library instruction component is typically offered to six to eight levels of ELI classes at the start of each of these six semesters. Most ELI students are unfamiliar with the organization and use of libraries in this country.

To facilitate instruction and ease of use, at the start of each semester, library staff are given accurate enrollment information. The personal information required for building the library patron database for the necessary circulation and contact purposes is provided before

Information Literacy (IL) instruction is scheduled. In addition to each student's university ID number, address, phone, and e-mail contact information, the library faculty member is given their country of origin, educational background, interests/expertise, language comprehension level, individual class instructor names, and the topics to be covered. ELI classes are grouped according to the individual student's comprehension level and not according to their educational or professional background. The schedule for library instruction is mutually convenient and changes with each semester since it occurs during the student's reading/writing class. Each ELI instructor is present and involved. These instructors recognize, as do many university professors who regularly schedule library instruction, that they, too, learn something new along with their students each semester.

The library staff designed the original instructional program that was initially offered in summer 2002. Since this was new territory for both departments, it was agreed that there would be a combined library/ELI evaluation at the end of that first summer semester that would result in inevitable and acceptable revisions.

As stated earlier, this bibliographic instruction program has been revised several times in the last three years in order to improve the student comprehension, retention, transfer of knowledge, and ease of use. In addition, the need for a permanent instruction area that would comfortably seat thirty students became apparent and eventually a reality. However, the first instructional program was offered at a time when the Education Library had neither a classroom nor an instruction area. ELI instructors voiced their preference to remain close to their classrooms rather than take their students across campus to the main library's instruction areas. Consequently, in order to accommodate the average ELI class of fifteen students, that first two-hour session consisted of separating the class into two smaller groups. One group met with a library technical assistant (paraprofessional) who led them on an informative tour of the two-story facility. At the same time, one of the Education librarians assembled the other group for a demonstration of the Online Public Access Catalog (OPAC) and two social science databases. After thirty minutes, the two groups changed places.

The first stop during the tour of the library was at the circulation desk where each ELI student's university ID card was activated for future use in any of the nine UF libraries. All students must prove their affiliation with the UF to access proprietary databases and services. Signing on with a validated ID card is always the first step when accessing the UF Libraries holdings electronically. Most students were too new to the system and, therefore, needed to have their individual cards activated so that they could check out materials and use the OPAC. While on the tour, an Education Library staff member explained the purpose of various service desks, available equipment, the locations, and organization of the specialized collections. Numerous printed handouts were distributed and explained. At every stop during their tour, questions were encouraged and immediately answered. In addition, the staff emphasized that the entire facility and staff were available to them seven days a week, that they were welcome and encouraged to ask for assistance at any time, remembering that "small towns and villages in other countries may have no libraries, those places with a library may have only books that may be out of date and/or not available for circulation."[5] Many ELI students come from countries that lack open access to free library materials or open facilities, even in their universities. There is no browsing of resources in a closed collection. Consequently, this tour and initial explanation of the basic services found within a major university library was an important first step that helped to make them feel welcomed as official members of the UF community. In many countries, people are unfamiliar with the concept of library services because there are no reference librarians, interlibrary loan, course reserves, etc. "The idea of self-service and of independent library research is a totally new concept to many foreign students."[6] They were grateful to stop in the reference area and be shown the location of dictionaries, handbooks, thesauri, TOEFL, GRE, and GMAT preparation materials. Other collections and equipment, including the ready availability of individual lockers, were pointed out as well as the ease of wireless connectivity on both levels of the library. The Library of Congress (LC) classification scheme was briefly explained since the majority of the materials housed in the Education Library consist of education-related titles. A brief explanation of the organization scheme for the business, fine arts, mass media, music collections, etc., found in the eight other libraries on campus, was also given.

As mentioned, while the first group was offered a tour of the library, a second group assembled for the demonstration of the OPAC and two social science databases. Since there was neither a classroom nor an instruction area in the Education Library at that time, and since half the class amounted to only seven or eight students on average, the demonstration of database searching was on a single, standalone computer on the second floor. The students, engaged in this new learning experience, did not mind standing since they could easily see the monitor. Although most of the ELI students were computer literate, they were amazed at the amount of information provided by primarily social science databases demonstrated by the librarian. The demonstration lasted thirty minutes and the students readily asked questions. They did not seem to mind the rather informal instructional setting and they asked questions without hesitation. When they changed places with their classmates and proceeded on a tour of the facility, their positive curiosity and eagerness to learn continued during the remainder of the two-hour class. It was a pleasure for all involved to work with these ESL students who were genuinely grateful for being shown the rudiments of these rather daunting research processes.

After both groups completed the tour and electronic demonstration, students assembled on the first floor at individual public terminals where they each completed a two-page assignment developed by the librarian that would eventually be corrected, but not graded, by library staff. They were asked to demonstrate what they had just learned and they were eager to do just that with the helpful assistance of supportive staff. Working at public terminals, they spent the remainder of the class searching for specific information and answering the questions in writing. The two assigned library staff members assisted individual students as needed. ELI instructors also remained and assisted their students when they could. The instructors frequently commented on how they learned something new each time as they assisted students with locating the information needed for individual assignments.

By the next semester, both departments agreed to a change in location in order to provide immediate hands-on experience while the librarian demonstrated the use of electronic databases. The information literacy classes were relocated from the Education Library directly downstairs to a conveniently located university computer lab. It quickly became apparent that allowing the students to access the databases while the librarian explained and demonstrated searching was not an improvement. Individual students had individual keyboarding skills and typing speeds. Some students had difficulty reading the screens and as a result some students could not keep up with the others. "Each individual has preferred ways of organizing what he or she sees, hears, remembers and thinks about . . . these preferences can be unique and specific to a cultural group . . . not every nationality learns alike."[7] The computer lab was not a satisfactory environment. The nearby lab was set up without a demonstration terminal in front which required conducting the class while sitting among the students. Their once revealing faces were now hidden behind monitors. It soon became obvious that many students could not comprehend the instruction and could not duplicate the search process themselves. This unsatisfactory experience was explained to the library administration and they agreed to set up a permanent instruction area in the Education Library for all future library literacy sessions. A separate, enclosed classroom was not feasible due to a lack of space. An instruction area was set up that included a new workstation, projection equipment, wall-mounted screen, and the addition of thirty chairs.

It was also discovered during summer 2002 that some ELI students had unexpectedly decided to remain for an additional semester at UF. Since they had already participated in the organized IL class it was unnecessary to repeat that class. Instead, instruction for the "advanced" group was revised to include additional databases, without a tour or written assignment. Alternative advanced instruction is offered whenever there is a return of ELI students.

All ELI students are now taught in the instruction area on the first floor of the Education Library. After introductions, a welcome, and a brief chat about student backgrounds and interests, including countries of origin and professional goals, the entire class embarks on the already described tour of the facility. Students return to the library instruction area for a demonstration of search strategies, using the OPAC, and searching several databases. The final thirty minutes of the two-hour session are spent completing their written assignment which is basically a search for specific authors and titles in the OPAC and a subject search in two or three social science databases. If completed, students turn in their papers at the end of class, or submit them to their instructor later in the week if additional time is needed. All papers are corrected, but not graded, by library staff. Positive comments are written on each paper regardless of the number of right or wrong answers.

RESULTS

There were inevitable problems in the beginning. An unacceptable number of students were either absent or arrived late to class. Some students were not in the habit of being punctual, some had not adjusted to an American education schedule, and some were not aware of the value of library instruction. It was soon made clear that attendance was not optional, each class needed to begin and end on time whether it began in their usual classroom or in the Education Library. For a short time in the beginning, ELI instructors were either indifferent or not overly receptive to sharing their class time. The ELI administrative team discovered that the teachers, like the students, needed encouragement and a bit of convincing to give up two hours of their class time for library literacy instruction. However, after accompanying their class to the library they discovered that the experience was positive and valuable for students and instructors alike. Their students were enthusiastic once they had an opportunity to work at the public terminals and start their own literature searches. Those who have lived in another culture and have had the opportunity to use a foreign language on a daily basis know well "how tiresome speaking in another language is, how much effort is required to use the jargon of a foreign language . . . [ESL learners] may require more time at the desk, in the classroom, or any setting where requests for information are made."[8] Many suggestions from the ELI instructors were implemented including better preparation for the instructors, more timely notification of scheduled library literacy instruction, implementation of the necessary fifteen-minute break at the beginning of the class so that the librarians could continue uninterrupted, adherence to the punctual ending of the class, and adequate time for hands-on activities.

One basic but important requirement was that each student, once they located the bibliographic record for a specific book in the OPAC, had to locate that exact volume on the shelf and bring it to the library instructor. This elementary but key step gave them a sense of accomplishment since they had to go off by themselves into the open stacks on another level of the library, find the correct collection, use the classification scheme to locate the exact call number, and return with the volume. This was not an easy task for a new foreign student. Some took quite a while to find the right book but once they did, a very real sense of accomplishment was obvious on their faces.

Computer-based research instruction is especially daunting for a foreign student even when a librarian uses appropriate language and speaks more slowly. The students were amazed at the amount of information provided by a few databases. Their hands-on involvement increased successful learning and they benefited from active interaction rather than passive observation. ELI students worked on their individual assignments with enthusiasm. This last phase of the library literacy class helped the students to overcome their shyness and gain the confidence needed to pursue their own research interests at a public terminal, alongside American students. They now knew how to sign on, develop a search strategy, read the screens, navigate basic databases, and locate specific materials in a large library system. They developed confidence and independence. Some instructors provided post-instruction academic activities that reinforced the library experience.

Watching a demonstration on how to enter a computer system, access specific databases, use Boolean expressions for searches, and interpret the numerous fields of information could easily be lost on the students if not for the immediate opportunity to apply this new knowledge. This training was much more than just a tour of the library; it was a valuable instructional and linguistic experience. Assignments gave students insight into their own degree of understanding without the pressure to attain a certain grade. As mentioned, grades were never given; comments and corrections gave students a positive sense of accomplishment.

CONCLUSION

The successful collaboration between two UF departments (ELI and the Education Library) resulted in hundreds of foreign students developing information literacy skills that will continue well into their academic and professional lives. The ELI administrative team has made the library information literacy skills component a mandatory part of the ELI curriculum due to the quality of instruction and the obvious opportunity for ELI students to experience another "real language" activity while learning about the complex organization and use of a major academic research library (ARL) system.

NOTES

1. Marcus, Sandra. "Multilingualism at the Reference Desk, Keeping Students Connected." *College and Research Libraries News* 64 (May 2003): 322-336.

2. Koehler, Boyd and Swanson, Kathryn. "ESL Students and Bibliographic Instruction: Learning Yet Another Language." *Research Strategies* 6 (Fall 1988): 148-160.

3. Jacobson, Trudi and Williams, Helene, eds. *Teaching the New Library to Today's Users.* New York: Neal-Schuman Publishers, Inc., 2000.

4. Chau, May Ying. "Helping Hands: Serving and Engaging International Students." *Reference Librarian* 79/80 (2002/2003): 383-393.

5. Jacobson, Trudi, p. 18.

6. Zhang, Wei-Ping. "Foreign Students and U. S. Academic Libraries." *College Student Journal* 28 (December 1994): 446-451.

7. Wayman, Sally. "The International Student in the Academic Library." *Journal of Academic Librarianship* 9 (January 1984): 336-341.

8. Sarkodie-Mensah, Kwasi. "Dealing with International Students in a Multicultural Era." *Journal of Academic Librarianship* 18 (September 1992): 214-217.

Chapter 13

Planning, Building, and Assessing a Library Instruction Tutorial

Megan Oakleaf

INTRODUCTION

Each fall, first-year students arrive at colleges across the country with widely varying abilities to complete library research assignments. Some students enter higher education as veterans of the information-seeking process, armed with strong school library media preparation and ready to conquer any research assignment. However, more first-year students are over-reliant on Internet resources, confused about distinctions between scholarly and popular sources, daunted by scores of article databases, and mystified by the Library of Congress (LC) classification system. Academic librarians face the challenge of establishing baseline information literacy skills in all students, often with limited time and resources. One way to confront this challenge facing academic librarians is to develop an online information literacy tutorial.

SETTING

North Carolina State University (NCSU) is an urban, research-extensive university with an enrollment of 23,000 undergraduates. Typical entering classes at NCSU include 4,000 students. More than half are male, 80 percent are white, and 90 percent are in-state residents. Many first-year students major in engineering, management, life sciences, social sciences, or humanities.

Library Instruction for First-Year Students

NCSU librarians partner with faculty across the university to facilitate the integration of information literacy instruction into the undergraduate curriculum. One example of this information literacy integration occurs in ENG 101, a first-year writing course, which is the only course required of all NCSU students. In ENG 101, instructors are required to teach and assess specific learning outcomes. One of these outcomes states that students should "demonstrate critical and evaluative thinking skills in locating, analyzing, synthesizing, and using information in writing or speaking activities."[1] To teach and assess this information literacy outcome, ENG 101 instructors look to their librarian colleagues for assistance.

NCSU librarians and first-year writing instructors are longtime partners in information literacy instruction. In the early 1990s, librarians created workbooks that encouraged first-year writing students to practice locating information in the library. Later that decade, librarians concluded that the face of library research changed faster than they could update the workbooks. As a result, they replaced the workbooks with an online tutorial that focused on broad information literacy concepts and required less maintenance. At first, this tutorial was well-received by ENG 101 instructors. However, by 2001 it was deemed overly conceptual, linear, and text-heavy. As a result, ENG 101 instructors ceased using the tutorial. Some instructors eliminated information literacy content from their courses entirely, while some attempted to teach library skills independently, and many others requested librarian-led workshops. As there were more than 200 sections of ENG 101 given each academic year, the librarian assigned to the first-year writing program was overwhelmed with requests. Even when additional librarians were enlisted to teach ENG 101 workshops, only 40 percent of the sections received library instruction. Librarians who taught information literacy workshops in other NCSU courses noted the impact of this uneven coverage. In these courses, students who had experienced library instruction in ENG 101 were bored, while those who had not were frustrated and confused. In late 2001, NCSU librarians acknowledged the need to develop a new information literacy tutorial for ENG 101.

Before starting work on a new tutorial, NCSU librarians searched the library literature to confirm the effectiveness of online approaches to information literacy instruction. The literature supplied adequate reassurance that online library instruction can be effective. According to Russell, no significant differences between learning outcomes from online and in-person lecture instruction can be documented.[2] Germain, Jacobson, and Kaczor concluded that there is "no difference in the effectiveness of the two types of instruction, Web and live,"[3] and both Holman[4] and Kaplowitz and Contini[5] supported this conclusion.

The review of the library literature also confirmed the value of online information literacy instruction. Online tutorials can be used whenever and wherever students find it convenient, as they are accessible remotely and supply independent, self-paced instruction. Online tutorials also ease the burden of generalized, drop-in instruction.[6] Use of online tutorials by first-year students allows librarians to "guarantee that freshmen are familiar with fundamental concepts and prepared for the more advanced research skills of their academic careers."[7]

In January 2002, NCSU librarians commenced development of a new information literacy tutorial called Library Online Basic Orientation (LOBO). They envisioned a tutorial that would balance conceptual and practical skills; be modular, interactive, and easily integrated into the ENG 101 curriculum; and be completed by August 2002.

OBJECTIVES

Development of the LOBO tutorial <http://www.lib.ncsu.edu/lobo2/> began with an analysis of the objectives of the three stakeholder groups impacted by the proposed online information literacy tool: ENG 101 students, ENG 101 instructors, and librarians.

Students

ENG 101 students face the challenge of completing college-level research papers and navigating a large academic library for the first time. For these students, an information literacy tutorial needs to fit limited attention spans and include accessible language. ENG 101 students also prefer interactive learning activities and modular designs that permit them to jump between areas of interest. ENG 101 students expected the new library tutorial to teach them to (1) navigate the physical space of the library; (2) locate books in the catalog; (3) use LC call numbers; and (4) obtain print and electronic journal articles.

Instructors

As ENG 101 instructors consider library research skills necessary for good writing, they seek ways to teach their students these skills efficiently and effectively. Instructors wanted the new library tutorial to address a number of objectives, including teaching students to (1) observe the steps of the research process; (2) evaluate resources; (3) avoid plagiarism; and (4) contact librarians for help. They also expected the tutorial to be accessible to all sections of ENG 101; include resources provided by the NCSU Libraries; accommodate different instructors' teaching styles; show students "how to" accomplish common tasks; integrate into the context of ENG 101 course content; and help students complete a real ENG 101 assignment.

Librarians

All NCSU reference librarians teach classes and work at the physical and virtual reference desk. Although not all librarians teach ENG 101 students, they encounter these students when they teach library workshops in advanced courses and benefit from students gaining a baseline level of information literacy skills. As a result, reference librarians hoped the new tutorial would address a number of objectives, including teaching students to (1) distinguish between scholarly and non-scholarly sources; (2) use databases to locate articles and the catalog to find books; (3) build keyword search strings using Boolean operators; and (4) use subject headings. Librarians also wanted the tutorial to be available at students' point-of-need; be useful for one-on-one instruction at the physical or virtual reference desk; be interactive; portray librarians as friendly and helpful; and encourage students to contact librarians for help, in person, or remotely.

LEARNING OUTCOMES

In addition to considering the objectives of stakeholders, NCSU librarians used learning outcomes to guide the development of the

LOBO tutorial. The outcomes addressed by the LOBO tutorial (see Appendix 13.1) were derived from several sources. These sources include *Information Literacy Competency Standards for Higher Education,*[8] *Objectives for Information Literacy Instruction: A Model Statement for Academic Librarians,*[9] previous information literacy instruction approaches used in ENG 101, and ENG 101 curriculum.

METHODS

The development of the LOBO tutorial included six steps:

1. Assessing needs
2. Building a framework
3. Creating content
4. Applying technology
5. Building, testing, and launching
6. Assessing and planning for future development

These six steps were coordinated by the NCSU instruction librarian and accomplished by a team of five reference librarians and two systems librarians. As project manager, the instruction librarian orchestrated collaboration, facilitated communication, encouraged progress, and integrated the work of the LOBO team to build a cohesive tutorial. The entire LOBO team met weekly during tutorial development. As the project progressed, team members moved into a "work independently, see what another team member thinks of completed work, work some more independently, then present to the team" cycle. Over time, this cycle allowed librarians with different levels of experience, skills, and work styles to communicate effectively and balance workloads fairly. Individual librarians felt valued, developed a unified vision, and understood group expectations. Franks, Hackley, Straw, and Direnzo note that this behavior is often exhibited by librarians working to create an online tutorial.[10]

Assessing Needs

The first step of LOBO development focused on identifying all stakeholders and determining the learning outcomes to be addressed by the tutorial. Stakeholders for the LOBO tutorial included students, instructors, and librarians. The needs of these stakeholders were gathered to inform the rest of the stages of the tutorial development process. This stage of LOBO development also included careful consideration of the learning outcomes taught by the tutorial.

Building a Framework

According to Franks, Hackley, Straw, and Direnzo, most tutorials begin as an outline.[11]In January 2002, NCSU librarians developed a rough outline for the LOBO tutorial that organized the learning outcomes of the tutorial around the steps of the research process. This outline served as the planning structure and ensured that the tutorial would be driven by outcomes-focused content. Furthermore, the outline enabled librarians to share concrete plans with ENG 101 instructors and gain their commitment to the tutorial project.

Creating Content

Armed with a LOBO tutorial outline, librarians met with the director of First-Year Writing in April 2002 to ensure that the content of the proposed tutorial would support the ENG 101 curriculum. After agreeing that the LOBO tutorial would integrate well into the course, the director decided to require instructors to incorporate the tutorial in their courses and volunteered ENG 101 instructors to contribute content to the tutorial. As a result of the director's decision, sections of the LOBO outline were assigned to individual librarians and instructors for content drafts. After initial drafts were created, instructors and librarians worked in tandem to make level of difficulty and tone revisions.

Applying Technology

After creating the content of the tutorial, NCSU librarians searched the library literature for guidelines governing technological aspects of tutorial creation. According to Franks, Hackley, Straw, and Direnzo, information literacy tutorials should include "consistent use of titles and headers," "prominent use of navigational aids," "availability of help links," "proper use of white space, color, and fonts," "appropriate use of graphics," "effort to make all pages ADA compliant," "use of templates," and testing in various browsers, platforms, and monitors.[12] Dewald delves beyond appearance and navigation to list the components of successful online tutorials, including assignment-related instruction, active learning components, clear objectives, and focus on concepts rather than on mechanics only.[13] Dewald also notes the importance of creating an interactive, self-paced learning tool that capitalizes on the extrinsic and intrinsic motivations of students completing research-based assignments.[14] Association of College & Research Libraries (ACRL) includes clear objectives, interactivity, and a focus on concepts in their guidelines for tutorial construction. ACRL also recommends that tutorials have clearly defined structure, contemporary language and topics, and strong relationships to course content.[15]

With these guidelines in mind, the LOBO team designed a tutorial that was outcome-focused, modular, interactive, and centered on students' motivation to complete course assignments. One librarian used Qarbon ViewletBuilder to create "movies" that demonstrated database and catalog searches. A second team member developed "wizards" to guide students through databases and the catalog through the use of student-created search terms. A third LOBO team member developed a "keyword builder" to illustrate Boolean concepts and a "citation builder" to guide students through parsing database citations and generating works-cited citations in Modern Language Association (MLA), American Psychological Association (APA), and Council of Science Editors (CSE) formats. Finally, a link to the NCSU Libraries' virtual reference service was added to each page of the tutorial to ensure that students could easily request librarian assistance.

Building, Testing, and Launching

In July 2002, librarians inserted all of the LOBO components into the tutorial Web template. Next, the LOBO team revised the tutorial to improve the flow and to unify the tone of the tutorial. Finally, all interactive elements were tested, and the tutorial was made available to library staff for experimentation and training.

In August 2002, the team members presented the newly launched LOBO tutorial to ENG 101 instructors and offered tips for the inclusion of each module in the ENG 101 curriculum. Instructors were most excited by the interactive components (wizards, viewlets, and builders) as well as the practical focus on helping students complete actual research assignments. They also lauded the convenience of the "Ask a

Librarian" link that encourages students to contact a librarian in real time as they move through the LOBO tutorial. Since 2002, librarians have continued to offer training to new ENG 101 instructors to ensure familiarity with LOBO and best practices for integrating the tutorial into ENG 101.

Assessing and Planning Future Development

The library literature emphasizes the importance of assessing the outcomes of library instruction. Lindauer states, "an increasingly important concern for academic librarians is how to document and measure the ways that the library, learning resources, and computer services units make a difference in the academic quality of life for students and faculty."[16] Franks, Hackley, Straw, and Direnzo also underscore the significance of assessment in "meet[ing] accreditation standards, secur[ing] funding, maintain[ing] staffing levels, and achiev[ing] service and teaching excellence."[17] Thus, tutorials must undergo assessment "to provide validation of our instructional effectiveness . . . [and] convince library and campus administrators to continue to support these activities."[18]

Assessment of the LOBO tutorial is based on open-ended questions included throughout the tutorial to help students advance through the research process. These assessment questions help students analyze, synthesize, and evaluate material. Many tutorial questions focus on specific research topics. By the conclusion of the tutorial, students have answered questions that help them:

- identify and narrow a topic;
- select keywords and extrapolate synonyms and variants;
- search a database and the NCSU Libraries' catalog for articles and books on a topic;
- use Google to search for related Web sites;
- evaluate sources according to specified criteria;
- select appropriate support for arguments;
- decide when to paraphrase, summarize, or quote directly from sources; and
- develop citations to avoid plagiarism.

Students view their answers to the open-ended questions in the form of an online worksheet that they can print or e-mail to their instructors.

For instructors, the worksheets serve as self-checks, discussion starters, or evidence that students have explored all sections of the tutorial. For librarians, these stored answers are a rich source of assessment data. However, because answers to the open-ended questions in LOBO are specific to each student's research process, they are not scoreable as "right" or "wrong." Instead, NCSU librarians have developed "rubrics," or charts describing different levels of student performance, to aid in the assessment of answers. Each semester, librarians select one or two questions in the LOBO tutorial for assessment, and score a random sample of student responses to the question using the rubric for that question. Assessment results are used to describe information literacy skill level, isolate areas for improvement, and celebrate successes.

RESULTS

The assessment of the LOBO tutorial is an iterative process. Each semester, answers to new questions are assessed in order to make changes that improve instruction. For example, the LOBO question that elicits information about the ability to use authority as a criterion for evaluating a Web site has been assessed twice. The first time, librarians used a rubric to score fifty student responses to a series of questions about the authority of a Web site as a possible source for an academic paper or project. Librarians discovered that a majority of students were able to address the authority of a Web site (88 percent). Most students also demonstrated that they were able to refer to indicators of authority (90 percent). However, less than a third (32 percent) of students could give specific examples of authority indicators from the site they were evaluating. In addition, fewer than half (44 percent) could provide a rationale for accepting or rejecting the Web site for use in their assignment based on their assessment of the site's authority. The results of this first assessment were vital to the improvement of the rubric, the content of the tutorial (see Figures 13.1 and 13.2), and the open-ended questions that form the writing prompt (see Figures 13.3 and 13.4).

A year later, after both the tutorial and the assessment rubric were revised, librarians assessed the same LOBO question. This time, 100 percent of students addressed the authority of the site and 93 percent

---

Evaluate Web Sites—Authority

Determining who created a Web site is critical in being able to judge its quality. Anonymous information should not be used for academic research.

1. **Can you tell who (person or institution) created the Web site?**
   Look at the very top or bottom of the Web page for a name, e-mail address, or "About Us" or "Contact Us" link.

2. **Are the author's credentials listed on the site?** If you cannot find these details on a Web site, try typing an author's name into a search engine to get biographical information.

FIGURE 13.1. Instructional content before assessment revisions.

Evaluate Web Sites—Authority

The URL (Web address) and author information for a Web site reveal a lot about site reliability. Determining who created a Web site is critical in being able to judge its quality. Generally, anonymous information should not be used for academic research.

Consider the following questions when you're evaluating the authority of a Web site:

1. **What type of domain does the site come from?**
   Government sites use .gov and .mil domains. Educational sites use the .edu domain. Nonprofit organizations use .org and business sites use .com. Generally, .gov and .edu sites are considered more trust-worthy than .org and .com sites.

2. **Who "published" the site?**
   The name between http:// and the first / usually indicates what organization owns the server the Web site is housed on. Learning about the organization that hosts a site can give you important information about the site's credibility.

3. **Is it a personal Web site?**
   Look for the names of companies that sell Web space to individuals, like AOL or GeoCities. Also look for a tilde (~). Tildes are often used to signify a personal Web site. Personal sites are considered less reliable than sites supported by organizations.

4. **Can you tell who (person or institution) created the site?**
   Look at the very top or bottom of the Web page for a name, e-mail address, or "About Us" or "Contact Us" link.

FIGURE 13.2. Instructional content after assessment revisions.

Answer the questions above for the Web site you are evaluating. Overall, does what you know about the authorship of the Web site indicate that it is a good resource?

FIGURE 13.3. Writing prompt before assessment revisions.

Respond to the following prompts in the space below, using complete sentences:

- Identify the "domain type" of the site you are evaluating and explain why that is acceptable or unacceptable for your needs.
- Identify the "publisher" or host of the site and tell what you know (or can find out) about it.
- State whether or not the site is a personal site and explain why that is acceptable or unacceptable for your needs.
- State who (name the person or institution) created the site and tell what you know (or can find out) about the creator.
- Look for the author's credentials on the site. List his or her credentials and draw conclusions based on those credentials. If there are no credentials listed, tell what conclusions you can draw from their absence.
- Using what you know about the AUTHORITY of this Web site, explain why it is or is not appropriate to use for your paper/project.

FIGURE 13.4. Writing prompt after assessment revisions.

could give specific examples of authority indicators from a site they were evaluating. However, only 50 percent of students could provide a reason for accepting or rejecting a Web site for use in an assignment. Although this was an improvement over the previous year, students appeared to need additional instruction. In response, NCSU librarians designed a new lesson plan that ENG 101 instructors can use help students make final determinations about the usefulness and appropriateness of Web sites.

CONCLUSION

The effectiveness of LOBO as an information literacy instruction tool has been illustrated in multiple ways. The LOBO tutorial has been honored with the American Library Association's (ALA) Library of the Future Award and the PRIMO Site of the Month Award in 2003. In recent years, the tutorial has been the subject of conference presentations at EDUCAUSE, ACRL, and various national assessment conferences. In the three years since its launch, the tutorial software has been copied and adapted by more than ten other libraries in higher education.

In addition to external benchmarks of success, NCSU librarians continue to improve the tutorial. Each semester, the assessment of student responses to LOBO questions allows NCSU librarians to improve the tutorial and ensure that it continues to support the ENG 101 curriculum. These assessment efforts have also given rise to a suite of lesson plans that support ENG 101 instructors who wish to extend LOBO content in their classrooms. Technical improvements continue. Before the beginning of the 2006 academic year, NCSU librarians plan to migrate LOBO from a HTML-based Web template to a content management system so that recommendations resulting from assessment can be followed quickly and easily. Under watchful eyes, LOBO has a promising future as a flagship of information literacy instruction at NCSU Libraries.

APPENDIX 13.1 LOBO INFORMATION LITERACY SKILLS OBJECTIVES & OUTCOMES

Objective 1

The information-literate student will determine the nature and extent of an information need.

Outcome 1.1

The student will develop a realistic overall plan and timeline to acquire the needed information. (ACRL 1.3.c)

1.1.1 The student will describe the stages of the research process. (ACRL 2.2.a) I, NDM
1.1.2 The student will search for, gather, and synthesize information based on an informal, flexible plan. (ACRL 1.3.c) I, NDM
1.1.3 The student will act appropriately to obtain information within the time frame required. (ACRL 1.3.c) I, NDM

Outcome 1.2

The student will define and articulate the need for information. (ACRL 1.1)

1.2.1 The student will identify an initial research topic. (ACRL 1.1.d) I, P

1.2.2 The student will narrow or broaden the scope or direction of the topic to achieve a manageable focus. (ACRL 1.1.d) I, P

1.2.3 The student will list key concepts and terms describing the facets of the research topic that may be useful in locating information. (ACRL 1.1.e) I, P

1.2.4 The student will narrow, broaden, or refine key concepts and terms describing the research topic. (ACRL 1.1.e) I, P

1.2.5 The student will demonstrate an understanding of how the desired end product will play a role in determining the need for information. (ACRL 1.1.d, 1.4.b) I, P

1.2.6 The student will describe how the intended audience influences information choices. (ACRL 1.4.b) I, P

1.2.7 The student will explore general information sources to increase familiarity with the topic. (ACRL 1.1.c) I, TBD

Outcome 1.3

The student will identify a variety of potential sources for needed information. (ACRL 1.2)

1.3.1 The student will identify various formats in which the information is available. (ACRL 1.2.c) I, P

1.3.2 The student will identify the value and differences (e.g., purpose, audience) of potential resources in a variety of formats. (ACRL 1.2.c, 1.2.d) I, P

Objective 2

The information-literate student will access needed information effectively and efficiently.

Outcome 2.1

The student will construct and implement effectively-designed search strategies. (ACRL 2.2)

2.1.1 The student will identify related terms and synonyms for the research topic. (ACRL 2.2.b) I, P

2.1.2 The student will identify phrases to use as search terms for the research topic. (ACRL 2.2.b) I, P

2.1.3 The student will identify alternative endings, abbreviations, and multiple spellings of search terms for the research topic. I, P

2.1.4 The student will construct search statements using Boolean operators. (ACRL 2.2.d) I, P

2.1.5 The student will identify search terms to truncate, if appropriate. (ACRL 2.2.d) I, P

Outcome 2.2

The student will select the most appropriate retrieval method or system for accessing needed information. (ACRL 2.1)

2.2.1 The student will use different research sources (e.g., search engines, databases, catalogs) to find different types of information (e.g., Web sites, articles, books). (ACRL 2.3.a) I, P

2.2.2 The student will describe the differences between article databases and library catalogs and/or search engines. (ACRL 2.1.c) I, P

2.2.3 The student will distinguish among article databases, identifying what types (e.g., general, subject-specific) or subject coverage are most appropriate for a research topic. (ACRL 2.1.c) I, P

2.2.4 The student will identify differences between basic and advanced interfaces in search engines, when more than one interface is available. (ACRL 2.2.e) I, P

Outcome 2.3

The student will retrieve information online or in person using a variety of methods. (ACRL 2.3)

2.3.1 The student will use the LC call number system to locate resources within the library. (ACRL 2.3.b) I, P

2.3.2 The student will determine whether or not a cited item is available immediately. (ACRL 1.3.a, 2.5.c) I, P

Objective 3

The information-literate student will evaluate information critically.

Outcome 3.1

The student will apply criteria to analyze information, including authority, content, purpose, timeliness, and point of view or bias, to information and its source (ACRL 3.2.a, 3.2.c)

3.1.1 The student will articulate established evaluation criteria. (ACRL 3.2.a) I, P

3.1.2 The student will investigate an author's qualifications and reputation. (ACRL 3.2.a) I, P

3.1.3 The student will investigate a publisher or issuing agency's qualifications and reputation. (ACRL 3.2.a, 3.4.e) I, P

3.1.4 The student will describe the content of an information source. I, P

3.1.5 The student will describe the purpose for which information was created. (ACRL 3.2.d) I, P

3.1.6 The student will identify where to look for a source's publication date and, if possible, determine when the information was published. (ACRL 3.2.a) I, P

3.1.7 The student will articulate the importance of timeliness or currency and/or describe the impact of the age of a source or the qualities characteristic of the time in which it was created. (ACRL 3.2.a, 3.2.d) I, P

3.1.8 The student will recognize prejudice, deception, or manipulation. (ACRL 3.2.c) I, P

3.1.9 The student will articulate the impact of an author's, sponsor's, and/or publisher's point of view. (ACRL 3.2.c) I, P

3.1.10 The student will describe how cultural, geographic, or other contexts within which the information was created may bias information. (ACRL 3.2.d) I, P

3.1.11 The student will recognize the presence of one-sided views, opinions, emotional triggers, stereotypes, etc. (ACRL 3.2.c) I, P

3.1.12 The student will consider the impact of his/her own biases on his/her interpretation of information. I, P

3.1.13 The student will investigate a source's point of view or bias through comparison with other sources, including links, citations found in the source, or other similar sources. (ACRL 3.2.a, 3.7.c) TBD

3.1.14 The student will distinguish scholarly from popular sources. I, P

Outcome 3.2

The student will evaluate sources (e.g., article, Web site, book, journal, database, catalog) for use. (ACRL 3.4.g)

3.2.1 The student will determine whether or not various information sources (e.g. Web sites, popular magazines, scholarly journals, books) are appropriate for the purpose at hand, based on established evaluation criteria (see LOBO 3.1), and provide a rationale for that decision. (ACRL 3.4.g, 2.2.a) I, P

3.2.2 The student will indicate whether or not a specific, individual source (e.g., a particular Web site, article, book) is appropriate for the purpose at hand and provide a rationale for that decision based on established evaluation criteria (see LOBO 3.1). (ACRL 3.2.c) I, P

Objective 4

The information-literate student will use information effectively to accomplish a specific purpose.

ENG 101 instructors are responsible for setting and achieving outcomes related to this objective.

Objective 5

The information-literate student will use information ethically and legally.

Outcome 5.1

The student will integrate their research into learning products without plagiarizing.

> 5.1.1 The student will articulate the differences among the acceptable methods for integrating research (e.g., quoting, summarizing, paraphrasing). I, P
> 5.1.2 The student will identify when to use acceptable methods for integrating research. I, P

Outcome 5.2

The student will acknowledge the use of information sources through documentation styles. (ACRL 5.3.a)

> 5.2.1 The student will locate information about documentation styles. (ACRL 5.3.a) I, P
> 5.2.2 The student will select an appropriate or assigned documentation style among different styles. (ACRL 5.3.a) I, P
> 5.2.3 The student will identify citation elements for information sources in different formats (e.g., book, scholarly journal article, Web site, interview). (ACRL 5.3.a) I, P
> 5.2.4 The student will follow documentation style guidelines correctly and consistently. (ACRL 5.3.a) I, P

I = Introduced	NDM = Not Directly Measured
P= Practiced	TBD = To Be Developed

NOTES

1. *NC State Academic Programs GER—Writing, Speaking, and Information Literacy Rationale.* Available: <http://www.ncsu.edu/provost/academic_programs/ger/wrtspk/rat.htm>. Accessed: June 5, 2006.

2. Russell, Thomas L. *The No Significant Difference Phenomenon as Reported in 355 Research Reports, Summary and Papers: A Comparative Research Annotated Bibliography on Technology for Distance Education.* Raleigh, NC: Office of Instructional Telecommunications, North Carolina State University, 1999.

3. Germain, Carol A., Jacobson, Trudi E., and Kaczor, Susan A. "A Comparison of the Effectiveness of Presentation Formats for Instruction: Teaching First-Year Students." *College & Research Libraries* 61 (January 2000): 65-72.

4. Holman, Lucy. "A Comparison of Computer-Assisted Instruction and Classroom Bibliographic Instruction." *Reference & User Services Quarterly* 40 (Fall 2000): 53-65.

5. Kaplowitz, Joan and Contini, Janice. "Computer-Assisted Instruction: Is It an Option for Bibliographic Instruction in Large Undergraduate Survey Classes?" *College & Research Libraries* 59 (January 1998): 19-28.

6. Tricarico, Mary A., von Daum Tholl, Susan, and O'Malley, Elena. "Interactive Online Instruction for Library Research: The Small Academic Library Experience." *Journal of Academic Librarianship* 27 (May 2001): 220-223.

7. Dupuis, Elizabeth A. "Automating Instruction." *School Library Journal Net Connect* 47 (April 2001): 21-22.

8. American Library Association. *Information Literacy Competency Standards for Higher Education.* 2000. Available: <http://www.ala.org/ala/acrl/acrlstandards/informationliteracycompetency.htm>. Accessed: April 22, 2005.

9. Association of College and Research Libraries. *Objectives for Information Literacy Instruction: A Model Statement for Academic Librarians.* 2001. Available: <http://www.ala.org/ala/acrl/acrlstandards/objectivesinformation.htm>. Accessed: March 25, 2005.

10. Franks, Jeffrey A. et al. "Developing an Interactive Web Tutorial to Teach Information Competencies: The Planning Process at the University of Akron." *Journal of Educational Media and Library Services* 37 (March 2000): 235-255.

11. Ibid.

12. Ibid.

13. Dewald, Nancy H. "Transporting Good Library Instruction Practices into the Web Environment: An Analysis of Online Tutorials." *Journal of Academic Librarianship* 25 (January 1999): 26-31.

14. Dewald, Nancy H. "Web-Based Library Instruction: What Is Good Pedagogy?" *Information Technology and Libraries* 18 (March 1999): 26-31.

15. ACRL Instruction Section Teaching Methods Committee. *Tips for Developing Effective Web-Based Library Instruction.* Available: <http://www.lib.vt.edu/istm/WebTutorials/Tips.html>. Accessed: April 22, 2005.

16. Lindauer, Bonnie G. "Defining and Measuring the Library's Impact on Campuswide Outcomes." *College & Research Libraries* 59 (November 1998): 546-563.

17. See note 10.

18. See note 16.

Chapter 14

Information Literacy
for Nontraditional Students
at the University of Rhode Island

Joanna M. Burkhardt

INTRODUCTION

Traditional college students are usually between eighteen and twenty-three years of age. They typically begin college the September after graduation from high school. They often live on campus when they start college and this is usually the first time they have lived away from their parents. They frequently have no firm ideas about career goals and use the first two years of their college experience to determine where their interests and aptitudes lie. Many traditional students attend college with the financial support of their parents. With no firm goal in mind, some traditional students beginning college lack focus and motivation.

Nontraditional students are older than twenty-three years of age. Many nontraditional students return to academic endeavors after doing something else for a number of years, such as working, having a family, caretaking of elderly parents or small children, traveling, or any combination of activities. The nontraditional student usually has more real-life experience and returns to academic pursuits with a specific goal in mind. Often these students do not attend college full-time, but rather fit one or two courses into their schedules while continuing some or all of their other established activities. They generally pay for the cost of attending college themselves and are therefore motivated to get the most they can for their money. Nontraditional students have specific goals and expectations for the academic experience. Educators have identified components specific to how adults learn which resulted in adult learning theory, known as androgogy. This theory first appeared in the 1980s based on the seminal work by Malcolm S. Knowles.[1] Since Knowles' initial work, this theory has been applied to library-related teaching and reported in the literature. For example, Lawler offers applied strategies for teaching adults in general.[2] Carr applies teaching strategies in the library setting.[3] Sheridan offers applications specific to the academic library.[4] Harrison offers teaching strategies for library applications as part of the reference and instruction mission.[5]

SETTING

The University of Rhode Island (URI), chartered as the state's agricultural school in 1888, is the principal public research and graduate institution for the State of Rhode Island and a land grant, sea grant, and urban grant institution. The university enrolls approximately 13,000 Full-Time Equivalent (FTE) students and has approximately 700 faculty and 1,700 staff. The university has four campuses, each of which specializes to some extent. The main campus, located in Kingston, is where most of the undergraduate and non-marine oriented graduate work is conducted. The Narragansett Bay Campus houses the Graduate School of Oceanography and the Coastal Institute. The W. Alton Jones Campus houses the National Center for Environmental Education. The Providence Campus, officially known as the Alan Shawn Feinstein College of Continuing Education, is located in the state capital. This urban campus caters to adult students in selected undergraduate, graduate, and professional programs.

The Providence Campus

The Providence Campus, founded in 1942, enrolls approximately 5,000 mostly part-time students. The average student at the Providence campus is forty years of age. Eighty percent of the students work full-time and 30 percent are single parents. Students typically pay for their own education, with many making great sacrifices of time and re-sources to do so. Some students have returned to an interrupted college education after some time away, while others are starting college for the first time. In either case, most of the Providence Campus undergraduate students have been away from academia for five or more years. Many URI-Providence Campus students have specific career goals in mind. In addition to the undergraduate programs, students can do graduate work in a variety of subject areas including Psychology, Business, Clinical Laboratory Science, and Library Science. The Special Programs office at the Providence Campus offers noncredit courses in work-related subjects. Classes at all levels are offered in late the afternoon, evening, and weekend time slots to accommodate working students.

The Library

Most of the Providence Campus students eventually come to the library. Libraries have changed remarkably in the last ten years, and continue to change on a daily basis. For students who have not used a library in some time, these frequent changes make the task of learning how to use the "new" library just one more thing they had to master. In this respect, nontraditional students have more catching up to do than the traditional students who have never known life without high levels of technology. In addition, many Providence Campus students are first-generation immigrants and/or the first generation in their families to attend college. Some received their elementary/secondary education in another country and may not speak English as their first language. For all of these reasons, there is a high level of "library anxiety" among nontraditional students. This anxiety has been discussed in the library literature. For example, Mellon identifies reasons students may feel anxious when approaching a library-related task,[6] while Harrell discusses techniques that may reduce the level of library anxiety students experience.[7]

Library mission statements usually include the goals of serving and educating library users, as well as providing information as needed. Older students often have experience with in-person visits to libraries. Nontraditional students may turn to the library staff for assistance more readily than do traditional students because their previous library training took place at a time when the library was the principal place to acquire information. Many nontraditional students also re-member libraries as a place of refuge, comfort, learning, and accep-tance. For these reasons, many Providence Campus students overcome their library anxiety and voluntarily walk through the doors of the li-brary looking for information.

THE PROVIDENCE CAMPUS LIBRARY

The Providence Campus Library has a staff of four full-time employ-ees: one MLS, three full-time staff. A few part-time student assistants are hired each semester. The library houses some 25,000 monographs and subscribes to approximately 300 periodical titles in paper. As a "branch" of the main campus library, the Providence Campus library also has access to the online databases and electronic titles subscribed to by the main campus library. The University Libraries are members of a statewide consortium of ten academic libraries known as Higher Education Library Information Network (HELIN). The consortium supports reciprocal borrowing, shared online tools (such as an online Information Literacy Tutorial), and consortial purchase of databases. This allows the "branch" library to offer the same resources and ser-vices as those available at the main campus.

Since many Providence Campus library users are essentially "new" users, in that they have little or no experience with information in the electronic format, the library staff at the Providence Campus has a strong teaching mission. Teaching library users how to use the library tools to find the information they need, rather than just presenting them with answers, is a very important part of the library's mission. An equally important concept conveyed by library instruction is the trans-ferability of knowledge to other settings and situations. All students, once they leave the university, must alter their means of gathering in-formation to some extent because they will no longer have online ac-cess to the databases, journals, and other reference tools they used while students. Part of the library's teaching strategy is to help students to recognize the common elements among information tools in the elec-tronic environment so they can use any tool that becomes available to them after they graduate.

TEACHING IN THE LIBRARY

During the past ten years there has been a marked shift in reference work in the libraries at URI, requiring that librarians spend much more time teaching library users how to use the wide variety of tools available to them. Historically the University Libraries have had a strong program of library instruction in both general and subject-specific categories. However, by the late 1990s it became clear that something more was called for. A fifty-minute class simply did not allow enough time to cover even the rudiments of library instruction in the electronic environment. Many instructors were not able to give more of their class time to library instruction. There was no comprehensive means to ensure that every student received library instruction.

METHODS

The faculty of the University Libraries decided that a plan was needed to document the existing programs of library instruction and to expand that instruction to be more inclusive and more comprehensive. A comprehensive Plan for Information Literacy at URI was created and approved in 2000.[8] The goal of this plan was to include as many options as possible for providing learning opportunities for students to become familiar and proficient in the uses of information. Some of this comprehensive plan's options include a Web-based tutorial, subject-specific modules, and two credit courses in information literacy.

Of the two credit courses created, the first was built as a one-credit "lab" meant to be attached to a specific course. Initially the class was attached to Business 110, the first course that all students take once they declare a major in Business. The laboratory nature of the class offered the opportunity for students to explore business related research tools. This one-credit class can be adapted to any subject and has since been offered in several other disciplines.

The second course, the focus of this case study, is a standalone three-credit course. When first created, it was a free elective meaning that it was not attached to any other course, not a required course for any major, and not a course that fulfilled any requirement. Today, the course fulfills a general education requirement in English Communication.

The class is also offered as part of some freshman Learning Communities in the fall term each year. It has been received enthusiastically by administrators, faculty, and students alike. One section of this course was offered in fall 1999. In 2005/2006, six to eight sections were offered each semester and there is often a waiting list to get into the course. To date, more than 1,000 students have taken the class to date. The class is offered at both the Kingston and the Providence campuses. The sections offered at the Providence Campus cater to the adult student population there.

The first section of the three-credit course, "Introduction to Information Literacy," was offered at the Providence Campus on Saturday mornings during fall semester 1999. The section was team taught by two tenure-track library faculty members. The strategy for the course was to focus on the information needs of nontraditional students, teach them about the information resources and tools available to them, make them familiar with the process of doing research in the online environment, and demonstrate how the skills learned in the class are transferable to situations outside the university setting.

All ten students enrolled in the first class were female, adult, nontraditional students. The experimental nature of the class was explained to the class at the outset. The students were very enthusiastic, dedicated, and cooperative. While the classroom equipment was minimal, a PC, LCD projector, and a blank wall in the library classroom provided the rudiments needed for the class. To give students hands-on practice during this first semester, they left the library classroom and used public access computers elsewhere in the library.

The literatures of education and library science condone the use of a wide variety of approaches to accommodate different learning styles. For example, Howard Gardner has published extensively on the theory of learning styles.[9] Reid discusses techniques used in teaching students who were learning English as a second language.[10] Allen writes about learning styles as applied to post-secondary library instruction.[11] Druke discusses active learning in the classroom.[12] Keyser emphasizes the differences between active and cooperative learning.[13] "Introduction to Information Literacy" was designed to accommodate as many different learning styles as possible, avoiding the stereotypical lecture scenario. Examples used in class were geared toward situations that might be encountered in a workplace or as part of daily life as well as those likely to be encountered in the academic realm. Exercises included a variety of opportunities for students to use their own experiences to illustrate information-related tasks. Exercises and assignments were of a practical nature, but geared toward academic projects likely to be assigned in the future or real-life problems that people confront and solve on a regular basis. The original creators of the course eventually published a book giving thirty-five examples of assignments of this kind.[14]

The course begins with discussions about what information is, where it comes from, how people receive it, how the digital divide affects people's lives, and how to tell good information from bad information. The exercise (see Exhibit 14.1) given to illustrate the ideas discussed in class is called "Let's Buy a Car!" Students are asked to outline the process of buying a car and to list the information needed along with a source for that information. For example, a buyer might want to know which features are standard items on a particular car, safety ratings, insurance rates, known mechanical problems, blue book value, previous accidents, auto loan rates, and so on. For each of these items, students provide what they consider to be a reliable source of information (the dealer, *Consumer Reports,* auto mechanics, etc.).

Class discussion reveals reasons why people deem their information sources to be reliable, and the broader implications of finding appropriate information sources to fit the information need. For example, the car dealer may reveal good things about the car, but will he/she tell customers about its drawbacks?

The second topic of the course is the organization of information. Students usually agree that organization of information is essential. Different systems of organization are identified including clothing catalogs, college catalogs, inventory systems, and numeric systems such as social security or student identification numbers. Students are asked to organize any collection of ten things using a set of rules of their own construction in order to (1) define things that fit the collection; and (2) govern their placement in the collection. Another person must be able to apply the rules to add an item to the collection. Students organize the contents of refrigerators, CD collections, sock drawers, etc. Usually they find that making rules that allow someone else to add something to their collection is not as easy as it sounds.

Exhibit 14.1. Let's Buy a Car!
Information Defined

What is Information?

- How is it used?
- Where does it come from?
- Who produces it?
- Why was it produced?

Characteristics of Information

- Factual information = statement of a thing done or existing
- Analytical information = interpretation of factual information
- Subjective information = understood from one point of view
- Objective information = understood from reviewing many different points of view

Quality of Information

Is it good or bad information? How do we know?
Critically evaluate the information by asking:
What is the . . .

- Purpose?
- Audience?
- Authority?
- Currency?

. . . of the information?

The Information Chain

Primary Sources: Original materials which have NOT been filtered through interpretation, condensation, or evaluation by a second party. For example, the U.S. Constitution, the Magna Carta, a personal letter or diary.
Secondary Sources: Information ABOUT a primary or original source that usually has been modified, selected, or rearranged for a specific purpose or audience. For example, encyclopedia articles and biographies.
Tertiary Sources: Information which is a distillation and collection of primary and secondary sources. Twice removed from the original source, they include information found in indexes to periodical articles and bibliographies on a topic.

Let's Buy a Car . . .

What sort of information would you gather to determine what car to buy?

What do you need to know before you can buy the car?

1. Brainstorm the questions and types of information needs you might have in preparation to buy a car.
2. What kind of information is it? Use the Characteristics of Information to determine what kind of information each information need requires.
3. List a source for the information you need (i.e., the dealer, a brochure, your mechanic).

As an in-class active assignment, students are given a card with an author and title on it. They are instructed to go directly to the book stacks, without using any information resource such as the online catalog or the library staff, and try to find the book listed on the card. They are to return to the classroom after a set period of time. Most students are unable to find a specific book by browsing. This leads to a meaningful discussion of the organization of library materials and the online catalog. Students gain an appreciation for the complexity and versatility of the online catalog, and gratefully learn how it works.

The third topic discussed is research. Most students feel that research related to academic subjects is daunting, complicated, and incomprehensible. Even adult students, who solve complex and intricate problems every day at work or at home, are initially overwhelmed by the prospect of doing academic research. In an exercise created to dispel this illusion, the class was divided into pairs or small groups that were each given a task. For example, a task might be to plan a weeklong camping trip in Acadia National Park. Students make a list of things they need to know to accomplish this task: where is Acadia National Park, when to go, whether reservations are needed, kind of equipment needed, and so on. Then students identify the tools they need to get answers to each question: get a listing of national parks from the Chamber of Commerce, find a map of the area at the library, map a route from the starting point to the park and back using MapQuest, go to park's Web site for the park to find out the dates of operation and the rules and regulations, and so on. The plans are presented in class and students are asked to point out things the presenters might have forgotten such as checking the weather and/or suggesting other sources of information. The point is that people do complex research every day and academic research is not very different from those everyday projects.

The discussion then moves on to different types of academic research tools such as general encyclopedias, subject-specific encyclopedias, books, journals (in paper and electronic formats), and Web sites. Less traditional sources of information are also explored by having students find organizations and experts for an assigned topic.

Students use a journal format to write about their experiences finding material for each of the assignments. Students write about how hard or easy it was, problems encountered, and what was learned. In this way, students get practice in writing. They identify problems and trouble spots. It is apparent from their journal entries that many students are initially leery and sometimes frustrated at the beginning of an assignment, but by the end they have mastered the tool, understood its usefulness, and have gained a measure of confidence in their abilities.

Several assignments require small group learning. For example, once students have learned to use a general periodical database, they are divided into small groups. Each group is assigned the task of learning how to use a subject-specific periodical database. The groups are given some class time but are also expected to work on this project on their own time as well. On the assigned day, the groups "teach" their database to the class. This exercise requires interpersonal skills and teamwork. It requires presentation skills and division of labor. It also makes all students aware that subject-specific databases exist and gives them firsthand experience with several of them.

Information collected for every homework exercise is applicable to the final project, called "The Paper Trail." This project is a portfolio that includes all the information a student would gather to write a ten-page research paper. A completed Paper Trail includes an outline of the paper that would be written, annotated bibliography of sources selected as appropriate for use, annotated bibliography of sources examined but not used with reasons for their rejection, title page for each source, journal entries for all exercises, and supporting materials that illustrate the journey. Students do not actually write the paper for this class, but may use the topic of a paper assigned for another class. This allows them to get credit for the research conducted in this class and write the paper for a grade in another class.

In the Paper Trail, students select an academically oriented subject and conduct some general background research on the topic. Students then learn how to craft a research question. Using the research question as their focus, students collect specific information from books, journal articles, Web sites, experts and organizations, government sources, and any other information source they feel is appropriate to their topic. Students learn how to find high quality information by examining authority, reliability, timeliness, and sponsorship.

The journal entries that accompany assignments, additional reflections about assigned readings, and a final summary about the process of becoming information literate are also part of this project. Required writing causes students to think about the process of doing research and to document its high and low points. Students are encouraged to be creative in the presentation of their portfolios, but most students submit a completed project on paper in a three-ring binder with dividers.

During one of the final classes, invited speakers talk about how they use information in their jobs, or to discuss/debate an information issue such as privacy. This emphasizes practical uses of information and shows students how the information learned in class can be transferred to uses outside the classroom.

Students take pre- and posttest assessment surveys, which are used to assess student outcomes for the course (see Appendix 14.1). Did students learn what the instructors wanted them to learn? Do they have the skills they need and can they apply those skills to an information need?

RESULTS

The surveys are used to help instructors improve the class and pinpoint trouble spots. In a recent analysis of surveys given over the past five years, results show that students realize significant learning gains from the course. In their voluntary comments, many students have indicated that they feel more confident in their ability to address research-related assignments. Former students frequently come back to the library after they have completed their degrees to tell their instructors how much the course helped them. This is high praise from students who rate their abilities at the beginning of the semester as almost nonexistent.

CONCLUSION

"Introduction to Information Literacy" was crafted for the needs of the nontraditional student, their concerns, and their time constraints. Demand for the course is high and the assessment results are positive, and the course continues to be offered every semester. By acknowledging life experience and emphasizing the transferability of skills learned in class to other academic and nonacademic situations, this course gives students the sense that their money has been well spent, and eases the anxiety that accompanies the start of any journey into the unknown.

APPENDIX 14.1.
INFORMATION LITERACY ASSESSMENT

Part I

1. What year are you? Circle one
   a. Freshman
   b. Sophomore
   c. Junior
   d. Senior
   e. Grad
   f. Nonmatriculated
   g. Don't know

2. Male   ❐   Female   ❐

3. Full-time student ❐   Part-time student ❐

4. What is your career goal? _____
5. I have had a class session on how to use the library:
   a. At CCE
   b. At Kingston
   c. At another college
   d. In high school
   e. Have never had a class
6. I used a library
   a. Less than one week ago
   b. More than one week but less than one month ago

c. More than one month ago but less than one year ago

d. More than one year ago

e. Don't remember

7. Do you use e-mail?

Yes ☐   No ☐

8. Do you use the World Wide Web/Internet?

Yes ☐   No ☐

Part II

1. The best place to look for an introduction to a topic such as astronomy is:

   a. The online catalog

   b. An encyclopedia

   c. A periodical

   d. Don't know

2. The best way to identify current and authoritative information for a research paper is:

   a. Search the World Wide Web

   b. Check an encyclopedia

   c. Consult a book

   d. Use a periodical index

   e. Don't know

3. For each information category at the left, place an X below the one best source to use to find the information:

Information Source	The New York Times	Encyclopedia of Associations	Journal Index	Encyclopedia Americana	Atlas of American History	Statistical Abstract of the U.S.	Don't know
Contact information for the Daughters of the American Revolution							
Borders of the former Yugoslavia							
Current research on cloning							
Unemployment data for 1996							

Information Source	The New York Times	Encyclopedia of Associations	Journal Index	Encyclo-pedia Americana	Atlas of American History	Statistical Abstract of the U.S.	Don't know
Latest presidential election results							
Description of Brazilian rain forests							

4. What information can you get from this call number? Circle all that apply.

QD 96 N8 P159 1979

a. Subject
b. Author
c. Title
d. Where the book is located
e. Which library owns the book
f. When the library acquired the book
g. Which cataloging system the library uses
h. How many pages in the book
i. The date of publication
j. Don't know

5. Read the following statement and answer the questions below.

"Describe the effects of acid rain on the environment."

What are the key concepts in the above statement?
a. Effects, environment
b. Environment, acid rain
c. Effects, rain

What source would best answer the question?
a. Dictionary
b. Map
c. Periodical index
d. Directory

6. If your keyword search in the online catalog on "public health United States" retrieves 827 books, what would be the best next step?
a. Add terms to the search and try again
b. Try searching under "United States public health"

    c. Try the search again with fewer terms

    d. Scan the list to choose the most relevant books

    e. Don't know

7. If you were writing a paper on crime in Los Angeles and you found a newspaper article with statistics indicating that there was a 10 percent decline in 1997, which of the following is the best next step?

    a. Verify the accuracy of the figure by comparing with last year's newspaper

    b. Check the statistics in a government source

    c. Use the data, being sure to cite the article in your paper

8. Suppose you are writing a research paper and you read an article on your topic. In which of the following instances would you write a footnote in your paper?

    a. When you copy a whole paragraph

    b. When you write over in your own words

    c. When you quote one sentence from the article

    d. All of the above

    e. None of the above

9. For your history class you must select a primary source and write a brief paper placing it in context. From the list below, choose the ONE best primary source on which to base your paper.

    a. Chapter in your textbook

    b. Journal article

    c. Scholarly monograph

    d. Collection of letters

    e. Critical biography

10. Which of the following would be a correct and complete citation for this item in a bibliography?

Meyer, Harris.

John Rother's Road trip. (studies managed care around the US) (Interview)

Hospitals and Health Networks v. 71 n.16 (August 20, 1997):23-25.

Pub type: Interview

Type D 1 AB to see abstract

    a. Meyer, Harris. "John Rother's road trip." *Hospitals & Health Networks* 71 (August 20, 1997):23-25

    b. Harris Meyer. *John Rother's* road trip. (Studies managed care around the U.S.) Hospitals & Health Networks, vol. 71, no. 16, August 20, 1997, p. 23.

    c. Meyer, Harris. "John Rother's road trip." Interview. *Hospital & Health Networks* 71(16), August 20, 1997

11. In an online database which search would retrieve the greatest number of records?
   a. Cognition and emotion
   b. Cognition or emotion
   c. Cognition not emotion

12. Suppose you perform a subject search in the library online catalog on the "French Revolution" and the computer retrieves zero results. Which one of the following best applies?
   a. Library has no books on the subject
   b. Adding more terms to the search will retrieve books on the topic
   c. Library's books on the topic are listed under different terms
   d. System is down

13. Decide whether each citation below (left column) refers to a book, a journal article, a Web site, or a government document. Make a check in the appropriate space to the right.

Citations	Book	Journal article	Web site	Government document	Don't know
Oaklander, C.I. Pioneers in folk art Collecting. *Folk Art* 17:48-55.					
Bay, C. Human needs and political education. IN Fitzgerald, R., Ed. *Human needs and politics,* 1-15.					
Winslow, Donald J. Thomas Hardy as a Subject of Biography. *THY* 5(1975): 15-21.					
Birks, L.S. Electron probe microanalysis. Wiley-Interscience, 1971.					
New Zealand. Dept. of Statistics. External trade: imports. 1973-74. Aug. 1977.					
University of Chicago Library. Slavic and East European Studies. <http://www.lib.uchigago.edu/ LibInfo/SourcesbySubject/ Slavic/>					
Cabinet Ministers and Parliamentary Government. Ed. M. Laver. Cambridge University Press, 1994.					

14. Which of the following Web site components would help you evaluate the authority and accuracy of the information it provides?
    a. browser name
    b. URL or Web address
    c. title of the Web page
    d. content of the page
    e. links to other sites
    f. "About Us" section of the page
    g. "Contact Us" section of the page
    h. date of last update
    i. author's biographical information
15. There are some problems in using the Web to do research. From the list below, circle all the items which might be problems when doing research.
    a. there are more than 2 billion Web sites in existence
    b. Web sites come and go without warning
    c. anyone can put up a Web site on any subject
    d. information may or may not be objective
    e. not all Web sites say where the information came from
    f. many researchers use the Web to publish cutting edge information
    g. some scholarly journals are only published on the Web
16. Scholarly journals are different from popular magazines. Circle the items that make scholarly journals a more appropriate choice when collecting information when doing research
    a. articles are printed on plain paper
    b. authors are usually experts in their fields
    c. articles are not interrupted by advertisements
    d. articles are usually longer
    e. articles include a bibliography
    f. articles use technical, hard to understand language
17. How could you locate an expert on a topic you are researching?
    a. look in the University catalog
    b. look in a directory of associations and organizations
    c. do a Web search on your topic
    d. ask a librarian

Thank you for completing this exercise.

NOTES

1. Knowles, Malcolm S. *The Modern Practice of Adult Education: From Pedagogy to Androgogy.* Chicago: Follett Books, 1980.

2. Lawler, Patricia A. *The Keys to Adult Learning: Theory and Practical Strategies.* Philadelphia: Research for Better Schools, 1991.

3. Carr, David. "Adult Learning and Library Helping." *Library Trends* 31 (Spring 1983): 569-583.

4. Sheridan, Jean. "Androgogy: A New Concept for Academic Librarians." *Research Strategies* 4 (Fall 1986): 156-167.

5. Harrison, Naomi. "Breaking the Mold: Using Educational Pedagogy in Designing Library Instruction of Adult Learners." In *Reference Services for the Adult Learner: Challenging Issues for the Traditional and Technological Era,* edited by Kwasi Sarkodie-Mensah. Binghamton, NY: Haworth Information Press, 2000, pp. 287-298.

6. Mellon, C.A. "Library Anxiety: A Grounded Theory and its Development." *College and Research Libraries* 47 (March 1986): 425-431.

7. Harrell, Karen J. "Reducing High Anxiety: Responsive Library Services to Off-Campus Nontraditional Students." In *Distance Learning Library Services: The Tenth Off-Campus Library Services Conference,* edited by Patrick B. Mahoney. Binghamton, NY: Haworth Information Press, 2002, pp. 355-365.

8. Plan for Information Literacy at the University of Rhode Island. University of Rhode Island. University Libraries. Available: <http://www.uri.edu/library/instruction_services/infolitplan.html>. Accessed: February 28, 2005.

9. Gardner, Howard. *Multiple Intelligences: The Theory in Practice.* New York: Basic Books, 1993.

10. Reid, J. M. "The Learning Style Preferences of ESL Students. *TESOL Quarterly* 21, no. 1 (1987): 87-111.

11. Allen, E. E. "Active Learning and Teaching: Improving Postsecondary Library Instruction." *Reference Librarian* 51/52 (1995): 89-103.

12. Drueke, J. "Active Learning in the University Library Instruction Classroom." *Research Strategies* 10 (Spring 1992): 77-83.

13. Keyser, Marcia W. "Active Learning and Cooperative Learning: Understanding the Difference and Using Both Styles Effectively." *Research Strategies* 17, no. 1 (2000): 36.

14. Burkhardt, Joanna M. et al. *Teaching Information Literacy: 35 Practical, Standards-Based Exercises for College Students.* Chicago: ALA Editions, 2003.

PART C:
LIBRARY INSTRUCTION IN HEALTH SCIENCES UNIVERSITY SETTINGS

Chapter 15

Turning Librarians into Teachers

Patricia C. Higginbottom
Lee A. Vucovich
Martha E. Verchot

INTRODUCTION

Providing library users with the skills they need to effectively and efficiently find and use information is an important service of every library. Who should do that training, when it should be done, and what methods should be used differs across types and sizes of libraries. At Lister Hill Library (LHL) at the University of Alabama at Birmingham (UAB), circumstances propelled a philosophical change from using the education coordinator model to one that involved all reference librarians in providing both formal instruction and capitalizing on informal teachable moments with patrons. Shifting from one method to the other required changes in viewpoints, skills, staffing, procedures, and responsibilities, and continues as an ongoing process. This chapter covers the circumstances that prompted these changes and describes the process of conversion and includes results and evaluation of education services under the new model.

SETTING

Lister Hill Library is an academic health sciences library that is part of the UAB. Although UAB is one of the institutions comprising the University of Alabama System, it is a young institution, having only existed as an autonomous campus since 1969. However, the medical school goes back much further than 1969, however. It was formed in 1859 and moved several times before settling in Birmingham in 1944 to associate with Jefferson and Hillman Hospitals. LHL was established in 1945 as the Medical College of Alabama Library.[1,2]

Today, UAB is an urban university categorized by the Carnegie Foundation as an institution of very high research activity.[3] With over 16,000 students in twelve schools, LHL supports much more than the medical school. Primary schools include dentistry, nursing, optometry, medicine, public health, health-related professions, and the joint health sciences. In addition, the library supports the clinical staff of a 900-bed hospital that include around 600 residents, and supports various other clinics and centers. As part of a public university and a resource library in the National Network of Libraries of Medicine (NN/LM), LHL provides support for health sciences faculty, staff, and students at other educational and research centers in the state and has an active outreach program to the general population of Alabama.[4]

LHL is staffed by fifty-five full-time equivalent (FTE) including eighteen faculty members. The library is contained within four floors of a six-story building that is currently open ninety-four and a half hours per week. Clinical staff are also served by a small branch library within the hospital. The print collection currently consists of just over 128,000 books and around 1,200 journal subscriptions. On-campus and remote access is provided to an array of additional electronic databases, including almost 300 books and over 27,000 journals.[5]

In 1993, LHL hired an education coordinator as part of the Reference Unit, reporting to the head of Information and Instructional Services. The position was created because of the increase in publicly accessible databases and the need to train end users to use them effectively. The education coordinator's primary duties included developing, scheduling, teaching, and managing end user classes, designing handouts and printed user guides, and evaluating and improving educational activities. In addition, the coordinator was a fully participating member in all other aspects of reference services. During this time period, as an outgrowth of educational activities, the coordinator also became responsible for the design and content of the library's Web site and for the maintenance of the library's online list of electronic journals. While the coordinator, in theory, organized the classes for others to teach, in reality, largely due to staff shortages, varying priorities, and perceptions among the other Public Services staff, this person did the vast majority of teaching. These sessions included basic orientations, library tours, "one-shot" targeted sessions on library research skills at the request of teaching faculty, and a monthly schedule of open classes on certain topics or tools such as the Internet, grant resources, MEDLINE, and EndNote/Reference Manager.

OBJECTIVES

In 1996, the library director initiated a strategic planning process to evaluate all aspects of the library's activities, programs, and services. After standard internal and external environmental scans, several strategy groups were formed to delve deeper into key areas. One group was the Education Implementation Team. This group was initially formed in 1998 with members from throughout the library, including the director, education coordinator, a reference librarian, a nonlibrarian IT systems specialist, head of the Instructional Technologies, and others. Unfortunately, after a year or so of work, several circumstances, including other priorities, a charge that was too broad, and the inflexible, diverse interests of some individuals involved, prevented this team from reaching any useful consensus on priorities. Ultimately the team faltered and failed to make recommendations. At the same time, the classroom component of the education program grew in numbers of sessions and attendees, including both a monthly calendar of open sessions and one- to two-hour, one-time, course-specific orientations but with very few opportunities for multiple-contact, course-integrated instruction. However, there were whole segments of the target population that remained unserved. Initiatives to enhance the educational offerings to include those target populations included:

- providing Category 1 continuing medical education credit for certain classes;
- teaching outreach sessions to health professional groups and groups of public librarians in the state; and
- offering a set of monthly classes as well as night/weekend classes.

Owing to the size and diversity of the UAB population and the reliance on a single librarian to teach, market, and evaluate instructional activities, it was impossible to add new and innovative programs, and the format of educational offerings continued to be provided as it had been for the previous six years.

By the beginning of the twenty-first century, several factors coalesced to focus the attention of library decision makers on the need to change educational strategies. The need for education beyond tours and demonstrations or hands-on sessions on a few major tools such as the catalog and MEDLINE exploded with the number and sophistication of online resources. The increased number of UAB blended learning and distance education classes, along with expectations for more individualized, point-of-need help, created situations in which people needed guidance on which resources to use, how to access them, and how to use them. Further input was solicited through an April 2002 LibQUAL+ survey,[6] focus groups, and Web usability studies, all of which revealed that people were not aware of the breadth of available library resources. Survey results revealed a common assumption of LHL users at that time that, "it is all free on the Internet." By this time, monthly library class session enrollments had sharply declined, resulting in the cessation of that part of the program. A new opportunity to create a one-week optional class within the School of Medicine curriculum offered the library staff the means to experiment with longer, more in-depth education methods. Finally, a medical crisis in the education coordinator's family in summer 2002 and the resulting leave of absence focused attention on how much the education program relied on one individual. It was clearly time to focus attention on the provision of educational services.

In 2002, the Education Implementation Team was reformed as the Education Strategy Team, with new membership, although it represented similar areas. This time, the charge was clear and focused. Goals for this group included conducting a needs assessment to develop "a prioritized list of educational objectives for LHL clientele" and to "identify one or more strategies for achieving" these objectives. The group met monthly for almost a full year. The first step was to systematically collect all information from previous needs assessments pertaining to education and training. Feedback from service point staff was gathered about the kinds of questions users were asking. While it was obvious that further needs assessments were unnecessary because the group had enough input to develop a definable list of educational objectives, it was clear that prioritizing the objectives would be difficult. Each team member was instructed to individually develop a prioritized list that would be compiled and evaluated by the team chair. From this process, two overarching goals were developed with a list of several accomplishing educational objectives. The LHL site features these goals in two tables (<http://www.uab.edu/lister/publications/ EducationGoalTable1.pdf> and <http://www.uab.edu/lister/publica tions/EducationGoalTable2.pdf>).

At this point, group discussion turned to finding the best ways to meet these objectives. As the group had been formed based on clear, organized, strategic planning methods, the team felt comfortable throwing out all assumptions on how things had been done in the past, how things should be done, or how difficult it might be to make changes. Open, frank discussion of needs and possibilities allowed them to develop a list of somewhat radical recommendations. In November 2002, based on the idea that every encounter with a library user is a "teachable moment," the group recommended the following:

- acceptance of the two goals with accompanying educational objectives;
- overall responsibility for provision of educational services be assigned to the associate director for Public Services;
- the position of education coordinator be eliminated, and all reference librarians were to be involved in the education program; and
- all Public Services staff would share responsibility for providing educational services to users, with specific activities assignable by someone in a supervisory role who could monitor and adjust workloads as necessary to accomplish these activities.

These recommendations were sent to the library director and senior administrative staff for review.

METHODS

Over the course of the next year, library faculty and staff discussed and debated the contents of the Education Strategy Team report. There was broad acceptance of the innovative new goals and objectives although some concern was expressed about how realistically staff would be able to implement them. On the other hand, changing the titles and responsibilities of staff members was more controversial. As this plan involved significant change, the library director met with public services staff a number of times to determine how staff could be retrained to take on these new responsibilities. While not every person supported the plan, it was accepted and the transition to the new model began during the 2003/2004 academic year.

Over the next two years, library staff began an incremental implementation process that involved training all reference librarians to be effective teachers. Administrative changes began immediately. With the elimination of the educational coordinator position, the associate director for Public Services took on organizational and class scheduling responsibilities, at first using the same procedures that were used before. The former education coordinator initially continued to teach most of the formal classes, although other reference librarians began to informally observe and assist these classes. There were also staff vacancies to be filled. For example, the position of assistant director for Reference Services remained open for a full year. Based on recommendations for expanded services supported by library administration, a new reference librarian position was created. Recruitment of reference librarians proved to have a major positive impact on the transition. Newly written job descriptions emphasized teaching and outreach roles, and during the interview process, candidates presented an actual class for the full LHL staff. By April 2005, there were three new members on the reference staff with strong interests and abilities in teaching.

Concurrently, LHL faculty undertook a new outreach initiative by creating an active liaison program. Reference librarians volunteered to be liaisons to each targeted school. While the objectives of the program encompassed far more than teaching, the group decided that the liaison would be the primary teacher for any sessions requested by their assigned schools. Even so, change did not happen overnight. The associate director for Public Services, assistant director for Reference Services, and the reference staff drafted a teaching plan of responsibilities and expectations (see Appendix 15.1). To prepare for the "fall rush" of students, they spent the summer of 2004 updating their teaching skills. This preparation focused on (1) making sure everyone in the unit was familiar with the major research tools; (2) ensuring that each frequently requested teaching topic had at least two individuals who felt confident enough to teach it informally or formally; and (3) improving the teaching and presentation skills of the group. Several activities addressed these areas. In summer 2004, each person in the reference unit planned and presented a fifteen- to thirty-minute session to the rest of the unit on one of the less common resources. This gave everyone practice in developing a class and also allowed practice of presentation skills. After each session, there was discussion and questions and constructive criticism was offered. Each librarian was responsible for reviewing a training video on adult learners.[7] A general outline and script of topics to cover in a tour or orientation (originally drafted by the education coordinator) was updated and shared within the group. The chair of the UAB Communication Studies Department provided a workshop to the reference unit on public speaking. Finally, as listed in the plan, Reference librarians were required to observe a class before they taught one and when they did teach, someone (usually the former education coordinator) would observe their class and help out if needed, plus offer feedback at the end.

RESULTS

The "fall rush" of classes in 2004 included thirty-three sessions, with all reference librarians as lead teachers. In fact, the trend of decreasing enrollment was reversed, and the total number of participants surpassed all previous years (see Figure 15.1).

Reference librarians were asked to give feedback on their instructional experiences in their quarterly and annual evaluations. The procedures were also discussed and refined in reference unit meetings. For example, when one person did most of the teaching, she was able to schedule and confirm classes quickly but scheduling and assigning classes with a larger group was problematic. Liaisons and the requestors both needed an uncomplicated system. A "Checklist for Teaching" was developed and the Web form for requesting classes expanded.[8] The two new reference librarians brought excitement, enthusiasm, and a fresh outlook as these guidelines were revised and updated, while the more experienced members of the unit shared their insight.

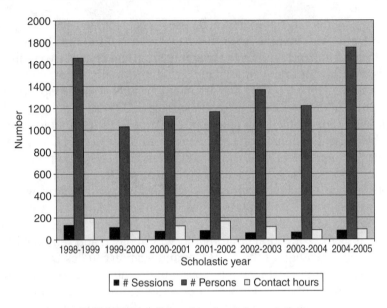

FIGURE 15.1. Educational sessions statistics.

With a new focus on classroom instruction targeted to user needs and a new excitement about educational methods, a small group of reference librarians recommended renovations to the computer lab used for teaching. New lighting, Nova stations, and an updated podium with digital Elmo document camera system have rejuvenated that space.

Collaboration has thrived. A resource library of presentations, handouts, and PowerPoint slides was created for use by all librarian instructors. Each librarian with work to share saves and updates their contributions. Groups or pairs of librarians have worked together on consumer outreach workshops, Personal Digital Assistant (PDA) instruction, and initiatives in integrating information management into the schools of medicine and optometry curricula. In addition, some librarians have experimented with new teaching techniques for the university's increasing distance learning population, while others focused on promotional activities related to the effective use of current and new resources for the users in labs, clinics, and offices. The entire unit has become flexible enough and staff members confident enough to embrace the changes needed to meet the diverse educational requirements of the schools that LHL supports.

EVALUATION

Statistics are kept on the number and type of classes taught. In addition, each librarian uses a standard evaluation form template that was developed collaboratively by the reference staff.[9] The purpose of the evaluation process is to (1) measure the effectiveness of LHL instruction in meeting faculty, community, and student needs; (2) suggest ways to improve/enhance the sessions; and (3) prove value of sessions to requesting schools, departments, and UAB. One key to the successful use of these evaluations was the unit guideline developed during this process. this education session evaluation process will be used to assess and improve the LHL instruction program and is not intended to evaluate an individual instructor's performance. Individual learning plans and the quarterly review/annual evaluation process instead will be used, where applicable, to suggest educational goals for LHL reference/instructional librarians.

Reference librarians are therefore free to experiment and discuss "learning experiences" as well as successes with their colleagues. Interesting and informative comments and suggestions from the evaluations are shared at departmental meetings and informal discussions. Student comments are summarized in a follow-up e-mail message to the instructor. In several cases, student requests for additional class time or sessions earlier in the term were implemented in following semesters. Finally, as they teach, reference librarians are observed by others in the unit and are consulted about their comfort level with teaching. Overall, the evaluations from students and faculty have been positive.

CONCLUSION

The participation in classroom instruction by all reference librarians has allowed each librarian to develop or maintain a classroom teaching skill set which has allowed LHL to increase its educational program flexibility. The most recent educational statistics for fall 2005 show an increase in both numbers of sessions (59) and attendees (765). In addition, the number of classes outside of the fall orientation period have increased. Classes taught outside of this fall rush period tend to be more course-integrated. As more instructors have been available and have felt more confident in classroom situations, team teaching and collaboration among members of the department have come more naturally to team members and occur more often. This greater flexibility has also enabled the unit to respond rapidly to new course-integrated opportunities coming from the School of Medicine and School of Optometry. This greater participation in the curricula has already helped to justify an additional reference librarian position. The reference unit staff are excited about the changes this new model has allowed, and are better positioned to initiate new kinds of learning opportunities.

Currently, reference librarians are involved in staff development programs to expand the knowledge base of other public services staff. This would allow the public services staff in the library to take advantage of teachable moments with library users, enrich the jobs of the public services staff and potentially help prepare the staff for possible policy shifts and newer trends involving the use of paraprofessionals in the provision of reference services.

APPENDIX 15.1. TEACHING PLAN REFERENCE SERVICES MARCH 2005

Serving As an Instructor

Tours

Everyone in the Reference Unit is trained and available to conduct basic library tours. Other interested and trained staff may also be available to conduct tours as needed.

Classes

Reference librarians are prepared to teach basic classes. Classes include:

- Basic library skills (introduction to the Web page; how to use the catalog; how to access online resources, including remote access)
- Basic research skills (how to find books and articles on a topic)
- MEDLINE (how to use Ovid and/or PubMed)

Other classes may be scheduled upon request. Examples include:

- EndNote/Reference Manager

- PDA Resources
- Web of Science

Scheduling

Sessions may be scheduled by direct contact with a reference librarian or by using the Web form <http://www.uab.edu/lister/register.htm> which sends the information to the Assistant Director for Reference Services (AD/RS).
The form can be completed by the requestor, or by one of the reference staff members if the information is taken by phone or email.
Upon receipt, the AD/RS schedules the electronic classroom then routes the request to the Reference liaison for that school. If that person cannot teach the class, the AD/RS works with other members of Reference to schedule it. **The AD/RS copies the Web form into the Educational Sessions calendar, including the instructor (and observer, when applicable) assigned.** Everyone trained to give tours and teach classes should conduct at least two sessions of each per year. The AD/RS will be responsible for handling any scheduling problems.
The person **who will be teaching** the class then contacts the requestor to confirm the session and clarify any details. Reynolds and Museum tours may be scheduled as part of an LHL tour or as a separate event. That part of the tour can be done by the assigned instructor or by Historical Collections staff. Extra time must be allowed when scheduling Historical Collections staff.
As soon as possible after confirming the class appointment, the assigned instructor will enter any additional information about the class in the Education Sessions calendar.
After the class, the assigned instructor will add notes, including the number of students attending, to the Educational Sessions calendar. Any handouts and notes should be placed on the S drive and linked to the Educational Sessions calendar entry, as applicable.

Training and Evaluation

Reference staff will design basic outlines for the above listed classes. Several training sessions will be provided, covering content, basic information, and public speaking skills. Before someone teaches his or her first session, she or he should attend at least two sessions as an observer. First sessions will be attended by a Reference staff member who can provide feedback and be available if needed. Refresher training sessions for staff will be held each June and July in preparation for the fall sessions. The AS/PS will send evaluations to the instructors after the session is completed. They will be reviewed by the instructor, AD/RS, and AD/PS.

Role of the Associate Director for Public Services

Responsible for providing staff training
Responsible for the quality of the educational sessions
• Sitting in on classes as needed
• Reviewing evaluation forms
Responsible for making changes to the education plan as needed

NOTES

1. *A Chronology of the University of Alabama at Birmingham (UAB) and Its Predecessor Institutions and Organizations, 1831.* Birmingham, AL: The University of Alabama Board of Trustees, 1996-2006. Available: <http://www.uab.edu/historical/uabchron.html>. Accessed: April 20, 2006.

2. *Lister Hill Library Historical Timeline—1945 to Present.* Birmingham, AL: Lister Hill Library of the Health Sciences, University of Alabama at Birmingham, 2006. Available: <http://www.uab.edu/lister/about/timeline.htm>. Accessed: April 20, 2006.

3. June, Audrey Williams. "College Classifications Get an Overhaul." *Chronicle of Higher Education* LII (March 3, 2006): A25-A27.

4. *UAB Lister Hill Library of the Health Sciences.* Birmingham, AL: Lister Hill Library of the Health Sciences, University of Alabama at Birmingham, 2006. Available: <http://www.uab.edu/lister/>. Accessed: April 20, 2006.

5. *Library Statistics.* Birmingham, AL: Lister Hill Library of the Health Sciences, University of Alabama at Birmingham, 2006. Available: <http://www.uab.edu/lister/libstat.htm>. Accessed: April 20, 2006.

6. LibQUAL+ Results of Library Users Survey. Birmingham, AL: Lister Hill Library of the Health Sciences, University of Alabama at Birmingham, 2003. Available: <http://www.uab.edu/lister/libqual/libqual_2002.htm>. Accessed: April 27, 2006.

7. Sutton, Helen. *How to Be a Better Trainer.* Boulder, CO: CareerTrack Publications, 1993.

8. *Checklist for Teaching a Class.* Birmingham, AL: Lister Hill Library of the Health Sciences, University of Alabama at Birmingham, 2006. Available: <http://www.uab.edu/lister/publications/teachingchecklist.pdf>. Accessed: April 20, 2006.

9. *Education Evaluation.* Birmingham, AL: Lister Hill Library of the Health Sciences, University of Alabama at Birmingham, 2006. Available: <http://www.uab.edu/lister/publications/educationevaluation.pdf>. Accessed: April 20, 2006.

Chapter 16

MeSHing with Medical Students: Effectiveness of Library Instruction Over Time— A Longitudinal Research Study

Kathryn E. Kerdolff
Maureen M. Knapp

INTRODUCTION

The end of the twentieth century saw a flurry of revisions to traditional medical education.[1] The drive to incorporate population health and medical informatics into the medical curriculum resulted in the redesign of the first- and second-year medicine course curriculum at the Louisiana State University Health Sciences Center in New Orleans (LSUHSC-NO) School of Medicine. The resulting program, Science and Practice of Medicine (SPM 100 and 200), is a two-year course which draws from population/community health initiatives outlined in *Healthy People 2010*[2] and includes active learning, computer-assisted learning, clinical skills, simulation, and small group work in the course curriculum:

> To be adequately prepared for the practice of population medicine, today's physician should have a working knowledge of epidemiology, biostatistics, evidence-based medicine, personal wellness, information management, healthcare policy, and health law. These are the concepts physicians will use to critically evaluate the literature about the health of their patient population and interventions to promote their well being.[3]

An Introduction to Instructional Services in Academic Libraries

As the sophomore clinical forums within the SPM program emphasized the need for physicians to critically evaluate the medical literature, LSUHSC librarians used the SPM 200 course description and syllabus to incorporate a formal library systems instruction program into the second year of medical school. The library program later expanded to include an orientation session for students in the first year, and a refresher class for students during their third year.

PURPOSE

The purpose of this longitudinal case study is to illustrate and report on the effectiveness of the planning, development, and instruction of a formal library systems course component that was integrated into a clinical education program for undergraduate medical students. This ongoing study also provides results from the assessment tools developed in-house to measure medical students' knowledge and retention of authoritative health information resources as gained from the library systems training.

The SPM 200 library systems course component was initiated in July 2003 for sophomore medical students in the graduating class of 2006. Librarians facilitated small group problem-based learning sessions with students, using the population and health topics assigned in the clinical forums as a launch pad to demonstrate good information-seeking behavior and appraisal skills. The small group sessions allowed the librarians to introduce the students to a variety of information resources, as well as guide the students in informatics training. The librarian-facilitated small group sessions continued through August 2005, when the LSUHSC Medical School was forced to relocate classes and adjust the curriculum due to Hurricane Katrina that devastated the area on August 29, 2005.

DESIGN

Pre- and posttests consisting of multiple choice questions were distributed to consecutive years of sophomore medical students in order to measure knowledge retention of health information resources over time. Vignette style questions relating to clinical forum themes and employment of primary resources, such as MEDLINE, evidence-based medicine, and the utilization of Medical Subject Headings (MeSH) were included on the students' midterm and final exams. An additional multiple-choice pretest was distributed to third-year medical students prior to a one-hour library review session. These assessment tools were used to measure information management skills and long-term knowledge retention, which could be used to forecast capabilities for lifelong learning.

SETTING

SPM 200 is a yearlong interdisciplinary course which continues the clinical education of students entering their second year of medical school. The course comprises computer-based cases, clinical experiences, and clinical forums. While computer-based cases and clinical experiences enforce fundamental clinical skills and knowledge, the clinical forums focus on health promotion and disease prevention in human populations. Library instruction was integrated into the clinical forums because of the emphasis on research skills, biomedical research tools, and lifelong learning.

Clinical forums are taught through a combination of didactic lectures and small group sessions. Lectures introduce topics ranging from disease prevention theory and epidemiology to medical informatics and evidence-based medicine. Small group sessions apply the topics to specific population health issues, which are presented as seven health modules (see Figure 16.1).

Ten to twelve students met regularly in small group forums throughout the year to discuss the health module topics. During small group sessions, students were presented with seminal papers, case vignettes, and research questions related to the module. Librarians facilitated these small group sessions by demonstrating how to conduct medical research and use various library resources in direct relation to the topic. Students then prepared a presentation based on their assigned research question for that module which was shared in a "symposium" format later in the month. Medical faculty moderated the symposium to discuss the major learning objectives. Figure 16.2 shows an example of the study topics encountered during the course.[4]

The core of the Library Resources Instruction program consists of instruction on library resources and information database systems;

> **The following public health problems will be discussed in the small group forums:**
>
> 1. Health Screening: The cornerstone of secondary prevention (early detection of disease).
>
> 2. Health-Related Physical Activity: A body in motion is a far healthier body.
>
> 3. Immunization: The cornerstone of primary prevention (prevention of disease).
>
> 4. Fuel—Necessity versus Desire: Too much of a necessary thing can lead to many disasters.
>
> 5. Substance Use and Abuse: People are always looking for an edge, but often risk "falling off."
>
> 6. Reproductive Health: Problems with sex hormones and sexually transmitted diseases.
>
> 7. Passport to Wellness: A study of your own health and how to maintain it.

FIGURE 16.1. Seven health modules of the SPM 200 clinical forums.

information access and retrieval processes; management, organization and presentation of biomedical literature; and locating current clinical trials and systematic reviews.

PARTICIPANTS

Three successive classes (2006, 2007, and 2008, respectively) of second-year medical students consisting of approximately 155 students per year (see Appendix 16.1) participated in voluntary and anonymous pre- and posttesting, which was conducted during the first and last clinical forum small group sessions of the yearlong SPM 200 course. The same students were given another anonymous and voluntary test during their third year of medical school.

INTERVENTION

Preplanning

Librarians held planning sessions to create a proposal for the LSUHSC School of Medicine undergraduate education committee regarding integration of library instruction into SPM 200. Using the

---

Study Topic #1: Screening for Osteoporosis, Obesity, and Diabetes
Instructions: Give a fifteen-minute PowerPoint presentation on the above topic. You may want to use the following questions as a guide. Consult the USPSTF Web site U.S. Preventive Services Task Force http://www.ahrq.gov/clinic/uspstfix .htm http://www.ahrq.gov/clinic/uspstfix.htm as well as other resources. At least one part of your presentation should involve the summary of one or more primary journal articles.

1. Briefly describe the prevalence and morbidity associated with osteoporosis.
2. Review the USPSTF recommendations about screening for osteoporosis in women. Include the sensitivity, specificity, and (if available) the predictive values of recommended tests.
3. Summarize the prevalence of obesity in the United States over the past few decades. How does Louisiana compare? Briefly describe the morbidity and mortality associated with obesity.
4. Review the USPSTF recommendations about screening for obesity. Does screening for obesity have an effect on mortality?
5. Summarize the prevalence of diabetes in the United States and describe changes over the past few decades. How does Louisiana compare? Are there ethnic or socioeconomic groups that are disproportionately affected?
6. Review the USPSTF recommendations about screening asymptomatic adults for diabetes mellitus or impaired glucose tolerance. What is the accuracy of screening tests? Are there effective lifestyle modifications if impaired glucose tolerance is detected early? Is there any evidence that this is beneficial? Cite some primary references and present an argument for or against routine screening for diabetes. *(Suggestion: if two students are giving the presentation, have one student argue for diabetes screening and one argue against routine screening for diabetes— each should try to convince the audience using data from the literature.)*

FIGURE 16.2. Study topic and instructions example.

AAMC objectives presented in *Contemporary Issues in Medicine: Medical Informatics and Population Health,* librarians created a mission statement and overall course objectives[5] (see Figure 16.3).

To generate learning outcomes for each module, a list of all library resources was compiled. Seventeen resources were identified as relevant to the module topics, and these resources were introduced to the class of 2006 (see Appendix 16.2). Following evaluation of the start-up year, ten resources were identified as essential tools for the classes of 2007 and 2008. The library acquired additional resources in 2004 and two of these were added to the essential list for the classes of 2007 and 2008 (see Figure 16.4).

Mission: **Prepare LSUHSC medical students for their future role as altruistic, knowledgeable, skillful, and dutiful physicians accustomed to lifelong learning.**

At the end of the Clinical Forums/Library Resources Instruction, students will be able to:

1. Recognize authoritative information sources.
2. Identify, locate, and retrieve relevant health information from biomedical books and journals, both print and electronic.
3. Recognize similarities and differences among various search interfaces.
4. Create bibliographies that substantiate and document research.
5. Acquire skills to remain current in health topics and research studies.
6. Search for and utilize evidence-based information to make clinical decisions that affect not only the individual patient, but populations as well.
7. Locate and participate in health research opportunities.
8. Organize information for presentation or publication.

FIGURE 16.3. Mission and overall course objectives.

---

1. Clinicaltrials.gov
2. Cochrane Library
3. InfoPOEMS and ACP Pier (evidence-based clinical decision-making tools)*
4. INNOPAC (library catalog/OPAC)
5. MEDLINE via Ovid or PubMed
6. MedlinePlus.gov
7. MeSH—Medical Subject Headings
8. MICROMEDEX
9. STAT!Ref
10. Web of Science via ISI Web of Knowledge

*Resources added for classes 2007 and 2008

FIGURE 16.4. Ten essential resources.

Resources were matched to the appropriate learning module(s). Learning outcomes were created based on the content of the module and mapped to the Overall Course Objectives. Figure 16.5 illustrates the learning outcomes for the Screening Module (presented in Figure 16.2), mapped to overall course objectives.

1. Identify, locate, and retrieve evidence-based research studies that evaluate benefits and risks of health care screening programs from both print and electronic resources. (1, 2, 6)
2. Locate and organize resources that identify recommended screening tests and screening programs. (1, 4)
3. Identify federal, state, and local health care screening programs and research opportunities and register to receive current and updated information about prevention programs and services. (3, 5, 7, 8)
4. Identify the leading health indicators and locate potential financial resources for health conditions and diseases identified. (2, 3, 5, 7)
5. Identify and organize screening recommendations, protocols, and guidelines from authoritative organizations to refer to in professional practice. (1, 2, 4, 8)

FIGURE 16.5. Library instruction learning objectives—module 1 screening. (*Note:* Numbers in parentheses refer to overall course objectives [see Figure 16.3].)

ANALYSIS

MeSH Assessment

This initial group of second-year students to participate in the library sessions comprised the 151 students in the class of 2006. Students were given a two-page posttest that included nineteen matching questions (see Appendix 16.2), eight course evaluation questions, and a number of "fishing" questions for the librarians to find out how the students responded to the library sessions. Analysis of the matching questions showed that the test was not as reliable an assessment tool as predicted. Many of the matching questions used confusing words. Multiple answers could have been selected. However, one valid question tested recognition of MeSH as the vocabulary to search MEDLINE. Seventy-two percent of the students matched answers to the correct response. The low number of correct responses indicated that the librarian sessions were not as effective as anticipated. Further evaluation of the assessment tool pointed out the problems not only with the testing instrument, but with the amount of material presented in the forums. Concepts such as systematic review, evidence-based study, and prospective study, while included in the library sessions, were unreliable terms when students needed to match the concept to a preferred resource.

Lessons Learned

Librarians limited the list of essential resources (see Figure 16.4) introduced to the next class of sophomore medical students (class of 2007). A one-page pretest/posttest was developed to measure knowledge retention before and after formal library systems training. Ten matching questions were used to identify knowledge of health information resources, including the same MeSH question as the previous year's test. Thirty-two percent of the students (class of 2007) responded correctly in the pretest. The posttest showed 82 percent of the students recognizing MeSH as the vocabulary to search MEDLINE. Reinforcing the effectiveness of the librarian instruction intervention, the same pretest given to the class of 2008 showed 60 percent of the students responding correctly to the MeSH question.

Another matching question assessed recognition of the library catalog as the resource to locate books and journals in the LSUHSC library. Seventy-five percent of the students in the class of 2007 selected the correct resource in the pretest and 95 percent of the students answered correctly in the posttest. Sixty-one percent of the students in the class of 2008 answered correctly on the pretest. The test developed for the third-year students (class of 2006), included abbreviated MeSH and catalog matching questions. Student answers indicated good knowledge retention for both. Ninety-one percent of the students matched to the correct answer for the MeSH question and 85 percent of the students correctly answered the catalog question.

EXAM QUESTIONS

SPM 200 course faculty included a single library resource question on the final exam given to the class of 2006. The question, written by the clinical instructor as a case vignette with four multiple-choice responses, was not valid because too many students answered it incorrectly. The format of the question inspired the librarians to create twelve vignette-style exam questions. Vignette-style questions were used to measure knowledge of the library resources and application of that knowledge in a clinical setting.[6,7] Both the midterm and final exams contained the MeSH and library catalog vignette-style questions. All the questions were accepted by SPM 200 clinical faculty and were included on the midterm and final exams for the class of 2007. All questions were counted in the exam scoring, and were computer analyzed for validity. Instruction on using MeSH was presented to the students in the third clinical forum. The midterm was administered to the students before MeSH training. Midterm results for the MeSH question (see Figure 16.6) showed that 77 percent of the students answered correctly. Ninety-three percent of the students answering correctly were from the upper third of the class. Sixty-three percent of the correct answers were from the lower third with a Discrimination Index of 0.30. The midterm catalog question (see Figure 16.7) had 88 percent of the class answering correctly, 93 percent in the upper third of the class and 80 percent in the lower third. The final exam used the same MeSH question and rendered 94 percent of the students giving correct responses, with 98 percent in the upper third and 79 percent in the lower third (Discrimination Index 0.17).

Analysis of the valid questions from pre-and posttesting identified increased resource knowledge after participating in a formal library

---

Which of the following is a controlled vocabulary of biomedical terms that is used to facilitate searching the medical literature?

A. INNOPAC—Library catalog   C. MEDLINE

B. Clinical trials   D. MeSH—Medical subject headings

FIGURE 16.6. MeSH exam question.

You need to consult a book for an anatomy assignment. Which resource would you use to see if the LSUHSC library has access to *Atlas of Human Anatomy* by Frank Netter?

A. INNOPAC—Library catalog   C. MEDLINE

B. Clinical trials   D. MeSH—Medical Subject Headings

FIGURE 16.7. Catalog exam question.

instruction program. Responses to exam questions confirmed the effectiveness of the intervention. Responses from the third-year students' test indicated stable knowledge and retention of resources from the second to third year.

CONCLUSION

Development of a long-term formal library resources instruction program in a large urban medical school's curriculum is an ongoing process. The number of hours of instruction on the various systems is inadequate for the number of resources available. Librarians struggle to provide sufficient training for understanding and accessing myriad resources. Librarian instruction and training and continued reinforcement of using health resources are effective in strengthening student knowledge and retention of those resources.

Constant changes and upgrades to systems and resources combined with the addition of new databases create a great need for continuous updating and revisions to the library instruction program. The overall mission and course objectives of integrating librarian instruction into the clinical curriculum emphasizes the importance of good information habits and encourages students to remain skilled and informed users of new and changing technology.[8]

Future Plans

Major revisions to the formal library instruction program are in the final stages of redevelopment. The effects of Hurricane Katrina prompted a restructuring of the instruction format. Second-year medical students in the class of 2008 will receive an electronic copy of the posttest at the end of the school year. These students received one online tutorial for Ovid MEDLINE instruction, and only one librarian-facilitated clinical forum session before the storm. Results of the posttest should provide more feedback about the effectiveness of the instruction program. To be more accommodating to the students after Katrina, the librarians are preparing online instruction and testing of the second- and third-year students (classes of 2009 and 2010) and plan to initiate the program after returning to campus for fall classes in 2006.

APPENDIX 16.1

LSUHSC Medical Students graduation class participating in formal library instruction.

Class of 2006—(2003/2004)	Posttest after library instruction (second year medical school)
	One final exam question (second year medical school)
	Test (third year medical school)
Class of 2007—(2004/2005)	Pretest (second year medical school)
	Posttest (second year medical school)
	Midterm exam questions (two forums completed—second year medical school)
	Final exam questions (second year medical school)
	Test (third year medical school) (only one group of sixteen students tested)*
Class of 2008—(2005-Aug 2005)*	Pretest (second year medical school)
	(Completed one clinical forum)*

*Interrupted by Hurricane Katrina

APPENDIX 16.2

***Essential Resources for Class of 2006 Evaluation
of Library Resource Sessions for SPM 200 (Posttest distributed
to second-year medical students following one full year
of librarian intervention)***

Select one letter corresponding to the library resource that would *best* locate the requested information. Put the letter of the resource on the line. Some library resources may be used more than once.

___ Book on a health topic
___ Journal article to back up a clinical decision
___ Journal article on immunization
___ Electronic, full-text general medicine text
___ Disease information to give your patient
___ Prospective study recruiting patients
___ Drug information
___ Systematic review
___ Substance abuse statistics

__ Genetic diseases
__ Medical dictionary
__ Evidence-based study
__ Articles that cited one of Dr. Bazan's papers
__ Vocabulary to search MEDLINE
__ National health priorities
__ Mental health journal article
__ Infectious disease statistics and reports
__ Books and journals available in the library
__ Louisiana health statistics

	LIBRARY RESOURCES
A	CDC Web site
B	ClinicalTrials.gov
C	Cochrane Library
D	Healthy People 2010
E	INNOPAC-Library Catalog
F	Louisiana Health Report Card
G	MDConsult
H	MEDLINE via Ovid
I	MedlinePlus
J	MeSH—Medical Subject Headings
K	MICROMEDEX
L	OMIM
M	PubMed
N	PsycINFO via EBSCOhost
O	STAT!Ref
P	U.S. Department of Health & Human Services Sites: NIH, SAMHSA, etc.
Q	Web of Science via Web of Knowledge

NOTES

1. Trevena, Lyndal J. and Clarke, Rufus M. "Self-Directed Learning in Population Health: A Clinically Relevant Approach for Medical Students." *American Journal of Preventive Medicine* 22 (January 2002): 59-65.

2. U.S. Department of Health and Human Services. *Healthy People 2010: Understanding and Improving Health.* 2nd ed. Washington, DC: U.S. Government Printing Office, November 2000.

3. *Overview of Sophomore Clinical Forums.* Louisiana State Health Sciences Center, School of Medicine, 2005. Available: <http://www.medschool.lsuhsc.edu/ medical_education/undergraduate/spm/SPM%20200%202004-2006/Overview %20 of%20Sophomore%20Year%20Clinical%20Forums.2005-06.htm>. Accessed: February 15, 2006.

4. Ibid.

5. *SPM 200 Module 1—Study Topics.* Louisiana State Health Sciences Center, School of Medicine, 2005. Available: <http://www.medschool.lsuhsc.edu/spm/ 200/module1/studytopics.asp>. Accessed: February 15, 2006.

6. LSUHSC Reference Librarians. *LSUHSC Library Resources Instruction— Science and Practice of Medicine 200 Curriculum.* Louisiana State Health Sciences Center Library, 2005. Available: <http://www.lsuhsc.edu/no/library/services/refer ence/L2Curr0506.pdf>. Accessed: February 15, 2006.

7. Connor, Elizabeth. "Using Clinical Vignette Assignments to Teach Medical Informatics."*Medical Reference Services Quarterly* 22 (Winter 2003): 31-44.

8. *Report II Contemporary Issues In Medicine: Medical Informatics and Population Health.* Washington, DC: the Association of American Medical Colleges, 1998. Available: <http://www.aamc.org/meded/msop/msop2.pdf>. Accessed: February 15, 2006.

Chapter 17

Preparing an Advanced Information Literacy Curriculum for Graduate Students

Daniel G. Kipnis
Anthony J. Frisby

INTRODUCTION

In fall 2005, Education Services staff of the Scott Memorial Library at Thomas Jefferson University located in Philadelphia, Pennsylvania, were invited to teach "tool box" classes as part of the curriculum for "GC550 Foundations in Biomedical Sciences." GC550 is an entry-level course for PhD candidates in the College of Graduate Studies. Teaching this course allowed medical librarians and instructional designers to develop hands-on exercises in database searching, literature evaluation, bibliographic management software, and presentation skills and software. This chapter will outline the objectives, methods, results, and conclusions in preparing an advanced information literacy curriculum for biomedical graduate students.

SETTING

Founded in 1824, Jefferson Medical College, one of the largest private medical schools in the United States, has more living graduates than any other medical school in the nation. The academic medical center includes Jefferson Medical College, Jefferson College of Health Professions, Jefferson College of Graduate Studies, and Thomas

Jefferson University Hospitals, a 900-plus bed teaching facility. Scott Memorial Library serves the three colleges in the university and is the library for the hospitals. The library's collections include nearly 200,000 print volumes, over 4,900 e-journals, and 265 electronic books.

Academic and Instructional Support and Resources (AISR) staff participate in teaching a graduate course that prepares students to be active members of the life sciences research community. GC550 is designed to build on basic knowledge of biochemistry, genetics, molecular biology, and cellular biology and the course has two primary objectives. The first is to convey knowledge of the molecular and cellular mechanisms controlling cell, tissue, and organ function. The second objective is to familiarize students with the powerful technologies that are available to today's research laboratory and currently utilized at Thomas Jefferson University. Approximately twenty-five students were enrolled in this course during the fall 2005 semester. Enrolled students pursued a variety of program disciplines including genetics, molecular cell biology, neuroscience, tissue engineering, and biochemistry.

The course met three times a week, Monday, Wednesday, and Friday from 9 a.m. to 11 a.m. and 2 p.m. to 4 p.m. and was divided into three components:

1. Traditional lectures (100 hours) of integrated Biochemistry, Genetics, and Cell Biology.
2. The "tool box" component that provided an orientation to technologies that are broadly utilized in biomedical sciences.
3. Less formal lectures (eight hours) on communication skills, literature review, scientific writing, oral presentation, and information retrieval.

OBJECTIVES

Graduate students are often highly focused on their own research and may not be aware of the diverse demands that will be expected of them as active participants in the research community. GC550 helps prepare Jefferson graduate students for these expectations by providing a forum for learning how research affects society and a researcher's responsibility to the public. Students initially overestimate the information skills they have already acquired, which is consistent with the findings by Oblinger and Oblinger reported in *Educating the Net Generation.*[1] In the library literature, information literacy is seen as a higher order function, not just library skills. A typical information literacy curriculum addresses lifelong learning "because they are able to locate the information required for any endeavor or decision that confronts them."[2] AISR's role in the GC550 course is to affirm students' information searching skills, literature evaluation skills, and presentation skills. The bottom line is to "stress that classroom instruction is intended to provide learners with information and skills that they will need sometime in the future when the instructor is not present."[3]

METHODS

Through a series of hands-on workshops, AISR staff teach students the skills of library research, literature evaluation, citation management, and research presentation. Each workshop is structured with specific examples appropriate for new researchers and includes time for students to work on finding content relevant to their own research interests, or practicing the skills for presenting their research finding.

Library staff were allotted nine lecture hours, of which five hours were used for teaching the graduate students tools such as PowerPoint for presenting their research findings and four hours for teaching information searching and citation management skills using a combination of: PubMed (one hour), Scopus (one hour), and RefWorks, a Web-based bibliographic management software application (one hour).[4,5] An instructional designer taught the five hours of PowerPoint instruction and a senior education librarian taught the databases and bibliographic management application. This chapter includes only the information searching and citation management aspects of the course.

Session 1

The first hour focused on PubMed search skills. A hands-on runthrough of the fundamentals of searching scientific literature was presented along with a search manual. After one hour of learning about PubMed, the students were given a series of practice questions to complete in class (see Appendix 17.1). Discussion on how the students answered the questions allowed the workshops to become more interactive. The students were also provided with suggested answers to their practice questions for review (see Appendix 17.2).

Session 2

The second session introduced Scopus. Students learned about "cited by" analysis and how it helps track scholarship overtime and pinpoints important articles. Students also set-up e-mail alerts on current research interests.

Session 3

The third session presented RefWorks. Extensive handouts, a company-produced tutorial, tips and tricks documentation, and online demonstrations were made available to the students from the library help page <http://jeffline.jefferson.edu/Education/edservices/refworks/help.html>.

Session 4

The final session gave students an opportunity to demonstrate what they had learned by completing a pass/fail in-class assignment (see Appendix 17.3). Research has shown that information literacy competencies cannot be simply taught, but must be reinforced with repeated opportunities to use the information resources, which is why AISR staff assigned an exercise that was completed in class.[6] The students performed a specific search in PubMed, exported citations into RefWorks, and then produced a bibliography. All students who completed the assignment received comments via e-mail about their search strategies and bibliographies.

RESULTS

Student and faculty feedback have been very positive. Following this course, students reported an improved understanding of literature research methodologies, citation management, and confidence in their abilities to organize and professionally present their research outcomes. In an informal poll before the lectures, the majority of the students had not been taught the fundamentals of MeSH, truncation, search field tag searching, limits, cited by analysis, or bibliographic management software. This explains why the lecture evaluations support the positive feedback received by the students. The students learned an entirely new approach to searching the databases that they will be using as graduates. The introduction to bibliographic management software made them aware of existing options for collecting, organizing, and generating bibliographies. See Table 17.1 for evaluation of the RefWorks assignment and Table 17.2 for comments about PubMed and Scopus

TABLE 17.1. RefWorks and practice assignment evaluations.

Question	Score[a]
To what extend did the content/subject matter meet your information needs?	4.5
Effectiveness of instructor's presentation?	4.6
Clarity and appropriateness of the distributed materials?	4.5
My expectations were met	4.5

N = 23 evaluations received.
[a]1 to 5 Likert-style scale: 1 = Poor, 3 = Average, 5 = Excellent.

What did you find most useful from this workshop?

Sharing of information

Learning how to use RefWorks since it will allow me to never have to type out my references ever again!

I found RefWorks to be very useful. I typically use EndNote and now have an alternative when I am away from my laptop

Makes making bibliography easier

Never knew of RefWorks before this

The hands-on example where we integrated info from the PubMed lecture was very useful

Applications that linked RefWorks to Word via Write-N-Cite. I was previously unaware of the connection

Learning how to use RefWorks will be beneficial to my research

The creation of the bibliographic page was easy

The program, RefWorks, seems extremely useful

What changes/improvements would you suggest for future classes?

No changes

None, it went well

I would change nothing! The class was very informative and I look forward to using what I have learned today throughout my graduate career

TABLE 17.2. PubMed and Scopus evaluation comments.

Question	Score[a]
To what extent did the content/subject matter meet your information needs?	4.3
Effectiveness of instructor's presentation?	4.4
Clarity and appropriateness of the distributed materials?	4.5
My expectations were met	4.3

N = 21 evaluations received.
[a]1 to 5 Likert-style scale: 1 = Poor, 3 = Average, 5 = Excellent.

What did you find most useful from this workshop?

It was amazing to find that there were many other helpful features and applications that I could use on programs like PubMed etc.

Did not know about cubby registration or how to do specific PubMed searches . . . GREAT (smiley face)

I use PubMed all the time and I never knew about any of these helpful features. This is going to make my research so much easier. I plan to share this info with my labmates. The cubby info was the most helpful. Thanks. (smiley face)

I thought I knew how to use PubMed, but now I realize the many methods I can use to accelerate searches

All information was helpful

Useful search techniques for popular biological search engines

What changes/improvements would you suggest for future classes?

Shorter time blocks
It was good
None, good stuff
None, it was great!

assignments. The comments from the evaluations support the claim that "98 percent of the doctoral students and 93 percent of supervisors think that information literacy skills are an important part of doctoral studies; however, 45 percent of the students and 43.5 percent of the supervisors admitted that they were lacking in information literacy skills."[7]

CONCLUSION

Working with future researchers provides library staff with a unique insight into their needs and future responsibilities. Experience with graduate students has resulted in new ideas for faculty workshops and outreach opportunities to affiliated research fellows, who may not have had a similar preparation in their graduate programs. Future workshops for graduate students may include Photoshop and Illustrator, statistical programs such as SPSS and SAS, using blogs and wikis for scholarly communication and collaboration, and more database/Internet searching.

Student and course coordinator feedback will help determine the needs and requests for future graduate students at Jefferson. Continued review and planning for all future information literacy courses are essential to success. The experience with GC550 is no different. Each year the staff has learned new techniques, content, and instructional methods that benefit students.[8,9] Currently, there are more study data available on undergraduates than on graduate students, but with continued collaboration with graduate curriculum committees, the needs of graduate students can be better understood.[10]

APPENDIX 17.1. PUBMED PRACTICE QUESTIONS

1. How far back can you search with the MeSH term, "Recombinant DNA"?
2. What is the preferred MeSH term for drooling?
3. Find citations to articles discussing the surgical or drug treatment of osteosarcoma in children. Limit to studies involving the drug, Cisplatin. Also limit to English-language articles.
4. Find reference to articles about Jocelyn Elders.
5. Create a hedge with the following MeSH terms: bioterrorism OR biological warfare OR chemical warfare OR vaccine OR smallpox OR anthrax OR allied health personnel in *New England Journal of Medicine* and save it in My NCBI. (Hint: Use Preview/Index)

APPENDIX 17.2. ANSWERS
TO PUBMED PRACTICE QUESTIONS

1. How far back can you search with the MeSH term, "Recombinant DNA"?
   Use the MeSH database and enter the term "Recombinant DNA: 1977."
2. What is the preferred MeSH term for drooling?
   Use the MeSH database and enter the term drooling: Sialorrhea.

3. Find citations to articles discussing the surgical or drug treatment of osteosarcoma in children. Limit to studies involving the drug, Cisplatin. Also limit to English-language articles.
Use the MeSH database and select the MeSH term "Osteosarcoma." Check drug treatment and surgery and click on Send to search box with AND, enter Cisplatin, and click on Go. Send to search box with AND. Search PubMed. Choose All Child and English.

4. Find reference to articles about Jocelyn Elders.
Elders j[ps]

5. Create a hedge with the following MeSH terms: bioterrorism OR biological warfare OR chemical warfare OR vaccine OR smallpox OR anthrax OR allied health personnel in the *New England Journal of Medicine* and save it in My NCBI. (Hint: Use Preview/Index)
"bioterrorism" [MESH] OR "biological warfare"[MESH] OR "chemical warfare"[MESH] OR "vaccine"[MESH] OR "smallpox"[MESH] OR "anthrax"[MESH] OR "Allied Health Personnel"[MESH] AND "the new england journal of medicine"[Journal]
Click on "Save Search," login to My NCBI account and proceed by setting up e-mail alert schedule.

APPENDIX 17.3 IN-CLASS PUBMED SEARCH AND REFWORKS ASSIGNMENT

LIBRARY WORKSHOP ASSIGNMENT—GC550

Due date: Monday, October 31st, end of class (4 p.m.)
Grading criteria: Pass/Fail
In order to receive credit for your work, make sure you include your name and e-mail address on your document.

• Word document with search strategy from PubMed. Cut and paste from History tab.
• Bibliography with at least 10 citations from your PubMed search in APA format fifth edition (the first APA option) using RefWorks.

Topic to research: Locate randomized controlled trials published in English from 2000 onward on vaccination treatment for HIV and AIDS.

Note: This assignment requires that you work independently. Search history and bibliography can be on the same Word document.

When finished print out to LRC printer (Laser Jet 8000 DN), staple documents and hand to me before leaving, along with your workshop evaluation which is the last document in your packet.

RefWorks access page from JEFFLINE: <http://jeffline.jefferson.edu/Education/edservices/refworks/>

Need a RefWorks refresher?
Online tutorial for RefWorks: <http://www.refworks.com/tutorial/>

NOTES

1. Oblinger, Diana G. and Oblinger, James L. *Educating the Net Generation.* EDUCAUSE, 2005. Available: <http://www.educause.edu/educatingthenetgen>. Accessed: December 14, 2005.

2. "Information Literacy Competency Standards for Higher Education." Chicago: Association of College & Research Libraries, 2000. Available: <http://www.ala.org/ala/acrl/acrlstandards/informationliteracycompetency.htm>. Accessed: December 12, 2005.

3. Halpern, Diane F. and Hakel, Milton D. "Applying the Science of Learning to the University and Beyond." *Change* 35 (July/August 2003): 36-41.

4. AISR Education Services. "Searching PubMed Handout." Available: <http://jeffline.jefferson.edu/SML/helpaids/handouts/PubMed.doc>. Accessed: February 27, 2006.

5. AISR Education Services. "Scopus handout." Available: <http://jeffline.jefferson.edu/SML/helpaids/handouts/scopus.html>. Accessed: February 27, 2006.

6. Jacobs, Susan Kaplan, Rosenfeld, Peri, and Haber, Judith. "Information Literacy as the Foundation for Evidence-Based Practice in Graduate Nursing Education: A Curriculum-Integrated Approach." *Journal of Professional Nursing* 19, no. 5 (2003): 320-328.

7. Franklin, Kimberly Y. "The Importance of Information Literacy: Insights From the Next Generation of Scholars." ACRL Twelfth National Conference, 2005. Available: <http://www.ala.org/ala/acrl/acrlevents/franklin05.pdf>. Accessed: December 13, 2005.

8. Hunt, Fiona and Birks, Jane. "Best Practices in Information Literacy." *Portal: Libraries and the Academy* 4, no. 1 (2004): 27-39.

9. Middle States Commission on Higher Education. "Sustaining the Momentum of Information Literacy: An Overview." In *Developing Research & Communication Skills: Guidelines for Information Literacy in the Curriculum.* Philadelphia: Middle States Commission on Higher Education, 2003. Available: <http://www.msche.org/publications/devskill050208135642.pdf>. Accessed: November 1, 2006.

10. Barry, Christine A. "Information Skills for an Electronic World: Training Doctoral Research Students." *Journal of Information Science* 23, no. 3 (1997): 225-238.

Chapter 18

Graded Online Pharmacy Assignments

Julia Shaw-Kokot
K. T. L. Vaughan

INTRODUCTION

Today's huge array of information resources, student skill levels, and packed curriculum challenge even an established, course-integrated pharmacy instruction program. Online assignments serve as a way to meet the goal of providing online instruction and evaluating information and computer competencies. This chapter will discuss the evolution of the University of North Carolina at Chapel Hill's (UNC-Chapel Hill) curriculum-integrated instruction for first-year pharmacy students over the past two decades, with an emphasis on the current iteration of online assignments using Blackboard, a course management system. Issues related to planning, presenting, and evaluating instruction, as well as future instructional opportunities, will be covered.

Library instruction for pharmacy students has been documented in the literature for fifty years. An early article by Martha Zachery from the H. Custer Naylor Library at the Southern College of Pharmacy in Atlanta identified the steps in library orientation as lecture, labs, and follow-up assignments.[1] In 1980, Winifred Sewell et al. discussed course integration and competency-based education in the University of Maryland's pharmacy program.[2] Sewell's eleven competencies range from the ability to find a known item to being able to evaluate conflicting information. At Yale in the late 1980s, Naomi Ikeda looked at the impact of literature search training for third-year pharmacy students four years after graduation from the PharmD program.[3] A 1990

An Introduction to Instructional Services in Academic Libraries

article articulated the integrative collaboration of the University of Southern California's Norris Medical Library with the School of Pharmacy.[4] More recently, a 2005 chapter on informatics instruction at the University of California, San Francisco emphasized an intensive lecture and hands-on lab approach.[5] In this half-century of scholarship, content matter has remained stable while methods of delivery have changed from paper to electronic. Over time, UNC-Chapel Hill's Health Sciences Library (HSL) has built a program based on the reported literature and on experience with the university's School of Pharmacy (SOP).

The terms "course integration" and "competencies" are as important to instruction today as they have been in the past. What makes instruction course integrated? The UNC-Chapel Hill HSL uses the following criteria as identified by Francesca Allegri:

> (1) faculty outside the library are involved in the design, execution and evaluation of the program, (2) the instruction is curriculum-based, in other words directly related to the students' course work and/or assignments, (3) students are required to participate, and (4) the students' work is graded or credit is received for participation.[6]

Although Allegri initially suggested that meeting three out of the four criteria would qualify as course-integrated instruction, HSL now considers all four vital for a successful learning experience.

Libraries, including UNC-Chapel Hill's HSL, have developed information competencies to serve as instructional markers and to help develop outcome measures.[7,8] In the area of pharmacy student instruction, Sewell's article identified eleven basic competencies needed by all students before they began to specialize in specific roles.[9] At HSL, information competencies are considered to be stable over time, even as the methods used to help students develop the skills change. For example, finding information related to a specific area of interest once required looking at print indexes and card catalogs in a library. Now these tasks are accomplished via online databases from anywhere in the world. The need to know how to find the information still exists but the tools continually evolve. With these two concepts as guiding principles, HSL staff have enjoyed support from faculty and students for integrating core competencies in the first-year SOP curriculum online assignments. The current approach of using online assignments to measure student skills has proved successful in integrating both information and basic computer competencies.

SETTING

UNC-Chapel Hill is a large academic institution that supports undergraduate and graduate education for health affairs students in dentistry, medicine, nursing, pharmacy, and public health as well as a large teaching hospital complex. Established in 1897, the SOP has offered a Doctor of Pharmacy (PharmD) degree at the professional level since the mid 1990s. After at least two years of required prerequisites, students must complete four years of study before obtaining a PharmD degree. Approximately 150 new students with various backgrounds and degrees enroll each year in this program; prior to its implementation, UNC-Chapel Hill's terminal pharmacy degree was a BSPh. In 2005, the SOP began a satellite program at Elizabeth City State University (ECSU). ECSU is a sister UNC system institution in the eastern part of North Carolina approximately five hours from Chapel Hill.

Along with the PharmD, other doctoral degrees are awarded in the areas of Medicinal Chemistry and Natural Products, Molecular Pharmaceutics, Pharmacotherapy and Experimental Therapeutics, and Pharmaceutical Outcomes and Policy. There are approximately sixty PhD candidates studying under SOP faculty at any given time.

To address the issues related to the change in the entry-level professional degree, the school established an External Doctor of Pharmacy Program, a distance education program to assist pharmacists in the state with upgrading to the new degree. This program graduated its last classes in 2006. Efforts are increasingly geared toward planning and implementing distant campus programs such as the one at ECSU. Two other pharmacy schools exist in the state: the School of Pharmacy at Campbell University, a small private university and Wingate University School of Pharmacy, which admitted its first students in 2003. Even with three schools, there is a growing need for pharmacists in North Carolina.[10]

Although the SOP is physically located across the street from the HSL, students are away from campus after the first year for rotations and work experiences. Off-campus, students are considered "distant" and have the same privileges as those enrolled in off-campus programs. Distant students require detailed knowledge of use of electronic resources, off-campus access to materials, and document delivery methods. However, most students live and work off campus and require "remote" access to the HSL throughout their enrollment.

OBJECTIVES

The primary objectives of the integrated pharmacy assignments are to provide hands-on experience using a number of resources that the students will encounter throughout their professional careers, and to measure information literacy skills at two points during the first year of pharmacy school. By the end of each assignment, the students will have demonstrated their abilities to find resources that answer specific questions, and to explain why they selected the given answer. A secondary objective, to provide practice with online applications, was added in the late 1990s. The delivery and content approaches have also changed over time to reflect the new information resources.

METHODS

HSL staff work intensively with the first-year students during their PY1 (postgraduate year one) Pharmacy Skills Lab course. The coordination of this block formatted course started in the mid-1980s. The course's basic setup has been slightly modified over the years, but the format has changed to reflect the evolving environment of education and information seeking.

Now, as with the original course, a lecture demonstration by a librarian each fall is followed by a two-hour hands-on recitation with librarians present to answer questions and to teach students how to use key pharmacy information tools. These tools are now exclusively the electronic versions of indexes and abstracts as well as other drug information resources, texts, and specialized databases. In 2005, simultaneous Macromedia Breeze sessions were held for students at ECSU. Breeze <http://www.macromedia.com/software/breeze/> is a Web-based multimedia communication tool that allows distance education students to see and hear both the instructor and supporting materials such as slides, Web pages, or documents. Since 1999, there has also been an unmediated spring assignment with the same requirements. From the beginning, students have been given assignments which require them to use the resources presented and submit their answers within a week of the instruction. After completing the assignment, students can view the "gold standard" answer. The assignments are graded by the pharmacy librarian and returned with feedback to the students. The pass/fail grade is factored into their grades for the semester.

The assignments have changed from questions based on practice interests to "hot" topics. Originally, SOP students were grouped according to practice areas after the first year, and, as stressed by Sewell,[11] this was a good way to maintain interest in the assignment. With the advent of the PharmD program and the more global approach to pharmacy education, the course instructor and librarian pick topics that are in the news and that relate to pharmacists and/or reflect block course content. Past topics have included FluMist flu vaccine, performance-enhancing drugs, and the use of melatonin for insomnia. An example of a fall assignment is featured in Appendix 18.1. As a rule, of the five to six assignment topics assigned per assessment period, each student must complete one.

Assignment formats have evolved from paper to e-mail to Web-based. As the students used e-mail for their courses and the implementation of a local MEDLINE system in 1992 enabled e-mailing of search results, the faculty member and librarian decided to require submission of assignments via e-mail. Sending and receiving the assignments by e-mail was challenging. It was necessary to know keyboarding and how to correctly type an e-mail address. The students often did not put the correct e-mail addresses in either the "to" or "from" lines which made grading and feedback a challenge, but students quickly learned to use e-mail, and satisfaction assessments showed that they enjoyed the learning opportunity. As with all technology, there were glitches beyond the control of either the librarian or the students. For example, the e-mail system once went down when the afternoon assignment began and did not come back up until the day it was due.

The World Wide Web arrived at a time when PY1 students' skills with e-mail were well developed and all the HSL's key pharmacy resources were electronic. In 1999, the assignment moved to the Web. Initially, assignments were scripted into a Web page, but students still sent in answers by e-mail. As technology improved, students could enter and submit answers in a Web form. Students received the recommended answer by e-mail after the assignment was completed.

The most recent change came with the selection of Blackboard as the campus course management program. Blackboard <http://www.blackboard.com> allows instructors to arrange all of the components of a class, including readings, assignments, and the gradebook, into an online shell. Again, the course instructor and librarian conspired to incorporate Blackboard skills as well as information searching skills into student assignments. By spring semester, students were very comfortable with both Blackboard- and Web-submitted assignments and could concentrate more on their information-seeking skills. In recognition of this, spring assignments are much less directed.

Designing assignments based on "hot" topics requires more preparation than basing them on the block subjects. The SOP faculty member and others suggest topics, but not all good topics make good assignments. As the topic is explored in multiple resources, each one has to be tested to make sure it retrieves the type of information desired from each resource used. The level of the information is another consideration. Since the students are in their first year, they may not be ready for a very detailed and research-oriented assignment. Once a topic has been selected, a "gold standard" answer is selected. This allows the students to compare their answers to the answers selected by the librarian. When the librarian is in doubt about which answer to select, the course instructor serves as a consultant. The lead course instructor relies on the librarian for this assignment and contributes on an "as needed" basis. She or he appreciates the reduction in her or his teaching load during the assignment.

The questions are designed both to find answers and to make the students think. Students are asked to explain their responses, allowing for a better understanding of their information skills and critical thinking. Since the assignment is pass/fail, one might expect students to take it less seriously. However, SOP students are notoriously competitive from the beginning of their program. Some students complete more than one assignment, and many are very quick to defend their answers if they do not match the "gold standard." There is little working together and copying of answers. In some years, students were asked to work together, and even then they came up with different answers. The librarian uses these assignments to identify students who are having problems and contacts them for one-on-one assistance. The fall assignment also helps point out areas that need reinforcement in the spring assignment.

The spring assignment measures skills development and growth. While students complete this assignment without librarian assistance or reinforcement, they may ask the librarian questions. While the format is the same as the fall, it is much less guided. An example of a spring assignment is featured in Appendix 18.2. Some students do not appreciate the second assignment, but most agree that it helps reinforce skills gained in the first year.

Faculty and teaching assistant responses also play a big role in evaluation. Before Blackboard, SOP support staff reported more technical and logistical difficulties. With Blackboard, the main problems are with student access to online resources. The monitoring of these factors continues to be important.

RESULTS

Online assignments are both fun and challenging to design and grade, and students find that they can "shop around" to find the "best" topic. Blackboard has improved the delivery and management of the assignments by offering a fairly stable platform and familiar system. The time involved at both the instructional and student levels is about the same as with the original paper-based assignments.

The integrated pharmacy instruction has been informally evaluated since the beginning. Many of the changes made in the assignments and objectives have been related to the feedback from these assessments. In spring 2001, Clista Clanton, then a UNC-Chapel Hill School of Information and Library Science student, completed the first formal evaluation of online course modules. Clanton found that 86 percent of the students who completed the survey preferred online assignments to written ones and were able to finish the assignment in less than one hour.[12] This was pre-Blackboard, so the process of completing the assignments was likely to be more problematic. The Clanton survey was slightly modified and given again with the fall 2005 assignment.

At that time, 97 percent indicated a preference for this type of assignment. Almost all of the students required over an hour but less than two hours to complete the exercise. This works well since the fall recitation sessions are two hours in length.

The assignments themselves are evaluation tools. For example, if few students match the recommended answer, the reasons for this are discussed. Students often have excellent reasons for selecting their article. Their thinking can be incorporated in future assignments. The evolution in resource selection and use over the period of one year are evident. For example, in the fall assignment, students are more likely to match the "gold standard" Web page than the "gold standard" PubMed article. This probably reflects their comfort with Web searching. In the spring assignment, students tend to use an appropriate resource based on their previous library assignment and other assignments that require them to use information resources. This shows a shift related to knowledge, comfort, and skills gained with using a variety of tools. The spring assignments are more open-ended, and students are asked to select the best resource for the task. They may try various options, but the final selection is based on content rather than under the librarian's guidance.

As students must explain why they select resources and answers, librarians not only learn how resources are used, but also what works well and what can be confusing in each resource. Students are asked which of the resources they prefer and why. While this information is not used for collection development, it does provide interesting insights into drug programs and search tools. For example, from the beginning students have not found *International Pharmaceutical Abstracts* (IPA) useful in any available format. They do not tend to use the database to find answers unless directed to use that tool. Reasons include the difficulty in matching terms and the large number of meeting abstracts. Because of this, IPA has been dropped from the fall assignments.

CONCLUSION

Online assignments are well worth the time and effort required. The assignments have also forced librarians and HSL graduate assistants to learn how to teach via Blackboard. The ease of setting up assignments, making them available, and enforcing the due date has been enhanced with this software. Even with Blackboard, these assignments are time intensive at both ends; each topic takes about eight to ten hours to create, while grading takes approximately an hour per dozen students.

The online assignments allow students to work at their own pace and experiment with topics, resources, and formats before submitting their answers. The fact that some students complete multiple topics "for practice" before turning in the best one, shows both their competitiveness to submit a perfect assignment and the desire to test different approaches to focused questions. The ability to offer "gold standard" answers to compare with the submitted answers allows for almost instant feedback. It also lets students contact the librarian and make a case for their answer(s). This means that the librarian does not feel rushed to get the grades back to the students.

Just as pharmacy education has changed over the last fifty years, online assignments allow librarians to combine Zachert's steps[13] into one learning moment. Yet HSL's library instruction still follows Zachert's model by using lecture, labs, and follow-up assignments. While the basic information content of information needs has changed little over the last fifty years, the instruction delivery and evaluation modes have changed greatly. Online assignments work well for librarians, pharmacy faculty, and students because they incorporate changing technology and interests.

APPENDIX 18.1. FALL ONLINE ASSIGNMENT

There has been a lot of discussion this summer about whether the use of sunscreen inhibits the body's production of vitamin D. It has even been suggested that people should not use sunscreen for this reason. You know that you will have parents coming into your pharmacy asking if they should stop using sunscreen on their child(ren) to ensure they are getting enough vitamin D. You decide to do some research.

Use the databases suggested to answer the following questions. You are welcome to ask the librarians monitoring your lab for help.

1. You would like to look up some research on whether people in the U.S. are getting enough vitamin D. Find a review article that discusses the dietary intake of vitamin D. Search PubMed MEDLINE, and paste the citation for the best article that you find in the box below.
2. Why did you choose this article?
3. Is this article available online via PubMed?
4. Paste your search strategy in the box below by copying and pasting the search from the Details tab in PubMed.
5. Look in the UNC Online Catalog for this journal. What years are available in print (if any) and in which library?
6. Look in the E-Journal Finder for this journal. What years are available online (if any)?
7. You have been given this article:xxxx It is a few years old, so you would like to see if anyone has used it in their research. Look this article up in the ISI Citation Databases (Web of Science). How many times has it been cited?
8. Is the article available online?
9. You would like to get specific information on whether vitamin D is known to interact with other drugs. Look in BOTH the Natural Medicines Comprehensive Database and eFacts drug information databases. What (if any) may vitamin D interact with?
10. What is the difference between the information in the two databases used to answer question 9.
11. Which of these databases do you prefer?
12. You are interested in contacting the officers of Pharmavite, the manufacturer of Nature Made brand vitamins. Using Business and Company Resource Center, find the names of the CEO, chairman, and two vice presidents.
13. Go to an Internet search engine such as Google to see if there is some good information about vitamin D, particularly for teenagers (since this is a group that spends a lot of time out in the sun.) What is the title and URL of the best page you find?
14. Why did you choose this page?
15. What terms did you use to find this page?
16. According to this Web site, why is vitamin D important for human health?
17. Look in MedlinePlus for similar information. What is the title and URL for the best page that you find?
18. Is the page found in MedlinePlus the same as the one you pick from the Google search?
19. Why did you choose the page in MedlinePlus?
20. What terms did you use in MedlinePlus?
21. How did your search in Google and your search in MedlinePlus differ? Which do you prefer?

22. You are interested in finding information about vitamin D and rickets. Since you need some basic background information, you want to check a book out of the library. Look in the UNC Online Catalog for books on this topic. What is the best book available to you at Carolina?
23. Why did you choose this book?
24. Where is the book located? Please give both the library and call number.
25. What terms did you use to search for the selected book?

APPENDIX 18.2. SPRING ONLINE ASSIGNMENT

In this assignment you will be searching for consumer, scholarly, and drug information. During the flu vaccine shortage, one of your clients mentioned that she had seen a flyer for a second type of vaccine.

1. You want to get more information on what this second type of vaccine might be. Since it is being released to the general public there should be guidelines or other consumer-appropriate information on the Internet. In a different window from this one, do a search for good information for your client. What online source(s) did you use?
2. What term(s) did you search to find the information?
3. Paste below the URL and title of the BEST page you find. What is the brand name of the intranasal vaccine approved by the U.S. government?
4. What makes the page you selected better than the others you saw?
5. Find some clinical trials-based evidence to use in evaluating your client's particular situation (pediatric case). You want to find an article or two from a reputable, scholarly source that talks about this type of influenza vaccine. What online source(s) did you use?
6. What term(s)/limit(s) did you search to find the information you wanted?
7. Paste the citation information of the BEST article you find in the box below?
8. What makes this article better than the others you saw? Where did you find the citation? Where can you find the article?
9. What are the contraindications and drug interactions for FluMist, the brand name for this vaccine? Search one of the drug databases (there are three). Which database and terms did you use? Why?
10. Paste the contraindications and drug interactions information that are applicable to a pediatrics case in the box below.

NOTES

1. Zachert, Martha Jane K. "Threefold Library Teaching Plan." *Bulletin of the Medical Library Association* 43 (April 1955): 296-299.

2. Sewell, Winifred, et al. "Integrating Library Skills Teaching into the Pharmacy School Curriculum." *American Journal of Pharmaceutical Education* 44 (February 1980): 65-74.

3. Ikeda, Naomi R. and Schwartz, Diane G. "Impact of End-User Search Training on Pharmacy Students: A Four-Year Follow-Up Study." *Bulletin of the Medical Library Association* 80 (April 1992): 124-130.

4. Wood, Elizabeth H., Morrison, Janet L., and Oppenheimer, Phillip R. "Drug Information Skills for Pharmacy Students: Curriculum Integration." *Bulletin of the Medical Library Association* 78 (January 1990): 8-14.

5. Owen, David J., Persily, Gail L., and Babbitt, Patricia C. "Informatics Course for First-Year Pharmacy Students at the University of California, San Francisco." In *A Guide to Developing End User Education Programs in Medical Libraries,* edited by Elizabeth Connor. Binghamton, NY: Haworth Press, 2005, pp. 129-142.

6. Allegri, Francesca. "Course Integrated Instruction: Metamorphosis for the Twenty-First Century." *Medical Reference Services Quarterly* 4 (Winter 1985/86): 47-66.

7. Blumenthal, Jane L., et al. "Defining and Assessing Medical Informatics Competencies." *Medical Reference Services Quarterly* 24 (Summer 2005): 95-102.

8. Moore, Margaret E. and Shaw-Kokot, Julia. "Core Competencies." *Medical Reference Services Quarterly* 19 (Winter 2000): 99-103.

9. See note 2.

10. Fraher, Erin P., et al. *The Pharmacist Workforce in North Carolina.* Chapel Hill, North Carolina: Cecil G. Sheps Center for Health Services Research. 2002. Available: <http://www.shepscenter.unc.edu/data/nchpds/pharmacy.pdf>. Accessed: January 14, 2006.

11. See note 2.

12. Clanton, Clista. *Faculty and Student Perceptions on the Effectiveness of Online Course Modules: Are Modules a Hindrance or Help?* Chapel Hill, NC: Master's Paper for the MSLS, 2001, pp. 1-54. Available: <http://ils.unc.edu/MSpapers/2660.pdf>. Accessed: April 4, 2006.

13. See note 1.

Chapter 19

Information Literacy for a College of Nursing

Sally Carroll-Ricks
Debra Shelton
Diane Graham-Webb
Susan T. Pierce
Laura Aaron
Debbie Moore

INTRODUCTION

Information literacy (IL) is critical to the provision of evidence-based practice (EBP) in today's health care environment. A university group of nursing and allied health faculty at Northwestern State University of Louisiana were concerned that student knowledge and skills were not to the depth and degree necessary to practice EBP effectively in their respective professions. As a result, a grassroots movement, initiated by this group, set out to develop, implement, and evaluate an IL program. This chapter describes the process utilized to make that plan a reality.

SETTING

Northwestern State University of Louisiana is a publicly funded, rural university serving a diverse population. The College of Nursing provides multiple, articulated programs that include associate's, bachelor's,

An Introduction to Instructional Services in Academic Libraries

and master's of Science degrees in Nursing, a Bachelor of Science degree in Radiologic Technology, a Registered Nurse-Bachelor of Science in Nursing (RN-to-BSN) program, and opportunities for Licensed Practical Nurse (LPN-to-RN) transition. The College of Nursing is located on three campuses geographically distant from the main campus in order to better serve the needs of students and to provide access to urban health care facilities. An academic library with approximately 350,000 books, journals, and documents is located on the main campus,[1] and a nursing and allied health library with approximately 10,000 books, 4,000 microform, and 200 print subscriptions is located on the primary College of Nursing campus.[2] Electronic subscriptions pertaining to nursing and allied health ensure access by students and faculty regardless of their location. A smaller library, located on one of the rural campuses, serves other programs as well. Together, these three libraries serve the health care provider programs. Library services and resources are provided to all nursing and allied health students and faculty from the nursing and allied health library, regardless of an individual's geographic location. Courses are supported by Blackboard course management software and delivered through traditional classroom and clinical methods, through compressed video, and through the Internet. To strengthen program outcomes and communication, interactivity and collaboration among the approximately fifty-four faculty[3] and 2,500 students[4] across campuses are encouraged.

OBJECTIVES

The primary objective and overall mission of the IL program are to produce graduates who legally and ethically access, appraise, and integrate information from multiple sources and systems to influence their practice of health care whether it is nursing or radiologic technology. Secondary objectives are for students to:

- determine the nature and extent of information they need;
- access needed information effectively and efficiently;
- evaluate information and its sources critically and incorporate selected information into their knowledge base, value system, and health care practice;

- compare new knowledge with prior knowledge to determine the value added, contradictions, or other unique characteristics of the information needed for health care decision making; and
- use information effectively to accomplish a specific purpose, whether or not they do so individually or as a member of a group.[5]

METHODS

The interdisciplinary group of faculty formed an IL Quality Circle to guide the development and implementation of a curriculum-based IL plan. The group consisted of nursing and radiologic technology faculty and the head librarian, all located on the College of Nursing campus. The Circle met frequently to discuss the problems encountered due to the students' lack of IL skills and decided to develop a plan to address the gaps in student knowledge. An initial assessment (a contest to define IL) determined the level of student and faculty knowledge of IL. As a large number of both faculty and students lacked a full comprehension of IL, the Circle concluded that a literature review, development of an action plan, and plan implementation was needed to improve faculty and student understanding of IL.

Literature Review

A comprehensive review of the literature examined primary documents from information science, nursing, and radiologic technology. The databases that generated the most helpful citations were CINAHL, PubMed, MEDLINE, and Library Literature and Information Science. Several online tutorials (general and discipline-specific) were examined. Except for one instance, no IL standards or competencies were identified for radiologic technology. The pertinent sources were divided into groups, beginning with the foundational primary sources for IL goals, objectives, skills, and competencies. The sources that were identified as guiding forces and primary documents were the IL-related recommendations of the Louisiana Board of Regents,[6,7] American Association of Colleges of Nursing for the baccalaureate program,[8] Competencies Task Force of the Council of Associate Degree Nursing for the National League for Nursing,[9] American Nurses Association,[10]

Joint Review Committee on Education in Radiologic Technology,[11] Association of College & Research Libraries (ACRL),[12,13] and American Library Association (1989).[14] Documents that described efforts at other universities in developing IL programs (several of which incorporated a curriculum-based approach) included the University of Northern Colorado School of Nursing,[15] Case Western Reserve University's School of Nursing,[16] San Francisco State University's School of Nursing,[17] Humboldt State University's Department of Nursing,[18] the University of Wollongong's Division of Nursing,[19,20,21] Ball State University's School of Nursing,[22] Massachusetts College of Pharmacy and Health Sciences,[23] and New York University's Division of Nursing.[24] Equally significant were the studies by Staggers, Gassert, and Curran that identified and validated competencies for nurses at four, graduated levels of practice.[25,26]

The review of literature provided information to develop a definition of IL as well as a mission and framework for the IL plan. The Circle defined IL as the ability to recognize when information is needed and to locate, evaluate, and use the needed information effectively. The mission developed focuses on producing graduates who legally and ethically access, appraise, and integrate information from multiple sources and systems to influence professional practice. ACRL's IL standards were combined and adapted into five standards that were deemed appropriate for the College of Nursing at Northwestern State University of Louisiana.

Development of Plan

As a result of the literature review, the Circle realized that the goal of the IL plan was more pervasive than preparing students for professional practice. Based on this growing understanding of the critical nature of IL, a comprehensive, succinct, and usable plan was developed that could be integrated across the curricula of various programs.

Framework

Circle members felt that faculty buy-in was critical. The literature review, professional knowledge, and expertise related to both the contemporary teaching and learning and the health care environments of the Circle, and the national needs assessments of nurses and colleges of nursing were synthesized to develop a conceptual framework <http://www.nsula.edu/watson_library/shreve/nurse_info_lit.htm> that guided the development of the IL plan. Elements evaluated to identify, appraise, and implement the plan's components included (1) environmental context elements of IL, EBP, quality care, cost-effective delivery of health care; (2) assimilation of standards and competencies for IL and EBP; and (3) best practices for nursing education in the twenty-first century. One important tenet of the plan was to demonstrate the close relationship among IL, EBP, and professional process. As students advance through the curriculum, represented by five levels, their skills develop along a continuum that can involve any of the skills pertinent to the nursing process, IL, and EBP.

Matrix

The plan involved the development of an IL matrix, use of online tutorials for students, and a workshop for faculty. The matrix consisted of five standards, each of which was associated with performance indicators that had outcomes, teaching content, and suggested learner activities. One example of a learner activity is a Search Strategy Planner <http://www.nsula.edu/watson_library/shreve/nurse_info_lit.htm> designed to help a person think critically think about locating relevant sources. The purpose of the matrix was to demonstrate visually how the standards and performance indicators were to be operationalized in core courses.

Online Tutorials

Another part of the plan was the use of online tutorials to improve and develop IL skills. The Circle searched the links for online tutorials provided on the Internet by the Library Orientation Exchange (LOEX) Clearinghouse for Library Instruction[27] and ACRL.[28] In addition, many general online tutorials were examined to find an existing resource that could be utilized "as is." It needed to be generic in nature and free of features unique to any particular university. The only tutorial found that completely met these criteria was the Texas Information Literacy Tutorials (TILT), created by the University of Texas Digital Library.[29] TILT had excellent content and allowed any person to register and take the three quizzes, which were graded instantly by the TILT software. It also allowed users to send grades to a specified e-mail address and print the test results. Purdue's Comprehensive Online Research Education (CORE) tutorials were similar to TILT except that some modules were specific to Purdue.[30] Nonetheless, permission was obtained from the University of Texas and Purdue to use their tutorials at no charge.

Two nursing-specific online tutorial models were found at Emmanuel College[31] and New York University.[32] Emmanuel College's tutorials contained no online quizzes but provided an excellent tutorial for teaching CINAHL, MEDLINE, LexisNexis Academic Universe, *Online Journal of Knowledge Synthesis for Nursing,* and Web sites. New York University created a self-paced tutorial, intended for graduate nursing students, that covered basic IL skills but, like Emmanuel College, it offered no online, self-graded quiz.

Faculty Workshop

As faculty buy-in and faculty development are essential elements for project success, the faculty development plan included a workshop designed to assist faculty with integration of IL content into their courses. The matrix was introduced to the faculty and their feedback was sought.

Implementation of Plan

Three key aspects of the plan implementation were a pilot study, faculty workshops, and evaluation.

Pilot Study

A pilot study, conducted during the fall 2004 semester, involved implementing the IL teaching and learning activities in the courses throughout the curriculum. Fortunately, the faculty who teach these courses or initial courses were all members of the Circle and they integrated IL activities in their courses to develop a foundation for the IL skills.

Faculty Workshop

Two faculty development workshops were conducted during the spring 2005 semester. The workshop began with a brief presentation by the Circle informing the faculty about IL research that had been examined by the group and introducing the matrix. Afterwards, faculty were divided into groups and asked to brainstorm teaching content and learner activities for the matrix outcomes. At the conclusion of the workshop, faculty came together and shared ideas they had discussed in their groups. One of the ideas generated was an IL Evaluation Tool <http://www.nsula.edu/watson_library/shreve/nurse_info_lit. htm> that faculty could use to determine whether IL skills were exhibited in submitted assignments. The workshop provided faculty with numerous ideas and strategies that could be used in their individual courses. In addition, the information gathered from faculty helped to validate the content in the matrix.

Evaluation

The evaluation plan for this project was twofold: (1) evaluating the process of planning, developing, and implementing the program; and (2) measuring learner competencies or outcomes. The process evaluation examined the content of the matrix by comparing faculty input to teaching content and examples of learner activities with the ideas generated by the Circle prior to the workshops. In addition, a questionnaire was given to faculty after the workshop. In order to evaluate learner outcomes, students were given an IL survey at the beginning and at the end of their clinical courses. The results of the survey were compared to determine if students' IL skills had improved throughout the course of the clinical program.

RESULTS

Integration of the IL plan into the curriculum, instituted in summer 2005 semester, progressed with positive outcomes reported from faculty and students.

Faculty Questionnaire

A twenty-item questionnaire was developed and distributed to faculty. The first part of the questionnaire elicited perceptions by faculty of their knowledge and input into the IL plan; the Circle's role as a resource; and their ability to integrate the IL plan into their courses. The second part of the questionnaire reflected faculty's perceptions of student work since the integration of IL into their courses. At the first faculty meeting in fall 2005, forty-five faculty members were asked to complete the questionnaire. Eleven completed questionnaires represented a 24 percent return rate.

On part one of the questionnaire, faculty agreed (100 percent, $N = 11$) that the Circle had communicated the mission and plan, that faculty were asked to provide input, and that the input was reflected in the plan. Ninety percent ($N = 10$) of the faculty perceived that the Circle had provided opportunities to increase their IL skills as well as improved their skills. In addition, the faculty perceived (90 percent, $N = 10$) that the Circle had provided resources to integrate IL into the College of Nursing and that the resources were useful to them.

All faculty surveyed ($N = 11$) reported improved integration of resource information into student assignments. Ninety-one percent ($N = 10$) reported an increase in information synthesis and in the use of electronic resources. Eighty-two percent ($N = 9$) of respondents reported increased use of scholarly journals by students.

Student Information Literacy Survey (SILS)

A two-part survey tool was developed to assess IL knowledge. The first part of the survey (nine questions) asked the students to (1) rate their skills and use related to e-mail, accessing the World Wide Web, university library, and full-text articles; (2) rate their overall ability to use a computer, MS Windows, word processing software, databases, and MS PowerPoint; and (3) report instruction or courses in databases or computers. The second portion of the survey consisted of twenty-five multiple-choice questions based on the five standards of IL formulated by the Circle. The survey was reviewed for content validity by a panel of content experts. The expected IL outcome for the second portion of the survey, which related to the five IL standards, was an 80 percent correct group average for the questions.

The survey was made available via Blackboard to three entering clinical groups and three groups completing their clinical courses in fall 2005. Students were informed of the purpose of the survey and participation was voluntary. The completion of the survey constituted students' consent to participate. All data were collected and reported as aggregate data.

Entering Clinical Groups (Cohort I)

The three entering clinical groups (Cohort I) totaled 157 students, 61 generic BSN students, 65 RN-to-BSN students, and 31 Bachelor of Science in Radiologic Technology (BSRT) students. One-hundred-and-forty surveys were completed for an overall return rate of 89 percent. BSN students had a 100 percent return rate. RN-to-BSN students completed fifty-three surveys for an 82 percent return rate, and BSRT students completed twenty-six surveys for an 84 percent return rate.

Ending Clinical Groups (Cohort II)

The three graduating groups (Cohort II), completing the SILS at the conclusion of their last clinical courses, totaled 119 students (49 generic BSN students, 36 RN-to-BSN students, and 34 BSRT students). Ninety-one surveys were completed for a return rate of 76 percent. BSN students completed thirty-five surveys for a return rate of 71 percent. RN-to-BSN students completed thirty-four surveys for a return rate of 94 percent, and BSRT students completed twenty-two surveys for a return rate of 65 percent. All of these students entered their respective program after integration of the IL plan.

Part 1 Results for Cohort I

Of the Cohort I respondents (entering clinical students) to Part 1 of the SILS, 71 percent rated their IL skills as three or higher on a scale of one (novice) to five (expert); 98 percent reported they used e-mail; 97 percent rated their ability to use the computer at 3 or higher; 96 percent said they had retrieved a full-text article from the library and they rated their ability to use MS Windows at 3 or higher; 92 percent said they used the World Wide Web; 91 percent rated their ability to use word processing software at 3 or higher; 89 percent indicated they had accessed the university library; 82 percent rated their ability to use MS PowerPoint at 3 or higher; 75 percent rated their overall ability to use computer programs and databases at 3 or higher; 62 percent said they had received some instruction on electronic databases from a variety of sources which included faculty, tutorials, computer courses, and librarians; and 66 percent indicated they had completed a computer course. All BSRT students were required to complete a computer course as part of their curriculum, accounting for 28 percent of the 66 percent of the students who had taken a computer course.

Part 1 Results for Cohort II

Results from Part 1 of the SILS indicate that 96 percent of Cohort II (graduating students) rated their IL skills as 3 or higher on a scale of 1 (novice) to 5 (expert); 100 percent indicated they used e-mail and the World Wide Web, and rated their ability to use a computer and MS Windows as 3 or higher; 99 percent said they had accessed the university library and had retrieved a full-text article from the library; 98 percent rated their ability to use word processing software at 3 or higher; 91 percent rated their overall ability to use computer programs and databases at 3 or higher; 90 percent reported they had received some instruction on electronic databases from a variety of sources which included faculty, tutorials, computer courses, and librarians; 88 percent rated their ability to use MS PowerPoint at 3 or higher; and 75 percent indicated they had completed a computer course. All BSRT students were required to complete a computer course as part of their curriculum, accounting for 32 percent of the 75 percent of the students who had taken a computer course.

Part 2 Results for Cohorts I and II

Cohort I and II results from Part 2 of the SILS (focused on the five IL objectives/standards) are detailed in the accompanying table (see Table 19.1). For Cohort I, the expected outcome of students able to determine the nature and extent of information needed (Standard I) was only met by the BSN group. No Cohort I group met the expected outcomes for standards II, IV, and V (accessing information, comparing new and old knowledge, and using information effectively). Both the BSN and the RN-to-BSN groups in Cohort I met the expected outcome for Standard III (evaluating and incorporating information).

In terms of standards I, III, and V for Cohort II, only the RN-to-BSN group met the expected outcome. Only the BSN group met the expected outcome for Standard II. The expected outcome for

TABLE 19.1. Percentage of correct responses to information literacy questions.

Group	N	I		II		III		IV		V	
		CR/TR	GS (%)	CR/TR	GS (%)	CR/TR	GS (%)	CR/TR	GS (%)	CR/TR	GS (%)
Cohort I (entering students)											
BSN	61	246/305	81	206/366	56	252/305	83	216/305	71	175/244	72
RN-to-BSN	53	194/265	73	165/318	52	222/265	84	184/265	69	166/212	78
BSRT	26	82/130	63	70/156	45	102/130	78	66/130	51	59/104	57
Total	140	522/700	75	441/840	53	576/700	82	466/700	67	400/560	71
Cohort II (graduating students)											
BSN	35	138/175	79	155/175	89	111/175	63	129/175	74	107/140	76
RN-to-BSN	34	137/170	81	161/204	79	147/170	86	117/170	69	110/136	81
BSRT	22	84/110	76	60/132	45	82/110	75	70/110	64	39/88	44
Total	91	359/455	79	376/511	74	340/455	75	316/455	69	256/364	70

Note: Part 2 (Questions 1-25) of the Student Information Literacy Survey tested the information literacy of respondents. Group scores of 80% or higher met the expected information literacy outcome (correct response). CR/TR (Correct Responses/Total Responses) = GS (Group Score).

Standard IV was not met by any group. Six questions on Part 2 of the SILS were answered incorrectly by a high percentage of Cohort II. These questions dealt with (1) narrowing a research topic; (2) evaluating books or articles for a paper; (3) identifying the rationale for including references in a research paper; (4) utilizing information from Web sites; (5) citing information from references without page numbers; and (6) interpreting "netiquette" rules.

CONCLUSION

According to the benchmark established by the Circle, the College of Nursing is on the brink of graduating information literate students. Long-term effects of the program cannot be determined at this time due to small sample size and lack of time to implement the plan.

Faculty

Even though the IL plan has been in effect for a limited time, faculty members are positive about educating students to legally and ethically access, appraise, and integrate information from multiple sources and systems to influence professional practice. As a result of the plan and faculty development, faculty feel prepared to integrate IL into the curriculum. Faculty members have also indicated that they have integrated IL activities. A variety of IL strategies have been implemented and faculty already perceive improvements in student work in terms of IL. Due to the limited time the plan has been in place, faculty members were not able to determine an improvement in the application of the American Psychological Association style or if incidents of plagiarism have decreased. The limited number of faculty who responded to the faculty questionnaire indicates a need for the Circle to foster ongoing dialogue and continued movement toward producing information literate graduates.

Students (Cohort I)

The majority of the students in Cohort I, who had taken a computer course, perceived themselves as being computer literate. Although the majority of these students rated their IL skills as average or higher, this perception was not supported by group scores on the SILS. The expected outcome was achieved only for Standard III (evaluating information sources critically and incorporating selected information into knowledge base, value system, and practice). As a cohort, the lowest group scores were reflected in Standard II (accessing information effectively and efficiently). The BSRT group scored the lowest of all groups for all standards despite the fact they all had taken a required computer course prior to entering clinical courses and taking the SILS. Completion of a computer course does not ensure an information-literate student. When averaging all group scores, entering students are not information literate in terms of the standards/objectives developed by the College of Nursing.

Students (Cohort II)

The majority of the students in Cohort II perceived themselves as being computer and information literate; however, this perception was not supported by group scores on the SILS. The RN-to-BSN group met the expected outcomes for three of the five standards; the BSN group, one standard; and the BSRT group did not meet any of the standards. The average of all group scores indicates that none of the standards/objectives were met.

The fact that the majority of RN-to-BSN students are, on the average, older than the two other groups and are currently engaged in practice may account for their higher results. Adult learners are self-directed and want to apply what is learned in the classroom immediately. Information management is a critical element of daily practice faced by these RNs in their clinical setting. The IL skills they learn in the classroom can be applied the next day at work.

One possible factor contributing to the BSRT group's lowest scores in Cohort II may be the fact that both the generic BSN and the RN-to-BSN groups have a required information management course in their curricula. The BSRT group receives IL knowledge and skills integrated throughout the curriculum. A factor that may account for the differences in Standard II between the BSN and the RN-to-BSN groups is the program delivery mode. Generic BSN students take traditional classes as well as Web-supported classes and, practice their skills in a supervised computer lab. RN-to-BSN classes are conducted over the Internet without the opportunity for supervised practice. In addition, low scores may indicate that content was not taught effectively or that some of the SILS questions were poorly written.

The SILS was completed by Cohort I students at various times during their first clinical course. In some cases, students had already received initial IL content. For that reason, the survey should be administered to entering students the first week of class. Faculty need to review the SILS to ensure that content covered is addressed in the curriculum. Questions on the SILS need to be reviewed for clarity, reliability, and validity. A pilot study should be conducted after revisions are made. As aggregate data were collected, individual knowledge and skills at entry and upon graduation could not be compared. Future data collection methodologies will allow for this comparison.

NOTES

1. Northwestern State University of Louisiana. "Eugene P. Watson Memorial Library." Available: <http://www.nsula.edu/watson_library/Webtour/>. Accessed: December 13, 2005.

2. Northwestern State University of Louisiana. "Shreveport Nursing Library." Available: <http://www.nsula.edu/watson_library/shreve/shrevetour.htm>. Accessed: December 13, 2005.

3. Northwestern State University of Louisiana, College of Nursing. "Faculty and Staff." Available: <http://www.nsula.edu/nursing/faculty.html>. Accessed: December 13, 2005.

4. Louisiana Board of Regents, Information Services Division. *Statewide Student Profile System: Student Headcount Enrollment by Declared Major (Detailed), Fall 2003-2004, Northwestern State University.* Baton Rouge: Author, 2004. Available: <http://as400.regents.state.la.us/pdfs/ssps/spring03/SPCIPD303.pdf>. Accessed: December 13, 2005.

5. Association of College & Research Libraries. *Objectives for Information Literacy Instruction: A Model Statement for Academic Librarians.* Chicago: American Library Association, 2001. Available: <http://www.ala.org/ala/acrl/acrlstandards/objectivesinformation.htm>. Accessed: December 15, 2005.

6. Louisiana Board of Regents, Division of Academic & Student Affairs. *Academic Affairs Policy 2.16: Statewide General Education Requirements.* Baton Rouge: Author, 2001. Available: <http://asa.regents.state.la.us/PP/Policies/2.16>. Accessed: December 15, 2005.

7. Louisiana Board of Regents, Division of Academic & Student Affairs. *Attachment IV: Louisiana Board of Regents Statewide General Education Requirements* [approved April 26, 2001, amended March 25, 2004]. Baton Rouge: Author,

2001. Available: <http://asa.regents.state.la.us/PP/Attachments/IV>. Accessed: December 15, 2005.

8. American Association of Colleges of Nursing. *The Essentials of Baccalaureate Education for Professional Nursing Practice.* Washington, DC: Author, 1998.

9. National League for Nursing, Council of Associate Degree Nursing, Competencies Task Force. *Educational Competencies for Graduates of Associate Degree Nursing Programs.* Revised edition by G. Coxwell & H. Gillerman. Sudbury, MA: Jones & Bartlett, 2000.

10. American Nurses Association. *Scope and Standards of Nursing Informatics Practice.* Washington, DC: American Nurses Publishing, 2001.

11. Joint Review Committee on Education in Radiologic Technology. *Standards for an Accredited Educational Program in Radiologic Sciences.* Chicago: Author, 2002. Available: <http://www.jrcert.org/pdfs/accreditation_process/standards/standards_%20for_an_accredited_educational_program_in_radiologic_sciences.pdf>. Accessed: December 15, 2005.

12. Association of College and Research Libraries. *Information Literacy Competency Standards for Higher Education.* Chicago: American Library Association, 2000. Available: <http://www.ala.org/ala/acrl/acrlstandards/informationliteracy competency.htm>. Accessed: December 15, 2005.

13. Association of College and Research Libraries, Institute for Information Literacy. *Characteristics of Programs of Information Literacy That Illustrate Best Practices.* Chicago: American Library Association, 2003. Available: <http://www .ala.org/ala/acrl/acrlstandards/characteristics.htm>. Accessed: December 15, 2005.

14. American Library Association. *Presidential Committee on Information Literacy: Final Report.* Chicago: Author, 1989. Available: <http://www.ala.org/ala/ acrl/acrlpubs/whitepapers/presidential.htm>. Accessed December 15, 2005.

15. Blankenship, L. and Fox, L. M. "Information Literacy—The Next Generation: Evolving with the Curriculum." *Colorado Libraries* 24, no. 4 (1998): 21-23.

16. Travis, L. and Brennan, P. F. "Information Science for the Future: An Innovative Nursing Informatics Curriculum." *Journal of Nursing Education* 37, no. 7 (1998): 162-168.

17. Verhey, M. P. "Information Literacy in an Undergraduate Nursing Curriculum: Development, Implementation, and Evaluation." *Journal of Nursing Education* 38, no. 6 (1999): 252-259.

18. Chadwick, S. *Nursing Information Literacy Skills, As Adapted from a Document by Corryn Crosby-Muilenburg.* Humboldt, CA: Humboldt State University Library, 1999. Available: <http://library.humboldt.edu/~chadwick/nursingcom petencies_498.htm>. Accessed: December 15, 2005.

19. Wallace, M. C. et al. "Integrating Information Literacies into an Undergraduate Nursing Program." *Nurse Education Today* 19, no. 2 (1999): 136-141.

20. Wallace, M. C., Shorten, A., and Crookes, P. A. "Teaching Information Literacy Skills: An Evaluation." *Nurse Education Today* 20, no. 6 (2000): 485-489.

21. Shorten, A., Wallace, M. C., and Crookes, P. A. "Developing Information Literacy: A Key to Evidence-Based Nursing." *International Nursing Review* 48, no. 2 (2001): 86-92.

22. Dorner, J. L., Taylor, S. E., and Hodson-Carlton, K. "Faculty-Librarian Collaboration for Nursing Information Literacy: A Tiered Approach." *Reference Services Review* 29, no. 2 (2001): 132-140.

23. Kaplan, R. B. and Whelan, J. S. "Buoyed by a Rising Tide: Information Literacy Sails into the Curriculum on the Currents of Evidence-Based Medicine and Professional Competency Objectives." *Journal of Library Administration* 36, nos. 1/2 (2002): 219-235.

24. Jacobs, S. K., Rosenfeld, P., and Haber, J. "Information Literacy as the Foundation for Evidence-Based Practice in Graduate Nursing Education: A Curriculum-Integrated Approach." *Journal of Professional Nursing* 19, no. 5 (2003): 320-328.

25. Staggers, N., Gassert, C. A., and Curran, C. "Informatics Competencies for Nurses at Four Levels of Practice." *Journal of Nursing Education* 40, no. 7 (2001): 303-316.

26. Staggers, N., Gassert, C. A., and Curran, C. "A Delphi Study To Determine Informatics Competencies for Nurses at Four Levels of Practice." *Nursing Research* 51, no. 6 (2002): 383-390.

27. LOEX (Library Orientation Exchange) Clearinghouse for Library Instruction. *Directory of Online Resources for Information Literacy: Tutorials,* edited by M. Dibble. Ypsilanti, MI: Author, 2004. Available: <http://bulldogs.tlu.edu/mdibble/doril/tutorials.html>. Accessed: December 12, 2005.

28. Association of College & Research Libraries. *Resources and Ideas, Information Literacy in Action: Tutorials.* Chicago: American Library Association, 2005. Available: <http://www.ala.org/ala/acrl/acrlissues/acrlinfolit/infolitresources/infolitinaction/iltutorials.htm>. Accessed: December 16, 2005.

29. University of Texas System Digital Library. Texas Information Literacy Tutorials. Available: <http://tilt.lib.utsystem.edu/>. Austin: Author, 2004. Accessed: December 16, 2005.

30. Purdue University. CORE: Comprehensive Online Research Information. West Lafayette, IN: Purdue University Libraries, 2001. Available: <http://core.lib.purdue.edu/>. Accessed: December 12, 2005.

31. Tricarico, M. A., Von Daum Tholl, S., and O'Malley, E. "Interactive Online Instruction for Library Research: The Small Academic Library Experience." *Journal of Academic Librarianship* 27, no. 3 (2001): 220-223.

32. New York University-Mount Sinai Libraries Nursing Tutorial Working Group. *Nursing Resources: A Self-paced Tutorial & Refresher.* New York: NYU Libraries, 2002. Available: <http://library.nyu.edu/research/health/tutorial/>. Accessed: December 16, 2005.

Chapter 20

Librarians in the Online Classroom: Proactive Bibliographic Instruction for Distance Education Students

Justin Robertson
Ellen Sayed
Linda Roussel

INTRODUCTION

The Internet has transformed the way information is created, compiled, and disseminated. This new technology has had significant ramifications for traditional instructional methods—effectively eliminating any distinctions between "around the corner" and "around the world." The virtual classroom's rapid growth and widespread acceptance has created a new, more efficient milieu for distance education, but it has also produced an array of unique and challenging issues for contemporary information professionals.

Several developments have caused the Internet, or more specifically the World Wide Web, to become the predominant mode of distance education. Technological advances and affordability have prompted the growth of undergraduate and graduate courses available online. Distance education software has developed rapidly providing increasingly sophisticated, yet easy to use, instructional platforms. Furthermore, widespread individual computer ownership nurtures an increasingly convenient and flexible learning environment, allowing individuals to plan around personal considerations such as work schedules, family responsibilities, and physical location.[1] The Web frees students to participate in both asynchronous and synchronous learning environments.

An Introduction to Instructional Services in Academic Libraries

Synchronous communication, characterized by classroom instruction or online live chat, occurs when involved parties exchange information simultaneously or in real time.[2] This format has been the standard model for traditional education for years, but it restricts involvement by requiring adherence to a set schedule. Online classes have established asynchronous communication as a viable and effective alternative educational strategy. E-mail and threaded discussions typify asynchronous communication, a situation where all parties involved do not need to participate at the same time for an effective exchange of ideas and information.[3] This method provides students with greater flexibility, allowing them to fit the educational experience within the parameters of their own schedules. The resulting popularity and efficacy of online education are borne out statistically. As of 2003, roughly 70 percent of all U.S. secondary education institutions offered some form of distance learning.[4]

SITUATION AND GOALS

Supporting the parent institution's mission remains the academic library's primary objective and the growing reliance upon the Web as an instructional platform presents unique challenges. For example, how does a library that supports a distance education program package deliver its traditional services and resources to a largely remote audience? What part should the librarian play in the online classroom? How does this new dynamic affect the "traditional" relationship between teaching faculty and librarians?

University of South Alabama's Biomedical Library in Mobile recognized that the school's burgeoning College of Nursing online program was creating a growing population of virtual users, making these questions a practical concern rather than a theoretical one. Although the library had supported online reference and document delivery previously, this rapid expansion required a more proactive approach. This chapter discusses the specific initiatives taken to address these issues.

LITERATURE REVIEW

Several professional organizations have addressed distance learning and other online education issues. Association of College & Research

Libraries (ACRL) and Southern Association of Colleges and Schools (SACS), the accreditation agency, have both established criteria for providing library services to off-campus students.[5,6] ACRL guidelines suggest a basic framework required for providing essential library services and resources to distance learning programs. These include reference assistance, computer-based bibliographic/informational services, institutional networks, consultations, library instruction, document delivery (via courier service or electronic delivery), reserves access, sufficient service hours, effective service/policy promotions, clearly stated regulations/procedures, and management of information sources.[7]

Similarly, SACS criteria specify that in addition to supporting online curriculum and instructional content, the library should offer remote access to its services, resources, and policies including reference, document delivery, and access to print resources. In addition, the library should inform prospective students of available services as well as the technological skills required to use them.[8]

These standards clearly demonstrate that the virtual classroom has not changed the librarian's primary duties, but it has irrevocably affected the methods and skills needed to successfully fulfill those duties. Among other things, this new paradigm requires employing innovative instructional designs and a willingness to collaborate closely with teaching faculty. The existing professional literature reveals several common trends about both the process and the means employed to accomplish these goals. For example, in 1997 when Duquesne University began developing its first online doctoral program, Milstead and Nelson identified hard copy access, document delivery, and information literacy as essential library services. To accomplish this, Duquesne library staff reviewed policies, implemented a fax document delivery service, and created an online orientation Web page. Students were also instructed to inquire about library services in their local areas.[9] The following year, Thomas Jefferson University launched an online epidemiology nursing course that included the library as an integral partner. Students attended an on-campus orientation that incorporated a library services overview and a computer skills assessment test, but subsequent student evaluations showed that this initial introduction to library services was largely ineffectual. Consequently, the librarians created an online quiz, course demonstration/overview, and Frequently

Asked Questions (FAQ) database that future students were required to review and complete before beginning their term.[10] Further recommendations included that libraries supporting distance learning should be prepared to provide interlibrary loan, courier services, and access to online materials on a full-time, 24/7 basis. Additionally, librarians must involve themselves in the earliest planning stages of off-campus courses, and designated digital reference librarian(s) should coordinate all online library instruction classes and/or tutorials.[11] The Ohio State University Library used their traditional service functions as a template for supporting their off-campus students. Subsequently they implemented an online "Ask a Health Sciences Librarian" Web form, electronic document delivery services (not including interlibrary loan), and electronic reserves. Future suggestions included supplementing on-campus library orientation materials and sessions with virtual counterparts that would allow online students to access this information at their convenience. The article suggests that proliferating online courses will create a library environment consisting of two distinct user groups, the local and remote patron, each having their own specific needs and demands. Providing satisfactory assistance to these patrons, through technology and enhanced service, will be a paramount responsibility for future academic librarians.[12]

Two key components of the University of Wyoming's online student library services are (1) making library resources readily accessible, and (2) integrating information literacy/bibliographic instruction into online courses. Specifically, the library provides reference services (via e-mail, nationwide toll-free number, and online chat), interlibrary loan/document delivery, and easy Web access to library catalogs, databases, electronic books, journals, and reserves. In addition, a designated librarian (versed in proxy servers, copyright, and Web site management among other specialized, technical skills) oversees all library outreach services. The library absorbs all costs associated with providing outreach services which are offered free of charge to distance learners.[13]

This is a very brief overview of the existing professional literature addressing and chronicling various initiatives libraries have taken to provide traditional library services to growing online student populations. Many of these ideas have been similarly employed by USA Biomedical Library, but several research-oriented College of Nursing courses (at the undergraduate and graduate level) demanded even more proactive service. Librarians formed a partnership with College of Nursing faculty to serve as guest instructors within several online classes. These librarians provided proactive, rather than reactive, services by giving research and access assistance within the online class itself.

SETTING

Located in Mobile on the Gulf Coast of the United States, the University of South Alabama is part of the state's higher education system. As of spring 2005 the University had roughly 12,000 students, of which 1,883 were enrolled in the College of Nursing program. The Biomedical Library is composed of three branches (campus site, Medical Center site, and Children & Women's Hospital site) and caters to three primary schools: the College of Nursing, Colleges of Allied Health Professionals, and College of Medicine.

For the last decade, the Biomedical Library has concentrated on developing the institution's online, full-text collection. By spring 2006 this collection contained 4,817 unique electronic journal titles and 358 e-books, all of which are available to all university students, both on- and off-campus. Library collections have been augmented by a vibrant, content-rich Web presence <http://southmed.usouthal.edu/library/> that provides relevant on and off-site information. In addition, several sections of the Web site have been specifically designed with the needs of online users in mind.

In fall 1999, the University of South Alabama initiated its online program by offering seventeen courses with a total of 250 registrants. A scant six years later, the university offered 116 online courses with a total of 2,343 registrants. The College of Nursing has been at the forefront of the university's distance education program, currently accounting for more than half of the classes offered as well as more than half of the total online registrants. Of the initial seventeen courses mentioned above, six were from the College of Nursing with a total of 130 registrants, and by spring 2005 the school offered sixty-three classes with a total of 1,386 registrants. In six years time the program's online component had grown by 95 percent (in terms of classes offered) and almost 94 percent (in terms of registered students). Currently the College of Nursing accounts for over 54 percent of all university online classes and 59 percent of registered distance education students.

In general, academic libraries embraced Web-based information access, conceptualized as the "virtual library," well before the ubiquity of online education. The advent of electronic journals and books was recognized as librarianship's manifest destiny, and integrating traditional collections with electronic content soon became a given aspect of the information professional's duties. The ascendant interest and popularity of Web-based instruction was certainly facilitated by increased access to electronic materials, but merely making information available is not enough. The librarian's ultimate goal is to make information accessible—a challenge in the brave new world of online content.

Since the University of South Alabama's first online offerings, Biomedical Library staff have strived to provide equitable services and resources to both distance education and traditional classroom-oriented students. Over the years the library has incorporated many of the services mandated by ACRL and SACS guidelines mentioned previously. Reference assistance has always been available for online students, initially in the form of e-mail and phone consultation and later with the addition of a live-chat service. Document delivery/interlibrary loan services are also readily available, and the librarians have worked diligently to create a content-rich Web site that includes various online interactive tutorials, FAQs, and specialized information pages. Collection development staff have also kept the online user in mind by ensuring that publisher licensing deals allow off-campus access to subscribed e-journals and books.

THE CLASSES

The University of South Alabama's College of Nursing classes overseen by biomedical librarians include:

- Advanced Nursing Research (NU 513)
- Evidence-Based Practice in Community Mental Health Nursing (CMN 514)

- Evidence-Based Practice in Adult Health Nursing (AHN 514)
- Evidence-Based Practice in Maternal Child Health (MCH 514)
- Nursing Administration Field Study (NU 566)
- Nursing Research (NU 304)
- Evidence-Based Practice for Advanced Practice Nursing (NU 690)

All of these classes included a significant research component. Librarians actively monitored the threaded discussions of each course and responded to relevant research and library-related questions. Their instructional goals were more ambitious than simply teaching effective literature searching methodology. They wanted to show students how to carefully compile and evaluate their findings, hopefully facilitating an understanding of how theoretical research can be translated into an actual evidence-based practice scenario.

METHODS

Research runs like a core thread throughout the professional RN program making it essential to introduce basic search techniques at all levels of study. This skill becomes even more valuable when an RN program focuses on evidence-based practice (EBP), a nursing theory built upon research, critical thinking, and informational synthesis. Professional nursing EBP competencies outlined by the Academic Center for Evidence-Based Nursing[14] state that simply understanding research methodologies is not enough—students must also know the practical "how, what, and where" of accessing timely, critical, and reliable evidence for the purposes of making clinical decisions. Essentials of Master's Nursing Education requires that students possess these core bibliographic competencies which prompted a teaching faculty/biomedical librarian partnership that focuses on integrating bibliographic instruction within online, EBP-based classes.

A task force was formed to incorporate EBP theory into the curriculum. Among this group's directives was to actively involve the College of Nursing's designated library liaison. While this individual had presented many classroom-based library orientation sessions, no prescribed infrastructure existed for extending equivalent services for distance education students. Previously most online users were assisted individually on an informal, "first come, first served" basis, but this approach's inadequacies became readily apparent when detailed bibliographic/research instruction was required. Initial meetings between librarians and nursing faculty identified core research skills that instructors expected of students:

- searching the literature for various levels of evidence,
- identifying and employing best search strategies and search engine(s) for finding relevant and reliable research materials, and
- evaluating levels of evidence for overall quality.

In addition to these core skills, graduate students were expected to search for all levels of evidence and determine any existing information gaps; make specific recommendations distilled from gathered research; and illustrate viability of recommendations using gathered information.

Several strategies were employed to meet these needs. For those students participating in hybrid nursing courses—those that combined traditional classroom time and online instruction—librarians conducted detailed, in-class, bibliographic training sessions. Ideally, these lectures consisted of a formal, prepared presentation and "live," online demonstrations of how to search relevant resources. In addition, print handouts summarized information presented in the class. Providing similar services to strictly online students required librarians to take a proactive role by regularly visiting the course's virtual classroom (generally in a threaded discussion format). Here librarians could field all varieties of relevant questions ranging from simple online access issues to complex research strategy assistance. These archived librarian/student threaded discussions served as an excellent forum for research information and peer feedback to all participating students, even for those who did not ask questions. Online equivalents to the print handouts, as well as various online tutorials, have also been created and maintained to close any unintentional information gaps between distance education students and their on-campus counterparts. Assuming these classes will be taught regularly (and perhaps continue to grow), further refinements can be made by analyzing student feedback and the firsthand experiences of participating teaching faculty and librarians. The ultimate goal is to ensure that online students receive library access and research training equivalent to those students attending classes on campus.

In preparation for the online classes, all of which included a significant EBP component, the librarians and nursing faculty met to discuss and clarify their goals and expectations. The librarians familiarized themselves with the theory and tenets behind EBP, particularly as it related to nursing and the professional literature. One article clearly delineated the difference between EBP and evidence-based medicine (EBM),[15] and another discussed evidence-based nursing information resources[16] made available online by librarians. While these articles were not required reading, students were strongly encouraged to look at them.

Further groundwork included reviewing the twelve Institute of Medicine topics from which the students were required to choose their research subjects.[17] From an information retrieval standpoint, these broad disease terms (hypertension, obesity, heart disease, and diabetes mellitus) can be narrowed down with related topics and/or specific limits (i.e., date ranges, data types). To broadly gauge the availability of pertinent information, as well as prepare for potential research questions, the librarians searched several relevant databases including (but not limited to): CINAHL (Cumulative Index to Nursing and Allied Health Literature), Cochrane Database, and HealthSTAR for periodical literature, and WorldCat for books. When appropriate, these searches were conducted using subject headings (in those databases indexed by a set or defined vocabulary), as well as general keyword searches. In addition, librarians created and posted topic-specific online pages providing the students with numerous useful tutorials, tips, and links.

Anticipating that students would use general Internet search engines (i.e., Google, Alta Vista) for information retrieval, librarians emphasized the importance of careful Web site evaluation skills when integrating Web-based health information into their work. These criteria were discussed and students were provided with a set of guidelines available both in print and online.[18]

RESULTS

As the classes began, the librarians began to carefully monitor the threaded discussions in each class. During the first two semesters, the research-related questions were combined with the main class threaded discussions; however, sorting out the relevant queries from the online conversations proved difficult. Future classes included a distinct "Reference Desk" thread, a separate forum for research-related questions.

With this infrastructure in place, the actual "virtual reference" assistance could begin. One issue that became immediately apparent was that the threaded discussions must be checked at least once per day. While there was a definite ebb and flow of inquiries that generally centered on initial research attempts, questions appeared throughout the duration of each course. The most common questions involved the actual search process. Due to differing skill levels and previous (or lack thereof) experience, the students had varying degrees of initial success. The research questions themselves generally fell into one of five distinct categories:

1. *Where and how to begin the research process:* In this case, librarians might suggest the creation of a specific research topic statement that takes into account all related terminology (including synonyms), types of information required, date ranges, etc. Students would be directed to the appropriate databases (usually CINAHL). Sometimes the librarians ran an initial search that served as a model from which research could proceed.

2. *What to do if unable to find any information on a topic:* If a student was unable to find any information on a topic, this generally occurred for one of two reasons: either the student did not look in the correct place with the correct terminology, or the information simply did not exist. The first reason could be addressed by suggesting refinements of the research topic statement (changing search vocabulary, subject headings and/or subheadings, expanding imposed limits such date ranges, etc.). Again the librarian would frequently run a refined search using the revised subject topic statement to get the student back into the research process. If topic revisions did not yield results, and if no information was available on a given subject, then the librarian would recommend speaking to the instructor about choosing a different topic.

3. *What to do if unable to find enough specific information on a topic.*

4. *What to do when finding too much information on a given topic.* Although issues three and four are different problems, the solutions suggested were generally the same. Search topics must either be

broadened (in the case of not finding enough information) or narrowed (in the case of finding too much information). Again, the librarian would run new searches with revised terminology and/or limits to get the student back in the right direction.

5. *How to access the full-text content for the information/citations found and related technical questions:* Falling into a separate category altogether were questions related to the technical side of using the online library. These questions ranged from simple password problems to more complex access issues concerning computers settings and the library's proxy server.

Naturally there were some questions that fell outside of these five categories, but generally these were not in the librarian's purview. For example, questions pertaining to actual research subject content, on-line classroom (eCollege program) technical questions, and/or specific class assignments were referred to the course instructor.

CONCLUSION

Although the library has instituted many changes since it began service to its online patrons, this can never be considered a static project. As these programs inevitably grow, and technology becomes increasingly sophisticated, information professionals will always have to treat online library services as an ongoing project. USA Biomedical Library and the College of Nursing have already begun to look forward by brainstorming future initiatives designed to enhance existing online bibliographic instruction programs. Plans already in motion include developing a Mediasite (canned video/audio presentation) orientation to the reference desk and the role of the biomedical librarians within the context of research and evidence-based nursing. In addition, the biomedical librarians plan to develop a self-study EBP tutorial certificate program. Working with clinical partners, biomedical librarians will also be included in future planning.

Finally, it should be noted that bibliographic instruction provided during these classes was intended as the means to an end, and not an end unto itself. In other words, the goal was to educate and empower students, not do their work for them. As research forms the backbone of evidence-based practice theory, nursing students must understand research methodology beyond basic information retrieval strategy. They must also gain an appreciation of the research process, including how information is gathered, grouped, and evaluated in order to understand how research theory moves into actual EBP.

Since these classes demanded the understanding of advanced research concepts, it was imperative that the librarians deliver advanced bibliographic instruction. Had these classes been presented in a more "traditional" classroom setting, the instruction could have been handled with one or more in-person training sessions. As these courses were held online, this situation presented the unique challenge of delivering extensive and comparable training to distance education students. While Biomedical Library staff have supported this online program since its inception, these new demands required a more proactive approach, necessitating an active partnership with College of Nursing teaching faculty that resulted in librarians regularly entering and teaching in virtual classrooms of several courses.

The historic popularity and current proliferation of distance education leave little doubt that this online community will continue to grow. Librarians must prepare for this eventuality by taking an increasingly proactive role in their institution's online programs. In addition to taking approaches such as electronic tutorials and Web pages, information professionals must develop new ways to provide equitable library services and resources for all students—regardless of location. Teaching in the virtual classroom is one way of bridging informational inequity, but establishing strong, collaborative relationships with distance education teaching faculty remains the most certain way. Participation in online learning cements the librarian's reputation as an invaluable educational resource and ultimately fulfills the information professional's main mission of providing patrons with the best and most readily accessible information possible.

NOTES

1. Morris, N., Buck-Rolland, C., and Gagne, M. "From Bricks to Bytes: Faculty and Student Perspective of Online Graduate Nursing Courses." *CIN: Computers, Informatics, Nursing* 20 (May/June 2002): 108-114.

2. Guillot, L., Stahr, B., and Plaisance, L. "Dedicated Online Virtual Reference Instruction." *Nurse Educator* 30 (November/December 2005): 242-246.

3. Milstead, J. A. and Nelson, R. "Preparation for an Online Asynchronous University Doctoral Course: Lessons Learned." *Computers in Nursing* 16 (October 1998): 247-258.

4. *Quality on the Line: Benchmarks for Success in Internet-Based Distance Education.* The Institute for Higher Education Policy. National Education Association, 2000. Available: <http://www.ihep.com/Pubs/PDF/Quality.pdf>. Accessed: December 20, 2005.

5. *ACRL Guidelines for Distance Learning Library Services*, June 2004. Association of College & Research Libraries. Available: <http://www.ala.org/ala/acrl/acrlstandards/guidelinesdistancelearning.htm>. Accessed: December 20, 2005.

6. *Best Practices for Electronically Offered Degree and Certificate Programs.* Commission on Colleges Southern Association of Colleges and Schools, 2000. Available: <http://www.sacscoc.org/pdf/commadap.pdf>. Accessed: December 20, 2005.

7. See note 5.

8. See note 6.

9. See note 3.

10. Frisby, A. J. and Jones, S. S. "The Initiation of Distance Learning at Thomas Jefferson University: The Library as Integral Partner." *Medical Reference Services Quarterly* 19 (Fall 2000): 19-37.

11. Mills, May Etta, Fisher, Cheryl, and Stair, Nola. "Web-Based Courses More than Curriculum." *Nursing & Health Care Perspectives* 22 (September/October 2001): 235-239.

12. Rodman, R. L. "Cost Analysis and Student Survey Results of Library Support for Distance Education." *Journal of the Medical Library Association* 91 (January 2003): 72-78.

13. Kearley, J. P. and Phillips, L., "Embedding Library Reference Services in Online Courses." *Internet Reference Services Quarterly* 9, no. 1/2 (2004): 65-76.

14. *ACE: Learn About EBP.* University of Texas Health Science Center at San Antonio. Academic Center for Evidence-Based Nursing, 2006. Available: <http://acestar.uthscsa.edu/Learn_model.htm>. Accessed: January 20, 2006.

15. Lavin, M. A. et al. "Essential Differences Between Evidence-Based Nursing and Evidence-Based Medicine." *International Journal of Nursing Terminologies and Classification* 13 (July 2000): 101-106.

16. Spasser, M. A. "Evidence-Based Nursing Resources." *Medical Reference Services Quarterly* 24 (Summer 2005): 71-84.

17. *Topics.* Institute of Medicine of the National Academies. Available: <http://www.iom.edu/CMS/2956.aspx>. Accessed: January 10, 2006.

18. *Pathfinder: Web Evaluation Criteria.* University of South Alabama Biomedical Library, 2006. Available: <http://southmed.usouthal.edu/library/ref/pathfinders/avocado.htm>. Accessed: January 20, 2006.

Chapter Exercises

Elizabeth Connor

PART A EXERCISES

Learning activities for library instruction in college libraries.

Reading	Chapters 1, 2, 3, and 4
Thinking Levels	**Learning Activity**
Knowledge	Define experiential learning. Define information literacy.
Comprehension	Explain how experiential learning or clicker technology can be used to improve learning outcomes. How can experiential learning be adapted to library staff development?
Application	Review ACRL information literacy standards and develop teaching goals/objectives for a current or future information literacy instruction session. Based on teaching goals/objectives for a current or future library instruction session, develop three questions that can be used to assess student learning of key concepts.
Analysis	Review various information literacy mission statements from small, medium, and large academic libraries. How do they differ? Review The Information Literacy Game <http://library.uncg.edu/de/infolitgame.asp> developed by librarians at the University of North Carolina, Greensboro or MLA Citation Style Simplified <http://www.umuc.edu/library/tutorials/mla_citation/> developed by librarians at University of Maryland University College. How can such resources be used or adapted by instruction librarians?
Synthesis	Develop a learning outcome related to an actual or hypothetical information literacy class session. How can this outcome be measured?

An Introduction to Instructional Services in Academic Libraries

(continued)

Evaluation	Develop a set of criteria that can be used to measure the success or failure of a specific instructional session. Using the criteria developed above, develop an instrument that can be used to rate library instruction sessions taught by yourself or a colleague.

Source: Adapted from Connor, E. *An Introduction to Reference Services in Academic Libraries.* Binghamton, NY: The Haworth Press, 2006, Table P.1.

PART B EXERCISES

Learning activities for library instruction in university libraries.

Reading	Chapters 5, 6, 7, 8, 9, 10, 11, 12, 13, and 14
Thinking Levels	**Learning Activity**
Knowledge	Define primary documents. Define learner-centered instruction. Define information literacy immersion. Define problem-based learning.
Comprehension	Explain how case studies can be used to improve learning outcomes. How does dualistic thinking affect student learning of library concepts and principles? Why is it or is it not necessary for the PBL students described in Chapter 9 to understand that they are using library resources to research class problems?
Application	Use <http://www.instructables.com/> to develop and share a simple set of illustrated instructions. Use the Research Guide discussed in Chapter 6 as a model for developing a guide useful for specific area of interest. Write a brief script for a university library orientation session.
Analysis	Search the Case Studies in Science site <http://ublib.buffalo.edu/libraries/projects/cases/ubcase.htm> for a case study that can be adapted and used in a future or hypothetical library instruction session. Compare librarian involvement/leadership in various first-year experience courses in small, medium, and large academic libraries. How can content scaffolding be used in library instruction?
Synthesis	Find a compelling news article and write a brief set of teaching notes that can be used to teach a library instruction class related to it. How can these notes be adapted for use with distance, ESL, or nontraditional groups of students?

(continued)

	Examine the document analysis worksheets developed by the National Archives, as mentioned in Chapter 14, and develop learning objectives related to their use or adaptation in an actual or hypothetical instruction session. Develop criteria that can be used to measure the success or failure of a specific instructional session.
Evaluation	Using the criteria developed above, develop an evaluation instrument for class participants to rate an instructor.

Source: Adapted from Connor, E. *An Introduction to Reference Services in Academic Libraries.* Binghamton, NY: The Haworth Press, 2006, Table P.1.

PART C EXERCISES

Learning activities for library instruction in health sciences university libraries.

Reading	Chapters 15, 16, 17, 18, 19, and 20
Thinking Levels	**Learning Activity**
Knowledge	Define medical informatics. Define evidence-based practice.
Comprehension	How does information literacy differ for undergraduates, health professionals, and graduate students? Explain how evidence-based practice can be applied to librarianship. What are the basic principles of evidence-based librarianship?
Application	Adapt the pharmacy assignments described in Chapter 18 for an actual or hypothetical library instruction session.
Analysis	Describe features common to each of the chapters included in this section. Search the library literature to find longitudinal studies of the effectiveness of library instruction. Compare these studies to articles related to the scholarship of teaching and learning.
Synthesis	Draw a diagram of the steps to follow to "turn a librarian into a teacher."
Evaluation	Attend three class sessions of a particular course and identify content areas that would benefit from library instruction.

Source: Adapted from Connor, E. *An Introduction to Reference Services in Academic Libraries.* Binghamton, NY: The Haworth Press, 2006, Table P.1.

Index